GREAT EXPECTATIONS FOR SMALL SCHOOLS

Praeger Studies in Ethnographic Perspectives on American Education

General editor: Ray C. Rist

GREAT EXPECTATIONS FOR SMALL SCHOOLS

The Limitations of Federal Projects

William A. Firestone

PRAEGER

PRAEGER SPECIAL STUDIES • PRAEGER SCIENTIFIC

Library of Congress Cataloging in Publication Data

Firestone, William A
    Great expectations for small schools.

    (Praeger studies in ethnographic perspectives on
American education)
    Bibliography: p.
    Includes index.
    1. School districts--South Dakota--Case studies.
2. Education, Rural--South Dakota--Case studies.
3. School size--Case studies. 4. Federal aid to
education--South Dakota--Case studies. I. Title.
II. Series.
LB2817.F57   370.19'346'09783   80-23199
ISBN 0-03-057397-1

Published in 1980 by Praeger Publishers
CBS Educational and Professional Publishing
A Division of CBS, Inc.
521 Fifth Avenue, New York, New York 10017 U.S.A.

0123456789   145   987654321

Printed in the United States of America

For Susan with love

STUDIES FOREWORD
Ray C. Rist

Our understandings of U.S. education are undergoing profound and swift changes. Instrumental in this process is the turning away from a near exclusive reliance on quantitative research methods as the only acceptable means by which to analyze and interpret the realities of education. In fact, one of the basic themes of this shift is that there are multiple ways of "knowing"; no one method can answer all our questions or offer all the necessary perspectives.

As those interested in education begin to explore alternative frameworks, one approach that is gaining increased attention and utilization is that of ethnographic research. This method of intensive, in-depth investigation by means of direct naturalistic observation has a long and honored tradition within the social sciences, especially in sociology and anthropology. Only in the past decade, however, has it gained new adherents who are applying it to the study of education. The impact has been immediate. The call for ethnographic case studies now comes from the academic community, from practitioners, and from policy makers. All are interested in the explication of the day-to-day realities of education, the microlevel issues influencing the lives of teachers, administrators, and students, and in the understanding of the school as a social system.

The present book is one in a series, Ethnographic Perspectives on American Education. The series is aimed at bringing together an exemplary set of recent studies employing ethnographic methods. What makes this collection of singular importance is that it will constitute perhaps the first "critical mass" of such studies of U.S. education. Further, the focus of the various volumes will span the formal organizational structure of the educational experience—from the early grades through higher education. The topics to be covered will be among the most pressing now confronting our educational system, for example, school desegregation, bilingual education, social class stratification, the future of rural education, and the preparation of teachers.

This series comes at a most opportune time. As the popularity of ethnographic research continues to increase, it is important for those concerned with education to have ready access to an outstanding collection of books employing this methodology, both to become more familiar with the approach and to study the insights it can provide. These studies seek not only to chronicle current conditions but to set forth explanations of why the situations are as they are. Each moves beyond the descriptive to the analytic. Their contributions reconfirm the absolute necessity of our continuing to observe U.S. education as it is and where it occurs.

I am pleased to include the present volume as the second in this series of ethnographic studies on education. It is a compelling analysis of the troubled, often tortured, effort undertaken to translate a new federal initiative into a viable local program. That we have over the past two decades witnessed a veritable explosion of federal interventions in education, and that so many of them have little or no match to what they were intended to be, suggests that the slippage between policy formation and program development is in need of cogent and insightful analysis.

Great Expectations for Small Schools is such an effort. It provides a unique contribution to our understanding of the implementation of educational programs instigated with the large carrot of federal dollars.

Federal incentives are successful only insofar as local communities and educational authorities choose to opt for them. But in saying this, an important point ought not be obscured. It is one thing for a local community to accept federal dollars. It is quite another for that same community to spend those dollars within the constraints and controls imposed by the giver. What makes this present study (and the broader federal initiative it examines) of exceptional interest is that the local community was promised funds "with no strings attached." This almost unprecedented promise by the federal government came about as part of the rhetoric of the Nixon administration to "turn government back to the people," and to allow local communities the autonomy to decide how best to respond to local problems. That the rhetoric was not translated into reality is one of the dramas played out in this book.

William Firestone is to be commended for his careful and painstaking documentation and analysis of one group of educators, parents, and local community members attempting to generate an "experimental school." His vivid protrayal of the cross-cutting agenda, of the multiple understandings of the project goals, and of the manner in which efforts at social change were transformed into further solidification of the status quo deserves our closest attention and study.

Through all of this Firestone writes with compassion and understanding for the individuals involved. As he notes, many were his friends. That this study has a human face, as it were, ought not to be minimized. Far too often social planners seem intent on instigating programs that are "person proof." Firestone has made it abundantly clear that any effort at social change that seeks to avoid the individuals involved is doomed to fail. There are no "quick fix" strategies for social change. People are at the very heart of any such effort—and change will come about only when they exercise the will to make it happen. Saying so at the federal level does not make it so at the local level.

PREFACE

There is much more of a national system of education in this country than there was even 25 years ago. An extensive federal bureaucracy is now devoted to setting and implementing federal educational "policy." A new federal program can have substantial impact in far corners of the country. Still, the real action in education takes place in local districts, schools, and classrooms. The chain of events, stretching from the announcement of a new program in Washington to the time when teachers do something different as a result, is long, and there can be many a slip between the cup and the lip. The final results are often quite different from what was originally expected.

This book describes the chain stretching from President Nixon's announcement of the Experimental Schools Program in 1969 to the midpoint of its implementation in the Butte-Angels Camp School District in 1976. The story is told in some detail to illustrate the complexities of the process—complexities that are not really well understood either by the people in Washington who design a new program or the people in schools who respond to it. The emphasis in this case is on what took place in the district. As a result, the story portrays the multifaceted context in which this project was implemented and the host of issues and special interests that became attached to it.

The actual story tells how the district's project was transformed into something that was very different from what was expected by program managers in Washington or by the district's superintendent and his staff who wrote the initial proposals that were funded. However, it provides an opportunity to explore a number of issues that concern those involved in change efforts at whatever level. These include questions like: How can new efforts be planned to ensure that they really address local problems and important goals? How can support for change be strengthened? What is the appropriate scope for a change effort? and How can the management of programs at the federal level ensure that change will be constructive, not disruptive? While these issues are addressed because they seem to be especially salient in this particular case, they are questions that recur frequently among those responsible for improving education at various levels. My hope is that this case study and my effort to draw lessons from it will provide some new insights and warnings to people who are considering or committed to change efforts.

I would like to thank a number of people who played an important role in this study's development. My wife Susan put off her own career aspirations and became active in the field work by helping to integrate us into the community, handling many of the special assignments from Abt Associates' main offices, and collecting field data through the informal contacts she developed. When this project started, we were a family of two, but now there are four. My daughters Cory and Becca have been very tolerant of my frequent weekend absences as the book neared completion.

The people of Butte and Angels Camp were most tolerant of my presence as they coped with a myriad of their own difficulties. Many close friendships developed that will not be forgotten.

At Abt Associates, Dr. Robert Herriott was an exemplar of the supportive project director and research facilitator. Stephen Fitzsimmons and Michael Kane helped us in dealing with the sponsoring agency and the company. Shiela Rosenblum provided access to her staff survey data. Other on-site researchers—most notably C. Thompson Wacaster, C. A. "Tony" Clinton, and Donald Messerschmidt—provided solace and support in our own internal processes of negotiation and exchange. Abby Freedman and Mary Schumacher provided valuable editorial assistance. My current employers at Research for Better Schools, most notably John Connolly and Keith Kershner, have been most supportive of my efforts to get this manuscript into print.

Harry Wolcott of the University of Oregon, Steven Bossert of the Far West Laboratory, and Howard S. Becker of Northwestern University provided useful advice early in the study. David Street of the University of Illinois Chicago Circle, Michael G. Trend of Abt Associates, and Elizabeth Eddy of the University of Florida all read the first draft and provided useful substantive critiques. Neal Gross of the University of Pennsylvania suggested a way to respond to those critiques and Terry Deal of Harvard University offered suggestions late in the revision process.

ACKNOWLEDGEMENTS

Portions of this book are based on material that previously appeared in the following publications, which the author gratefully acknowledges permission to reprint.

From Administrators' Notebook: "Between Two Communities: External Pressures on the Direction of Educational Change," by William A. Firestone, vol. 24, no. 6, 1976, pp. 1-4.

From The Journal of Applied Behavioral Science: "Participation and Influence in the Planning of Educational Change," by William A. Firestone, vol. 13, no. 2, 1977, pp. 167-83, NTL Institute for Applied Behavioral Science.

From The Dynamics of Planned Educational Change: "Butte-Angels Camp: Conflict and Transformation," by William A. Firestone, edited by Robert Herriott and Neal Gross. Berkeley, Calif.: McCutchan, 1979.

CONTENTS

LIST OF TABLES AND FIGURES

GREAT EXPECTATIONS FOR SMALL SCHOOLS

.

1

INTRODUCTION

Experimental Schools is the first program in the U.S.
Office of Education to offer support for long-term testing, documentation, and evaluation of comprehensive
change. . . . [It] provides the Nation with an unprecedented opportunity to find out whether new educational
programs, which address all parts of an educational system simultaneously, will be more effective than past reform efforts which have focused on only one or several
parts of an educational system at a time.

> Announcement of the Experi-
> mental Schools' Small
> Schools' Competition

It's one more thing to worry about. It has little relevance to what I do, and it's a pain in the butt.

> A teacher

On June 25, 1973, the Butte-Angels Camp School District* received notification that it was the recipient of a three-year, $734,000
award from the National Institute of Education's Experimental Schools
Program. An award of that magnitude would be a major event in any
small, rural school district with an annual budget of about $2.2 mil-
lion, climbing expenses, and the threat of a taxpayers' revolt. However, John Raleigh, the district's superintendent, must have been especially elated. The award was the result of an 18-month effort that
at times involved all staff in the district. For Raleigh, it was an unusual opportunity to put into practice the new approach to teaching that
he had advocated for some time. The district's proposal described
this approach as:

---

*Throughout this book, all names of places and people are pseud-
onyms. The only exception is when national figures instrumental in
setting national educational policy are mentioned.

1

> Personalized education (which) considers the academic,
> social, emotional, and physical needs of children and
> then provides for these in a way best suited to the child.
> A determination is made as to the needs, readiness . . .
> and interests of the child. A personalized program is then
> designed for the child with due consideration to the best
> utilization of staff, community, and its resources.

This was no casual effort. Every teacher in the district would become adept at new procedures for diagnosing and prescribing for individual students. As Raleigh later told his staff, he intended that this project become "a way of life."

Three years later, in the summer of 1976, the great expectations raised by the project had been dashed. John Raleigh had been pushed out of the district and replaced by a less innovative successor who had been a teacher when the project began. While the language of comprehensive, personalized education was still used, the project had become a congeries of separate efforts that interested specific teachers, counselors, and principals. Two-fifths of the project's expenditures over the first two years went to the purchase of teachers' aides and educational materials that did not differ significantly from what had been used in the district previously.

A similar transformation took place in Washington. The Experimental Schools Program (ES/Washington) was first announced in President Nixon's 1969 budget message to Congress. It received early support of Robert Finch, secretary of health, education and welfare; Daniel Moynihan, the president's special assistant for domestic affairs; and Sidney Marland, the commissioner of education. HEW planners expected that the program would spend $190 million over an eight-year period (Herriott 1979).

The program was an attempt to overcome a number of obstacles to federal stimulation of educational improvement that had been identified in the early 1970s. One of the most important to the program's staff was that existing programs were only intended to encourage "piecemeal" changes; they were aimed at special target groups, some of whom (for example, preschool children) were not even typically considered clients of public schools. The ES staff believed that these programs left the central instructional activities and managerial patterns of the school system untouched. While piecemeal programs could be started easily, it was just as easy to drop them since they had no effect on the district as a whole. Another criticism of previous programs was that the one-year funding pattern did not allow time for new developments to mature. Guaranteed continuity of support would, it was argued, increase the likelihood that new developments could be built into a district.

ES/Washington adopted the hypothesis that long-term, "comprehensive" change projects would be more effective than piecemeal efforts. A project would be comprehensive if it dealt with students of all ages from kindergarten through grade 12 and if it addressed five different issues ranging from curriculum to organization and management. In all, the program funded three waves of projects. The third wave was aimed specifically at rural school districts, partly because past federal efforts had ignored those schools, but also because it was believed that small districts would be especially amenable to the comprehensive approach. All systems in the nation with fewer than 2,500 students received the announcement of the competition for funding of districtwide change efforts; 319 districts responded to the announcement. The Butte-Angels Camp District was one of ten that were eventually selected to receive four to five years of support.

However, ES/Washington quickly lost touch with its rural districts as it faced problems of its own. In 1972 the program was transferred from the Office of Education (OE) to the new National Institute of Education (NIE), a much more hostile setting. A later review of the program concluded that

> ES had proposed one thing and produced another; ES had not delivered on the rhetoric of "comprehensiveness."
> . . . One reviewer cast the issue in sharp operational terms when he said, ". . . if we made a judgment concerning the program in terms of its comprehensiveness, I would say that we would have to shut it down." [Doyle 1975, p. 8]

By May 1976 ES/Washington was shut down, and responsibility for administering its final contract was spread throughout NIE. In all, only $55 million of the $190 million originally envisioned for this innovative program was actually spent.

RECENT FEDERAL EDUCATIONAL
CHANGE EFFORTS

The transformation of the Butte-Angels Camp Experimental Schools project and its funding agency was more dramatic than many recent attempts at educational reform, but in other regards it was fairly typical of recent change efforts. Since World War II, there has been a strong demand for educational change and a growing expectation that schools develop a planned, coordinated response to externally imposed requirements. Whether the concern was to increase the number of scientists and technicians being trained as in the 1950s, to increase equality of educational opportunity as in the 1960s, or to find ways to reduce the costs of educational and other government services as is increasingly the case today, the U.S. educational system has been expected to develop special approaches that can be rapidly disseminated among, and implemented by, local schools and districts.

As the demand for change accelerated, the federal government became the most important level of government in responding to that demand. Before 1957 the primary concern of the federal Office of Education was the collection and dissemination of information; the business of running the schools was the responsibility of the states and local communities. But with the passage of the National Defense Education Act that year, followed by the civil rights legislation and the Elementary and Secondary Education Act of the mid-1960s, the federal government began to play a major role in educational policy making. By 1973 when the Butte-Angels Camp project began, the government was spending an estimated $6.3 billion on schools. While this amount was less than 10 percent of state and local expenditures on education, almost all of it was intended to produce some kind of change (Kirst 1974).

In spite of the increased role of the federal government in producing change, the track record for developing, implementing, and institutionalizing innovative programs in local school districts has been poor nationwide. In the early 1970s, some private foundations reported that the money they spent on special projects often produced no change at all. In other cases the changes were small, cosmetic rearrangements that did not have any significant impact on students, and even these were often terminated when special funds were eliminated (Ford Foundation 1972).

Federal programs produced similar results. After the first blush of optimism in the mid-1960s, there was a growing sense that the substantial financial investment in education had not produced a commensurate amount of change. Evaluations of such widely heralded programs as Headstart, Title I, and others indicated that these attempts to increase the achievements of lower class and minority children were not meeting the expectations that program designers had for them.

More recently, an extensive examination of several federally funded innovative programs identified three outcomes of such attempts to implement new practices: nonimplementation; cooptation, requiring a major adjustment to the practice to fit local conditions; and mutual adaptation of the new practice and the local unit to each other. However, accurate replication of effective new practices in the local context as a result of learning and adjustment by the school staff simply has not occurred, and mutual adaptation has been a less frequent outcome than the other two (Berman and McLaughlin 1975).

The story of the Butte-Angels Camp Experimental Schools' project is a history of the processes that lead to nonimplementation and cooptation. It is also a useful supplement to the existing literature on planned change. While there is a growing body of research in this field, most studies treat the actual implementation of new projects as a "black box," comparing the outcomes of the change process with initial plans in order to evaluate the fidelity with which those plans were carried out (Fullan and Pomfert 1977). Less attention is paid to the events that occur between the decision to change and the time when outcomes are evaluated. The same holds true for planning efforts; the activities by which project objectives (the evaluation criteria against which outcomes are measured) and strategies for implementation are designed and approved remain a mystery.

The better descriptive studies of implementation in schools focus narrowly on the innovation itself. * Very little attention is paid to everyday administrative and instructional activities either to compare these routine activities with those related to the innovation or to examine the relationship between one set of activities and another. Moreover, most of the existing studies are confined to events in individual schools. There are very few studies that attempt to describe events related to the project at the district level or that examine districtwide change efforts even though such projects are so complex that they may be qualitatively different kinds of events. † Finally, even less attention is given to the district's local and national environment. Yet most innovations are imported, the incentive to adopt them is often special funding, and they may be affected by community reactions to them. Bringing the multitude of contexts in which a change effort takes place to the forefront helps to understand how change projects are derailed and to challenge current thinking about how to manage innovation.

THE RESEARCH OPPORTUNITY

The Experimental Schools Program provided an unusual opportunity to learn more about why planned change is so difficult for schools and to examine alternative strategies for school improvement. At the same time that the announcement of the Experimental Schools' competition for rural schools was distributed, ES/Washington issued

---

*These include the works of Gross, Giacquinta, and Bernstein (1971); Smith and Keith (1971); and Sussman (1977).

† For an exception, see the work reported by Herriott and Gross (1979).

a request for proposals (RFP) for "documentation and evaluation" of the districts' efforts so that it could examine the utility of this approach to effecting change.

The agency was open to the use of the case study approach to documenting the process of planned change, since it felt that unconventional evaluation methods would be needed to accommodate the ES Program's comprehensive, holistic nature. Moreover, the federal program designers hoped to avoid what they believed were major failures of previous evaluations, including fly-in/fly-out data collection, the black box approach to the analysis of implementation, and the failure to understand the context in which change takes place (Herriott 1974). Documentation of events in the district was to be a major component of the evaluation; the RFP specifically required that the winning contractor assign one person to live full time on each site.

Abt Associates prepared the winning proposal to conduct the rural Experimental Schools research. Its plan called for several studies including a case study of each project as the research evolved. Guidelines for the studies were developed that required that each provide information on the district's project, the district itself, and its community setting. The person recruited to live on site would be qualified to conduct such a study and would determine the balance among those three components in the final report. However, half of his or her time would be devoted to collecting data for the numerous cross-site studies being directed from Abt's main offices in Cambridge, Massachusetts. I was hired as the on-site researcher in the Butte-Angels Camp School District.

Case studies vary in the extent to which they are initially guided by a research problem. A study that focuses on a particular problem is most likely to emerge when the researcher begins with a set of interests, becomes familiar with several locations, and selects the one that presents an opportunity to develop that line of research. My situation was almost the exact opposite. I was placed in a situation and charged to make the most of it, even though I lacked the concrete knowledge about the Butte-Angels Camp District to anticipate what problems could be most fruitfully studied there. My task was inductive: to document conditions in the district and the history of the project and then to identify the lessons gleaned from that project for researchers and practitioners. I tried to make optimal use of the considerable resources available—including direct access to the district, a wealth of data, and extensive time on site—in a context characterized by competing demands within the project and shifting demands from the funding agency.*

---

*The way I conducted the study is described in Appendix A. Additional description is provided by Firestone (1975) and Wacaster and Firestone (1978).

I arrived in Butte-Angels Camp in August 1973 just before implementation of the ES project began and remained until funding for
my position was terminated in August 1976. The project continued for
two years after I left. During the three years I was in Butte-Angels
Camp, the project underwent its transformation from a comprehensive effort to implement personalized education to a collection of subprojects with no central focus. This transformation highlighted and
raised questions about a number of assumptions about how to produce
successful planned change.

The district offered an especially useful setting for examining
comprehensive change. One would expect that such efforts are most
likely to be successful in small, geographically compact districts
where the difficulties of controlling and coordinating a project are
minimized. The Butte-Angels Camp District was quite small when
implementation of its ES project began. Its 2,300 students were
served by 135 teachers and counselors working in 7 buildings: a high
school serving grades 9 through 12, a seventh and eighth grade junior
high, and 5 elementary schools. While the district comprised an area
of 430 square miles in a western mining region, most of the area was
sparsely populated. Six of seven schools were in the two towns of
Butte and Angels Camp, which were only eight miles apart. The
seventh school housed one teacher and fewer than ten students in a
community 20 miles away.

This district only provides a useful case for analysis if it is
typical of other school districts in most respects. While an enrollment of only 2,300 students may seen unusual, it is not often recognized that 74 percent of the school districts in this country have fewer
than 2,500 students. A fifth of the nation's students are served by
these small districts (National Center for Education Statistics 1978).
Moreover, the Butte-Angels Camp district resembled most others in
this country structurally. Its staffing pattern included an elected
school board, a superintendent, a business manager, six principals,
teachers, and a variety of specialists. It also faced most of the problems of resource utilization that beset all but the richest school districts in the 1970s—falling enrollments, a declining tax base, pressures from teachers to increase salaries, and demands from the community to lower taxes. Overall, the Butte-Angels Camp district was
fairly typical.

ASSUMPTIONS ABOUT EDUCATIONAL CHANGE

As I came to understand the district and its project better and
identified what was unique about the Experimental Schools Program,
I saw that thinking in the district and in Washington was shaped by
four assumptions:

- That new projects can be designed through a rational process,
- That participation can routinely overcome the biggest barrier to planned change—staff resistance,
- That the federal government is a major catalyst for constructive change, and
- That comprehensive changes can be implemented in schools.

The first two are routinely made by planners and experts on educational change; they are often built into federal and state policy. The third assumption is widely held in Washington, and the fourth was the central theme of the Experimental Schools Program.

As I considered these assumptions in light of the Butte-Angels Camp experience, I became more and more convinced that they were misleading. Some are true under special conditions, but all of them mask the complexity of the change process in ways that lead to faulty decisions. The remainder of this chapter will consider those assumptions in more detail. The body of this book will examine the extent to which they applied in Butte-Angels Camp and will offer reformulations that this district's experience suggests are more accurate.

Rational Project Design

Most policy making related to project design assumes that new practices are adopted in a district through a rational process: only rational adoption will lead to improved educational performance, and improved performance is assumed to be the purpose of change (Emrick and Peterson 1977). Commenting on the early Teacher Corps, Corwin (1973) observes that most policy makers assume that both schools and federal programs are more rational, potent instruments for policy implementation than is in fact the case. Educators have, for the most part, not examined the concept of rationality; but there have been several analyses in other areas that identify prerequisites for rationality that seem to be rare in school districts.

The essence of rational planning is the formulation of technically correct or accurate decisions based on clear goals and adequate information. Hage and Aiken (1970) describe this aspect of the change process as follows:

> The beginning of the process of organizational change occurs when organizational decision makers determine that either the organization is not accomplishing its present goals as effectively or efficiently as possible or when decision makers alter or amend the goals of the organization. . . . During the evaluation stage, decision makers

must assess the state of health of an organization, consider
alternative ways of correcting organizational problems, and
then decide on one alternative that hopefully will accomplish
the desired ends.

Rational planning, then, begins with a matching process. The organization's health is determined by examining discrepancies between
goals and performance, then alternatives are sought that best reduce
these discrepancies at the least cost.

Policy makers often assume that rational adoption is both useful and feasible. For instance, the state of New Jersey mandates that
its school districts provide a "thorough and efficient" education to
children. To do so each district must continuously move through the
following six-step process:

Goal development: The district develops district and school
goals with involvement of teachers, staff members, administrators,
board members, pupils, parents, and other citizens.

Establishing objectives: The district specifies, in writing, ob-
jectives/goal indicators and specifies the level of student achievement
desired.

Needs identification: The Local Education Agency (LEA) deter-
mines the difference between its current status and desired level of
proficiency.

Developing and installing educational programs: The district
school board adopts and implements an educational program for the
district and each school, which includes programs designed to improve the quality of education.

Evaluating educational program effectiveness: The district
measures the extent to which its educational programs actually fulfill
their expected purposes.

Budget review: The LEA budgets annually for its projected educational plan and programs (State of New Jersey 1976).

While this process goes beyond adoption, it mandates that program
decisions be predicated on the need to reduce discrepancies between
goals and performance.

Analyses of decision-making processes indicate that any organization trying to base decisions on this rational discrepancy analysis
must meet three prerequisites:

- A clear ordering of goals,
- The capacity to obtain information on its progress toward meeting
  these goals,
- The capacity to obtain information on all available alternatives for
  meeting these goals (Simon 1957).

Each of these prerequisites is problematic, but most attention has been given to the difficulties in identifying organizational goals. Two difficulties are often mentioned.

First, while the basic purposes of an organization are clear, they are too general to serve as useful guides for action. Schools are expected to promote a variety of student outcomes including knowledge of basic skills like reading and arithmetic, a strong self-concept, good citizenship, general aptitudes expected of workers, and specific job skills. In addition to these product goals, schools have numerous system goals (Perrow 1970) or internal operational needs—high morale, innovativeness, or efficient fiscal operations—that are intrinsically valued. Before goals can be matched to organizational conditions, they must be specified in a measurable form and prioritized, so that greatest attention will be given to those that are most important. The measurement problems are often complex, and the rank ordering is extremely difficult. Value judgments are often required in the absence of objective guidelines. Moreover, the prioritization of goals is not static but changes in response to external conditions (Lindblom 1959).

Second, individuals within the organization disagree about goals for several reasons. One involves the division of labor within the organization: units or departments are assigned specific tasks or subgoals, and members of the department adopt these subgoals rather than the organization's overall goals. When these subgoals come into conflict, for instance, when a choice must be made between allocating resources to research or to service, disagreement results (Simon 1964). Differences in occupational perspective also lead to disagreement. For instance, social workers will stress the importance of affective development of children while teachers emphasize the need for skills development. When members disagree about goals, selection by consensus is virtually impossible. This problem can be alleviated only if there is a unified administrative cadre that can agree on goals for the organization and has the authority to enforce its decisions. But if goals cannot be specified in a clear and consistent fashion, it is impossible to know what innovation will enhance overall goal attainment.

Less attention has been given to the problems of achieving the other conditions required for rational decision making, but they are also difficult to create. For instance, information on the organization's progress toward meeting its goals requires both outcome measures related to goals and measures of the behaviors that must take place to achieve those goals (Ouchi and Maguire 1975). Such outcome measures are only possible when goals are clearly stated and agreed upon, and when sophisticated measurement techniques are available. In human service organizations—schools, mental health agencies, and social work institutions—those conditions are often missing (Miles 1965). Information on behavior can only be collected when there is a clear understanding of which activities lead to desired outcomes. Without such an understanding, one does not know which processes to measure. Finally, information on all possible innovations that might be selected, and their consequences if implemented, is difficult to obtain because of time and energy limitations (Lindblom 1959).

There is relatively little research on the extent to which schools actually approximate rational program design. The clues that do exist suggest that rationality is the exception, not the rule. For instance, if the conditions for rational decision making are met, then the highest quality innovations will be adopted most frequently. Yet, quality does not affect rate of adoption. A study of 17 innovations adopted in urban secondary schools examined their quality and frequency of acceptance. A rank-order correlation of .34 was found between these two variables, and only two of the five highest quality innovations had been adopted by more than a third of the schools studied (Nelson and Sieber 1976).

Moreover, one of the few studies that examines the adoption process indicates that rational behavior is atypical. Almost no school districts search their environments systematically for innovations. A A few districts do adopt a limited problem-solving orientation whereby they identify a problem and select an innovation from among the few they know about that may solve the problem. They then seek federal funds to support their change effort. Most districts are opportunistic: they are more committed to obtaining federal funding than to actually implementing the project described in their proposal (Berman and McLaughlin 1975).

These findings come from large, national studies that did not include direct observation of planning. They do not indicate why rational planning does not take place or what kind of decision process takes the place of systematic goal matching.

Resistance and Participation

Resistance to change is the most frequently examined barrier to planned change. Research has been conducted on the topic in industrial settings since the 1940s, and the issue continues to be of interest for studies of change in a number of areas, including education. Four assumptions are often made about resistance, although they are not always explicit. First, resistance is typically seen as irrational. This view usually attributes irrationality to either a general personality trait or the result of a number of other traits, including intolerance for ambiguity, unwillingness to take risks, the strength of habit, personal insecurity, and the strength of the superego in the service of tradition (Watson 1969; Zaltman and Duncan 1977). The possibility that resistance is a rational response to the extra work and uncertainty caused by the innovation receives less attention. *

Second, resistance is typically assumed to be concentrated within the organization's lower staff. † The early studies of resistance to change were conducted by researchers and managers in industry who were intent on implementing innovations to increase productivity. A similar assumption is still common in studies of the implementation of educational change, where the problem is often seen as one of mo- tivating teachers to accept new practices (Chesler, Schmuck, and Lippit 1975). However, opposition could come from a number of other sources such as members of the administrative cadre, parents, or other governmental entities. Unfortunately, there has as yet been no attempt to develop a taxonomy of locations for opposition that examines the consequences of different distributions of resistance for the change process and outcomes.

Third, any opposition to the innovation that becomes manifest is assumed to be resistance to that change; the extent to which other or- ganizational factors or events contribute to opposition is rarely ex- amined. There may be several reasons for this omission. For in- stance, much of the writing on resistance has been done by change agents and consultants who were probably directed to focus on the change process itself. The research studies that are conducted often concentrate narrowly on change activities or on attitudes related di- rectly to the innovation. There is often no way to examine the extent to which attitudes toward an innovation are affected by already existing concerns about worker satisfaction, staff autonomy, teaching philoso- phy, or other issues because the necessary data are not collected (Coch and French 1968; Morse and Reimer 1956; Morris and Binstock 1966).

Finally, although the importance of resistance is frequently stressed, resistance is nonetheless assumed to take relatively pas- sive forms. The outcomes of resistance that have been measured or documented include reduced productivity, failure of the innovation to be incorporated into the organization's operating practices, and in- creased absenteeism. Other conceivable and more salient outcomes, such as turnover among the organization's top leaders or rank and

---

*See Gross, Giacquinta, and Bernstein (1971) for an exception.
† One exception to this view is the observation that resistance to training and organization development by top levels of the organiza- tional hierarchy will usually doom those programs to failure. This observation has not stimulated a general analysis of the location of resistance (Argyris 1969).

file or the substantial reallocation of authority among positions, are rarely discussed.

If resistance to change is taken to be the problem by most students of the topic, participation of potentially resistive parties is generally believed to be the solution. Giacquinta (1973) quoted studies arguing for a law that participation routinely overcomes resistance to change. In spite of the popularity of this law, there are important questions about the nature of participation, why it should reduce resistance, the conditions under which it is possible, and its possible consequences. One such question concerns the relationship of participation to influence. The term may refer to power equalization (Leavitt 1965) between levels of the organizational hierarchy, or it may mean simply that participants were present when decisions were made. *

Gamson (1968) identifies two explanations for the relationship between participation and reduced resistance to change, one based on shared influence and the other on social control. In the first case, staff support a change effort because they have designed it to meet their needs and interests; their influence is important primarily because it ensures that their needs are met. In the second, teachers' activities during the decision process rather than the change outcome are critical. Mechanisms like group discussion techniques increase the acceptance of management-stimulated change, partly by communicating the need for change as perceived by managers and partly by fostering a sense of ownership on the part of teachers or staff. For instance, Coch and French (1968, p. 350) argue that resistance can be overcome "by the use of group meetings in which management effectively communicates the need for change and stimulates group participation in planning the changes." However, it is not clear whether a sense of ownership can really be stimulated without the sharing of influence.

In spite of the general acceptance of the "law of participation," the research findings are ambiguous. The few studies of the relationships among participation, resistance, and outcomes of the change process have numerous methodological flaws and present results that are weak or even the reverse of what is expected (Giacquinta 1973; Dunn and Swierczek 1977). Equally important, few studies have examined the impact of participation on the design of change projects. If social control mechanisms indeed explain the relationship between participation and reduced resistance to change, then design is not an

---

*Throughout this study, participation will refer to presence during activities so the relationship between participation and influence can be examined rather than inferred.

issue because crucial decisions remain under the control of top management. If sharing influence is important, however, then the staff's interests must be considered; the change may have to be significantly modified. In the extreme case, initial objectives may be completely subsumed by a new agenda.

Similarly, relatively little attention has been given to the conditions necessary for staff participation. Administrators may easily create opportunities for teachers to participate in decision making, but there are a variety of barriers to actually sharing influence that have not been considered. These include:

Unequal distribution of time and skills: Teachers are occupied with their normal full-time workload. While they can attend some planning meetings, preparation for those meetings is needed, as is synthesis afterward to turn the varied inputs into a coherent program. The time and skills for this work usually rest with the central staff; a fact that offers the central staff an opportunity to shape the project's design.

The search for outside funding: Many innovations are supported by federal funds obtained through competitive proposal writing. Hence, district leaders may give more weight to the funding agency's ideas and priorities than to those of staff members.

Standard operating procedures (SOPs): Fixed procedures in the school district are the key to efficiency, but they may preclude consideration of new and creative ideas or a representative mix of "actors" (Allison 1971). SOPs determine who will handle liaison with the agency and when and how extensively teachers will participate. These liaison persons can commit a district to an idea before teachers ever become involved in the planning process.

The Government as Catalyst

In the last 25 years there has been a tendency to look to the federal government as a catalyst for constructive reform in education. The reasons for the federal government's prominence include its visibility and its enforcement powers, and the sheer volume of discretionary money at its disposal.

The high point of confidence in the federal government was reached in the mid 1960s when in two years, Congress passed both the Civil Rights Act and the Elementary and Secondary Education Act (ESEA). Referring to ESEA, President Johnson said, "No law I have signed or will ever sign means more to the future of America" (Halperin 1975). Since then, faith in the government's ability to reform education has dwindled, but efforts continue.

The government uses three modes to motivate change: legal enforcement; research, development, and the dissemination of results; and the provision of funding for innovations. The Experimental Schools Program is an example of the last approach. In using funding as an incentive for change, the government never provides schools with general grants. Rather awards are made for specific purposes such as providing assistance to identified target groups (the Handicapped Act) or in specific content areas (the Right to Read program). As a result, the recipient must anticipate the interests of the federal agency and adhere to its policies when using the funds. These pressures on the recipient are intensified when the agency uses a competitive procedure to allocate funds rather than a formula and employs a contract rather than a grant as the legal instrument for the award. ES/Washington did both.

Under these conditions, there are at least three prerequisites for the use of funding to facilitate change. First, the noise in the federal-district relationship must be reduced (Gideonse 1979). Noise can take a variety of forms. Federal regulations or guidelines can be unclear. The limits to federal authority or local discretion may be ambiguous. There may be delays in response to requests for information or approval from the local level, and funds may not flow from the agency to the local project on schedule. Under these conditions, school people will become confused and frustrated. They may spend a great deal of time trying to determine what they are supposed to be doing and what they are allowed to do. In the extreme case, considerable distrust and game playing may result.

The government uses a variety of media to communicate with local projects including regulations, grants or contracts, and written correspondence. However, especially with innovative programs, considerable ambiguity is bound to arise; and personal communication with someone in the agency who knows the site will be important. Typically, the agency will employ one or more project officers to maintain communication with the site, monitor the project's progress, and provide some level of assistance. Noise reduction will depend to a great extent on the project officer's skill, understanding of the federal program and the local project, and stability of position.

Second, the noise within the federal establishment must be minimized (Gideonse 1979). This noise includes competition for a program's funds and program staff, questioning of the basic premises of the program, and even threats to its survival. Outsiders tend to think of the federal government as a monolith with a single, ponderous purpose. Viewed more closely it turns into a massive, incoherent array of bureaus, programs, committees, and individuals with very diverse goals and styles for achieving them. There is a constant maneuvering for advantage. Whether this maneuvering is for altruistic or personal ends, it creates a fluctuating and sometimes threatening environment for any given change program. Yet, such programs must have stability and the absence of noise if they are to reduce the noise in their relationships with local projects.

Finally, the program must have a good idea. Noise reduction is only a way to ensure that good ideas come to fruition. Given the unstable environment, there are both technical and political requirements for a good idea. Technically, the idea must be based on a sound analysis of what is wrong with a part of the U.S. educational system or it must offer some way to make the system better. Moreover, the approach to improvement must be realistic in that it is actually implementable in schools. Politically, the idea must be appealing to some constituency that will fight for it in Washington. Often these technical and political prerequisites are at odds. In order to build support for an idea, its goals are made so broad and ambiguous that it is difficult to identify what the initial idea was and judge its technical quality (Tumin 1973).

Comprehensive Change

The Experimental Schools' Program's guiding idea was that comprehensive change is an effective approach to educational reform. The meaning of comprehensive change is not always clear, but Doyle et al. (1976, p. 30) say that the term was defined in internal memorandums for ES staff as "accounting for or comprehending all or virtually all pertinent conditions, e.g., including at a minimum all the significant elements of a formal education program." They point out that the idea reflects the view that schooling is not a set of discrete programs, but rather that all aspects of school operations and relations with the community must be considered simultaneously. Hence, change activities must encompass all aspects of the system—from curriculum, through staffing and governance, to the community. It should be noted that ES's idea of comprehensive change referred to the form of an innovation, not to its content. For instance, it was initially argued that U.S. education could, in principle, be improved by combining various promising practices believed to be attributable to several federal development efforts. However, an initial ES attempt to identify such practices was unsuccessful, and no analysis of how to combine disparate elements into a comprehensive program was ever made.

The rural school districts received their operational criteria for a comprehensive project in the announcement to which they responded in the spring of 1972.* It stated that:

---

*The whole announcement is reprinted in Herriott and Gross (19

A(n) . . . Experimental Schools Project must be comprehensive, that is, it must include at least the following
components:

(a) a fresh approach to the nature and substance of the
    total curriculum in light of local needs and goals;
(b) reorganization and training of staff to meet particular
    project goals;
(c) innovative use of time, space, and facilities;
(d) active community involvement in developing, operat-
    ing and evaluating the proposed project; and
(e) an administrative and organizational structure which
    supports the project and which takes into account
    local strengths and weaknesses.

An internal capacity to evaluate changes in the school system and its
project was later added to this list of required components. In addition, a comprehensive project would involve all students and teachers
in the system from kindergarten through grade 12.

Comprehensive change is a form of the "alternative of grandeur"
(Smith and Keith 1971). This approach is based on the alteration of
multiple components of a system in one major effort, and it generally
entails great risk. Change in each component should complement
change in other components so the sum total is a change effort of major
proportion that overcomes organizational inertia. The alternative of
grandeur has two distinct characteristics. First, it requires change
of the total system rather than of just some components. The requirements that all district staff and students, as well as the five activity areas listed in the federal announcement, be included in funded
projects ensured that this characteristic would be present in the ES
projects.

Second, the alternative of grandeur requires making all changes
at once. At best, the change process is divided into two phases, one
for planning and one for implementation. A single, linear development from plan to action then takes place. The notion of breaking the
intended change into a series of small steps or allowing different sub-
units to proceed at different rates in order to adjust their schedules
in response to initial implementation experiences is effectively ruled
out. ES established a number of procedural requirements that pressed
the rural districts to attempt this kind of single, massive change. For
instance, a single plan was to be developed before funding was approved. This plan established objectives for the five-year project
and the local evaluation component. The plan became legally binding
by being incorporated in a contract rather than a grant. * Further-

---

*Government agencies use contracts to specify in detail the
tasks to be performed. Grants are less binding; they provide fewer

more, the districts had to develop budgets that would reflect the sharp decline in federal funding after the first year, thereby precluding any phased approach to implementation.

The alternative of grandeur is in essence a shock tactic for changing a bureaucracy. One characteristic of bureaucracies is supposed to be that their parts are interdependent. Interdependence generally becomes a barrier to change, thus contributing to the conservatism of this kind of organization (Merton 1968). An attempt to modify any one part of the system requires changes in all others, and the inertia of parts of the system that are not targeted for change slows the process of change in the targeted part. The alternative of grandeur is intended to capitalize on system interdependence so that change in each part complements and reinforces change in the others. Without system interdependence, the complementary effect of multiple changes on different components will not occur (Smith and Keith 1971).

ES shared the assumption that school districts are highly integrated, an assumption that appeared in the agency's criticism of past change efforts—that districts include a central core that is not affected by the addition and subtraction of special services through federal programs. This assumption was also used to help explain why comprehensive change would be effective. According to Doyle et al. (1976, p. 31), ES staff held that such change "would have a synergistic effect, in that the comprehensive program's impact would be greater than the sum of each component's impact. Given compatible and mutually reinforcing components and a massive change in the total learning environment, it was believed that pupil performance would improve."

The assumption of linear project development was implicit in the program's procedures. This idea is embedded in traditional federal funding procedures that were adopted by the program. Most programs, especially those requiring competitive awards of funds for local projects, have two phases. In the first, local agencies develop program plans in the form of proposals or grant applications. In the second, the funded projects implement their plan. Federal project monitoring is geared to ensuring that those plans are followed and that funds are not used for other purposes (CPI Associates 1971). ES/Washington employed standard competitive funding arrangements for the most part. While the length of each project's funding period and the project officers' ideology that they were providing technical assistance to projects (Corwin 1977) permitted some development of initial plans, the agency never made provision for the possibility of project transformation or development.

---

mechanisms to observe for compliance and fewer penalties for violation of the agreement.

OVERVIEW OF THE VOLUME

This book describes the Butte-Angels Camp Experimental
Schools project and the setting in which it was carried out. The description is organized to clarify the four assumptions about how to
produce change. Chapter 2 describes the district's environments.
The district had to respond to contradictory pressures from two communities—the community of local residents and that of professional
educators. Each had conflicting ideas about what the district's program emphases and financial priorities should be. These pressures
precluded developing the consensus on goals necessary for rational
program design. Although the district did have some discretion because of the license granted it by the community and erratic public
scrutiny, this freedom was a weak base from which to plan.
Chapter 3 describes the internal operation of the district. Particular attention is paid to four issues that conditioned both attempts
to plan rationally and the likelihood of initial resistance to change.
These are:

• The differences in goals among individuals and groups on the staff,
• The way authority was shared among teachers and administrators
  and the extent to which exchange could be used to increase or
  decrease influence,
• Interdependence and information flows among staff and the impact
  of these factors on the coordination of action,
• The history of conflict in the district and its sources.

These factors are shown to affect initial orientations toward the project at the beginning of implementation and strategies used to overcome resistance to change.
The history of the Butte-Angels Camp ES project is presented
in Chapters 4, 5, and 6. Chapter 4 examines planning in the district
and in Washington. The mechanisms for staff and community participation are described along with the early development of the program
and initial federal-local negotiations. This description highlights a
number of barriers to rational program design and examines the impact of participation on staff orientations to the project. It also describes two kinds of noise affecting federal efforts to support change
in the district.
The fifth chapter describes the first year of project implementation. A number of barriers to implementation other than resistance
are identified and shown to have affected the development of the project's several components. After three months, conflict developed
between the superintendent and one faction of the faculty. This conflict expanded to include the school board and ES/Washington, and it

FIGURE 1.1

Timelines for Butte-Angels Camp ES Project

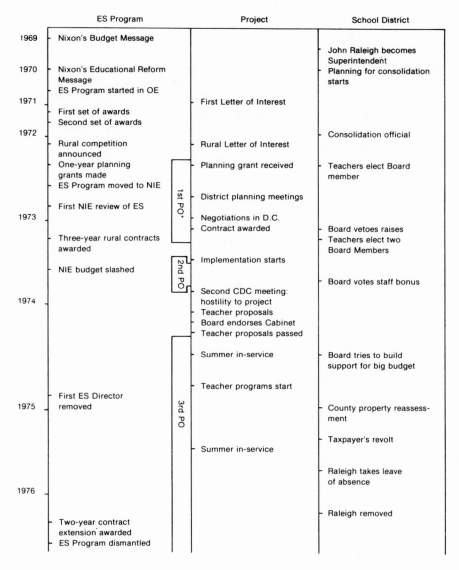

	ES Program	Project	School District
1969	Nixon's Budget Message		
1970	Nixon's Educational Reform Message ES Program started in OE		John Raleigh becomes Superintendent Planning for consolidation starts
1971	First set of awards Second set of awards	First Letter of Interest	
1972	Rural competition announced One-year planning grants made ES Program moved to NIE First NIE review of ES	Rural Letter of Interest Planning grant received District planning meetings	Consolidation official Teachers elect Board member
1973	Three-year rural contracts awarded NIE budget slashed	Negotiations in D.C. Contract awarded Implementation starts	Board vetoes raises Teachers elect two Board Members Board votes staff bonus
1974		Second CDC meeting: hostility to project Teacher proposals Board endorses Cabinet Teacher proposals passed Summer in-service Teacher programs start	Board tries to build support for big budget
1975	First ES Director removed	Summer in-service	County property reassessment Taxpayer's revolt
1976	Two-year contract extension awarded ES Program dismantled		Raleigh takes leave of absence Raleigh removed

1st PO*   2nd PO   3rd PO

*PO = Project Officer

precipitated the project's transformation. Chapter 6 describes the outcomes of the transformation of the ES project along with the unanticipated consequences for the whole district—a new balance of power.

The concluding chapter—Chapter 7—summarizes what has been learned. It suggests reformulations of assumptions about how to produce change and suggests implications for change oriented administrators and others.

To understand the events described in this study, it is necessary to follow three different trains of events: the history of the ES Program in Washington, the history of the Butte-Angels Camp District, and the development of the project. Figure 1.1 presents timelines for each of these histories to show how they are related. The reader may wish to refer to this figure during the course of the narrative that follows.

2

BETWEEN TWO COMMUNITIES

The dual nature of public school systems means that administrators must respond to two publics. Schools are, simultaneously, service organizations where children who cannot evaluate what they need are cared for by professional educators and commonweal organizations governed by popularly elected school boards (Zeigler and Jennings 1974). Hence, administrators must attend to both the local community that sends its children to school and pays taxes and to the professional community of teachers' colleges, researchers, professional associations, and state and federal agencies that provide special expertise, change ideas, and funds. The different outlooks of these communities led to contradictory ideas about what schools should do when the Butte-Angels Camp project began.

This tension was actually increased by ES/Washington. On the one hand, it assumed that community support for a project would facilitate implementation so it mandated community participation in planning. On the other, it expected each project to take advantage of advances in the state of the art in education (Herriott 1979). To understand the district and its project, it is important to know how the interests of the local community and national educators differed, the strength of pressures emanating from each source, and how they were reconciled.

After describing the history of the communities of Butte and Angels Camp, this chapter describes the community's interest in education and then looks at ideas emanating from the national level before identifying ways in which conflicting pressures were resolved.

THE COMMUNITY SETTING

The towns of Butte and Angels Camp are located in a mountainous region about 400 miles from Denver, the nearest major city. The steepness of the mountains, covered by rich stands of ponderosa pine and white spruce, precludes any extensive farming or ranching. About three-quarters of the district is national forest land managed by the National Forest Service for timber production. These outlying areas are sparsely populated, and it is doubtful that there would be any population concentration at all were it not for the mineral wealth of the mountains, especially gold.

Until the 1870s the region was an Indian reservation, but when gold was first discovered, white people came flocking in. Within a year, the population had jumped to over 15,000, and all the towns and hamlets that exist today had been founded.

Angels Camp and Butte were distinguished from other mining camps of the time primarily by their permanence. This area boasted a large vein of low-grade ore that extended into the mountains several thousand feet below the surface and ran right under the town of Butte. The mineral rights to this vein were quickly consolidated by the Deep Down Mining Company, and by 1912 the Deep Down Mine produced five times as much bullion as the other 18 mines combined. It continued to dominate until all competition disappeared in 1959.

The shift from prospecting to mining in the early 1880s brought a change in the social character of Butte and Angels Camp. Early prospectors who came to make a quick killing and get out fast rarely had families, but the miners who replaced them were seeking steady work and brought wives and children with them. Within two years of their founding, there were private schools in both Angels Camp and Butte and a public school in the latter.

During the prospecting period, Angels Camp was the major town of the region and Butte only a minor camp, but the development of the Deep Down Mine changed that relationship. By 1905 the population of Butte was 8,000 people and that of Angels Camp about 4,400. The growth of mining also affected the ethnic composition. While the earliest settlers were of U.S. birth or from the British Isles, they were joined in later years by European immigrants, so that, by 1890, Butte resembled a little Chicago or New York more than a Dodge City or a Cripple Creek.

The turn of the century marked the beginning of a fitful population decline. There was a major exodus in the 1920s when it was feared that the Deep Down vein had played out, but the 1930s brought a renaissance. The Depression provided a big impetus to the gold industry and the mine became by far the largest industry in the state and, for many people, the only hope of steady work. An executive order during World War II halting extraction of nonstrategic minerals closed the mine and almost emptied Butte, but most residents moved back in the immediate post-War period. The 1950 populations of Butte and Angels Camp were about 6,500 and 3,300, respectively. From then on, numbers fell. In 1970 the cities included 5,200 and

2,500; the population of the whole district was just under 10,000. Population declines have been reflected in the enrollments of the Butte and Angels Camp schools, which dropped from a peak of 3,000 students in 1966 to just over 2,300 when the ES project began in the fall of 1973. They would continue to decline throughout the project's history.

Since the region was so dependent on mining, these population shifts reflected predictions about trends in the local gold industry. In the 1960s its future seemed precarious. In the 1950s the Deep Down Mining Company began diversifying, and by the 1970s only about a quarter of its earnings came from the mine. Meanwhile, the cost of extraction increased as the vein was followed well more than a mile below the surface. At the same time, the fixed price of gold at $35 an ounce made it apparent that mining would soon be unprofitable. The decision to allow the price of gold to vary brought a new lease on life to both towns, but their future would continue to depend on the price of this single commodity.

The two towns differed in their dependence on mining. Butte's was much more direct. Three-quarters of those employed in that city worked directly in mining, and the mine itself physically dominated the east end of town. Three miles away, Angels Camp was more indirectly dependent. Only a fifth of its work force was employed at the mine; the town was essentially a regional shopping center. While about $2 million were spent annually on goods in Butte, five times as much was spent in Angels Camp. The latter town, because of its gold rush history and the rich recreational opportunities in the surrounding area, was also a tourist center. In addition, it housed the county seat. Some logging and ranching were conducted in the outlying areas.

A working class area, its school district showed neither grinding poverty nor great affluence. In 1970 about 10 percent of the families in the district had incomes below the poverty level, but only a little more than a fifth had family incomes over $10,000. Angels Camp had both slightly more wealth and poverty than did Butte. About half the population had graduated from college in each town. The district's population included a small group of American Indians, less than 5 percent, who had moved in to work at the mine, but it was essentially white. About 15 percent of the residents were second- or third-generation ethnics, with Scandinavians, Germans, and Britons predominating.

Unions have never been powerful in the school district. An early miner's union was ended by a lockout in 1910. After several attempts to organize after World War II, mine employees did vote to unionize in the middle of the 1960s. The union held its first strike six years later. Generally, however, the union has been relatively passive and has had much less impact on the community than on the mine. An attempt to organize newspaper workers in the early 1970s failed completely. In fact, the state as a whole has not been conducive to unionism; the strongest employees' association in the state is the State Teachers Association, an affiliate of the National Education Association (NEA).

Most nineteenth century miners were Democrats, and mining camps often supported political radicals. As late as 1908, Angels Camp had an active socialist party. The early mine management was Republican, however, and it set its stamp on Butte. Although the county went for Bryan in 1896, Butte did not. Since then Republicanism has grown: Republican presidential candidates carried the county every year after 1916. Voters traditionally favored Republicans in state and local elections, often giving losing candidates their largest county majorities in the state. As the ES project began, 62 percent of all registered voters in the county were Republicans, as were all state and county officials and the area's U.S. Congressman.

This Republicanism was only one indication of a pattern of fiscal conservatism that characterizes the district. While the cost of county services doubled in the 20 years preceding the start of the ES project, most of this increase was due to inflation. The county government resisted property reassessments for several years, and the Butte city government began laying off employees well before fiscal constraints became serious in other U.S. cities.

LOCAL INTERESTS IN EDUCATION

The community's orientations to the school district were shaped by the area's conservative heritage and declining financial base. They also reflected the fact that the community dealt with a number of governmental agencies at the town and county levels. Moreover, since the community consisted of voters who were not parents and since parents were concerned with more than just the schools' educational programs, local orientations toward schools included positions on a number of issues not normally considered by educators whose outlook is more specialized. Residents were concerned about three issues: the costs of schooling, the quality of schooling, and the nature of the district's wider impact on the community.

The Low-Tax Ideology

The recent history of the Butte-Angels Camp area indicates the presence of a strong low-tax ideology that is applied to schools and to other governmental agencies. This ideology has been noted in other rural areas of the nation, especially in times of recession and declining economic growth (Vidich and Bensman 1968). The mine's economic problems had placed severe constraints on local schools. In the 1960s Butte and Angels Camp had separate school districts, and the financial conditions of the two towns differed considerably. By 1967 the Angels Camp schools had overspent their income in three of the six preceding years, accruing a debt of $105,000. In 1964/65 they enrolled just over 1,000 students but had a tax base of only $8.5 million. In contrast, the Butte system, because of the Deep Down Mine, had about 2,000 students, but a tax base of $23 million. Still, it too was feeling the pinch. In the late 1960s it began spending its then considerable reserves to balance its operating budget. Consolidation of the two districts in 1971 was mandated primarily to equalize the tax base of the two towns, but the change was not successful. The Butte surplus was absorbed, and by the spring of 1974, the combined district developed a $134,000 debt on a $2.2 million budget.

The district's financial problems stemmed from three sources. First, although the state's budgets usually projected a substantial surplus of income over expenditures during this period, it was in the bottom tenth nationally in providing operating funds to local school districts. Only about 15 percent of the district's income came from state sources. Second, as part of the national forest, much of the property in the district was exempt from taxation. Although the Forest Service did pay a small amount to the county to support the schools, district representatives argued that the amount was much less than would be received if that land were taxable at state rates. During the course of the project, the school board began lobbying with the area's U.S. Representatives and Senators to get the Forest Service reimbursement rate raised.

Finally, over the years, the school board and superintendent argued that much of the property in the district had become underassessed and that the schools should be receiving more income from local sources than, in fact, they were. The county government assessed property, set mill levies, and collected taxes. The school boards in the county held that the government was not complying with state law, which required the assessment of property at 60 percent of its value, but rather following an unwritten custom in the state of assessing at about 40 percent of true value. The districts held that proper assessment practices would alleviate their financial problems and appealed to the county repeatedly for relief. They had no success until a major reassessment was conducted in 1975.

The district's recent history indicates that opposition to providing more support for schools was easier to mobilize into a political force than was support. The board felt it was in a financial crisis during the spring of 1974. Faced with its second straight annual deficit, projections of increased costs, and the probability that its income would not be increased, the board felt "squeezed between costs and the county," as one member put it. * A number of budget reductions, including the unpopular act of closing a school, had been suggested, but members felt that, "We're cutting to help the (county) commissioners." Before making those cuts, the board tried to create support for its requests for more money by publicizing its problems and holding a series of well-advertised public forums to which the commissioners and state legislators were invited.

The first forum, held in conjunction with the July board meeting, drew a little over 100 people, a number that did not impress a state legislator who commented midway through the meeting:

> You finally got a decent crowd here, but with as basic a
> problem as this is, the place ought to be jammed. But
> the feeling I get is that people feel there's too much
> taxes. That's all over, not just in Butte and Angels Camp.

This feeling was echoed by all but one of the speakers from the floor. For instance, one woman said, "I have three daughters in the school system. I think you should cut out extra offerings." Even parents from the endangered elementary school only mounted a tepid resistance. After this session, the school board voted approval of all proposed cuts. A second meeting the following month drew no public response at all.

The lack of attention to the board's attempts to elicit support for the school system is in marked contrast to the public response to an increase in property taxes six months later. The county undertook the first massive update of assessments in 20 years in 1974, and taxpayers were shocked when property tax bills were distributed in January 1975. Some increases of 50 percent to 100 percent were reported. In response, a grassroots movement to lower taxes and local government spending was started. Over 450 people attended each of two public meetings to quiz officials on government expenditures and taxing procedures. At these meetings, a Taxpayers' Association was organized and various actions, including recalling elected officials, were discussed, although no action was taken.

The Taxpayers' Association tried to pursuade government agencies to reduce their expenses and, in the case of the county, decrease taxes directly. Attention was focused on the city of Butte,

---

*Unless otherwise noted, inserted quotes are taken from the author's field notes or from personal interviews.

which was implementing a new garbage collection procedure to meet
Environmental Protection Agency requirements. This new service
required a new, direct monthly charge to residents of $3.50. The
Taxpayers' Association organized a meeting to discuss the issue. It
was attended by 300 angry citizens, and 50 percent of the city's voters
took part in a special referendum election that saw the ordinance for
the new system voted down 1,242 to 345.

As the largest local government operation, the school system
did not escape the attention of the Taxpayers' Association.* About
45 people attended the March 1975 board meeting, and 90 came to the
one in April. Their message was clear. As one of the group's leaders announced to loud applause: "I'm here for only one thing. I recognize that the schools are working on trimming their budget. I'm
telling you that you may have to cut programs you think you can't cut."

A review of the objections to increased tax rates voiced during
these meetings highlights the salient elements of the low-tax ideology.
At the same time, by providing illustrations of similar objections
made to other local governmental agencies, it is possible to show that
the low-tax ideology was a general feature of the local community,
not something that was school specific. As such, it was all the more
difficult to change.

The most frequent criticism of the schools was that they were
run wastefully and managed finances poorly:

> If you cut the budget and still go in the hole, your budget's
> no good.

> I wonder if the quality of the school system is keeping up
> with its budget. Frankly, I doubt it from the products
> I've seen.

These comments indicate a general concern that increased expenditures were not reflected in a better "product" and that good
business practices were not being used. The scheduling of school activities—the long summer vacation, short school day, and the "open
campus" at the high school that allowed students not taking classes to
leave the buildings—gave the impression that schools were especially
unproductive and led to comments that the "schools let the kids out
any time of day. That's not right 'cause we are paying for a full day's
education."

---

*In 1970 the combined budgets of the county government and the
cities of Butte and Angels Camp totaled $1.24 million, a figure equal
to approximately 60 percent of the school district's budget.

While schools seemed especially open to charges of waste, complaints were made about the inefficiency and poor management of other
government agencies. Specific practices, such as irregular collection
of back taxes, were frequently cited.

Graft and provision of unwanted services were believed to be
major sources of wasted tax money. The superintendent's house was
the most frequently cited example of graft in the district. Like other
school districts in the state, the Butte-Angels Camp schools owned a
house that the superintendent lived in rent free. This provision of
free housing to the superintendent seemed unfair to many, and it was
suggested that the school board sell the house "so people can see that
he's paying his own way." This house was also a source of frequent
rumors of alleged misuse of school funds. One school supporter said,
"I don't know what went on in the superintendent's house, but you'd
think he had a gold-plated bathtub."

This concern was not limited to the superintendent. A variety
of new developments in teaching were perceived as mere conveniences
to the teacher with no educational impact:

> Did [the school district] buy ten color TVs? Why? Were
> they needed? . . . I don't object to television if they are
> in the classrooms and not in the teachers' lounge.

> I don't think we should spend so much money on aides.
> Nowadays everything is prepared, and those aides are
> just a waste of money. Teachers should do more for
> themselves.

The suspicion of graft was voiced in noneducational areas as
well. For instance, the new garbage collection scheme for Butte was
opposed largely because the company that contracted to do the work
was headed by the recently resigned chief of the Butte police force.
Moreover, the city attorney was also the lawyer for the new corpora-
tion. Accusations that he was "sitting on both sides of the fence,"
and that various city officials were stockholders in the new company
were made repeatedly. Revelations of a kick-back scandal in Angels
Camp and the disappearance of funds from the County Treasurer's
Office in the ensuing months suggested that these suspicions were not
completely unfounded.

Aside from their suspicions that funds were misused, Taxpayers' Association members did not even want many services the district offered:

> I think you should cut out extra offerings and mini-courses.
> You have courses in Negro Studies, Southwest Asia, and

> Bible Studies. Ten years ago, these were all in American
> history and world literature. If the child is given a good
> background in the basics, he can learn what he wants to
> pursue later.
>
> The school district is the only government entity in debt.
> It will get money to pay off the debt . . . and put it into
> new tape recorders.

Plant changes that would facilitate the education program—including
a plan to build a combination gymnasium-cafeteria-library at the district's most crowded elementary facility—were also opposed.

Perhaps because it was one of the most visible parts of the system, the busing program received frequent complaints even before
the Taxpayers' Association organized. Busing Butte's junior high
children to Angels Camp and that town's high school students to Butte
seemed wasteful to the local community, as did the use of large buses
for long runs into outlying rural areas where very few children lived.

Outside the field of education, the most frequent complaints
about unwanted services concerned environmental protection. Federal regulations mandated that Butte and Angels Camp develop their
first sewage treatment facilities ever, as well as the garbage collection system previously discussed. During years of negotiations
between the local sanitary district, which was responsible for sewage
treatment, and state and federal authorities, local officials frequently
pointed out the problems and expenses government regulation caused.

Anger about the waste and mismanagement of public monies
was accompanied by a deep concern over the growing burden that increasing taxes placed on individual citizens. A county commissioner,
for instance, told the school board:

> I sat in a meeting of the Equalization Board to hear tax-
> payers' problems today. These problems mostly con-
> cerned homes. I'm a senior citizen. Many of them are
> being taxed out of their homes.

This statement reflected the feeling that, however legitimate specific
expenditures might be, the tax burden was becoming unbearable for
many people. Even before the Taxpayers' Association was organized,
fear of strong public reaction had kept local officials from raising
taxes substantially for many years. Moreover, they were especially
sympathetic to the position of many residents who, they felt, could
not afford higher taxes.

Another complaint about taxes directed specifically at the
schools was that people who do not use schools must still pay for
them. Most of the concern was for the elderly. Senior citizens were

a potent enough political force for two older county commissioners to publicly number themselves as members of that group. Senior citizens objected to paying for educational services they did not use because they were too old to have children, and the legitimacy of their objections was acknowledged by others:

> I know old folks who own property and pay large taxes to support the schools and other people who don't own property so their kids are educated free. That's not fair.

The argument was generalized from senior citizens to all property owners without children, and it was suggested that only families that use the schools should pay for them:

> It's wrong for property owners to support the schools. The people who send their kids should pay.

> I don't have any kids, but I still pay taxes. Maybe I and the people with no children should be exempt.

The low-tax ideology was part of the area's conservative, Republican heritage, as evidenced by a survey of residents conducted by Abt Associates in 1973/74. Its results show that the low-tax ideology was applied to the schools even before the Taxpayers' Association organized. In a pair of open-ended questions about the schools, 40 percent of the respondents mentioned that the district had financial problems, but most comments were opposed—63 to 48—to raising taxes in order to increase the schools' incomes. Moreover, the main themes of the ideology were repeated in the survey responses. There were 42 comments to the effect that the schools wasted the money they were receiving, and 21 complaints that taxes were too high or inappropriately collected even before property was reevaluated.

Education in the Basics

Educational goals are difficult to state clearly and to measure. Sets of goals are often contradictory because schools are expected to provide such a wide range of services. Educators have great difficulty in identifying and reconciling educational goals, so it is not surprising that residents' discussions of preferred goals are diffuse and difficult to interpret. The following notes record impressions of a discussion at the high school between lay people and teachers of a proposal to revise the district's mathematics program:

> I was impressed with the diffuseness of the parents' concerns. They were talking about independent study and

whether kids were getting enough supervision. They
talked about their experiences at Central School and the
Junior High as well as at the High School, and it was
very difficult for them to sit down and consider the actual
proposal, partly because their concerns are diffuse and
related to other things besides the math program per se.

Still, the conservative outlook that the community brought to financial
matters was also applied to the question of educational goals. Field
notes indicate:

A thread going through parents' comments of conservatism,
of "there should be more supervision of kids. . . ." Parents referred to their own experience about what they had
done in school. One guy made an analogy between teachers
and sergeants at a boot camp.

Central to this conservative outlook was an interest in the basics,
an interest shared by opponents and supporters of the district's
schools. For instance, one active lay supporter reported that:

Two of my kids have taken Mountain Survival now, and they
both enjoyed it. I'm all for having my kids enjoy these
things in school and enjoy themselves, but what about the
basics? Let's get back to the basics!!

As this comment indicates, one always "got back" to the basics instead of progressing toward them. Their importance was often emphasized with references to the old days, "when I was in school."
The basics refers to the content of instruction. The basics always
included reading, writing, and arithmetic, and they sometimes included standard government and geography courses. The basics were
preferred to the growing number of special social studies courses
focusing on different parts of the world and on minority groups in this
country, as well as to a growing number of electives in the high school.
As the leader of the Taxpayers' Association told a meeting, "I don't
believe mini-programs should be paid for by the school. They can
learn knitting at home." Parents, too, advocated limiting the number
of special courses. Even literature courses on such works as the
Bible came under fire.

There was only one area where community residents wanted an
expansion of the curriculum—vocational education. Said one mother:

The community is interested in vocational education. I've
heard it for the 12 or 13 years I've been here. They felt
that only the top percent of students are educated.

Since only about a quarter of the district's graduating seniors entered college and the area's mine-based economy offered opportunities for individuals with occupational training, vocational education was believed to have a practical value that most of the new courses being offered in the district did not.

Along with an interest in the basics, there was strong pressure for greater discipline.* Interest in discipline did not mean that children should always be treated in a regimented way that ignored individual differences,† but simply that more control of children was needed, especially in the upper grades.

The local community wanted more discipline partly because it was shocked and worried by the behavior of local youth. Complaints about vandalism and the use of drugs among young people and about high school girls getting pregnant were frequently linked to poor control of students by the schools. As one community resident wrote on a questionnaire, "Number-one problem is drugs, and second is discipline. New freedom given students have [sic] led to problems which are hard to resolve." While this concern about the behavior of local youth was general, there were numerous complaints about the high school's "open campus" policy that allowed students to leave school when they did not have classes. As one mother who generally supported the schools said:

> We have kids running around town all day and this, to my
> knowledge and in my opinion . . . , is probably the reason
> why we have so many kids getting pregnant in the high
> school.

At the same time, the local community disagreed with the professionals' concept of the student as a potentially self-motivated learner. Instead, they viewed children as recalcitrant and school

---

*Complaints about discipline were more frequent than anything else in the open-ended responses on the Abt Associates Resident Survey. Of 333 respondents, 83 specifically mentioned that the district's disciplinary policy was not strict enough or that children were wild and out of control.

† In responses to the open-ended questions on the Abt Associates Resident Survey, 27 respondents specifically indicated that they liked the kind of personal attention children received (before the Experimental Schools Program started) in this district, and another 26 indicated that they approved of the small classes and size of the schools because children were known to their teachers and not lost in the crowd.

work as a difficult activity that children would not undertake voluntarily:

> This may be what my one objection is to the school right
> now: They do not press upon those kids that they're going
> to have to spend some time outside school studying. . . .
> Any kid that hasn't grown up to being disciplined to get his
> head into the books after he gets out of school is really
> going to have a tough freshman year at college.

Without discipline, it was argued, students would not learn to work hard enough at school to get ahead in life. If the district intended to change its approach to discipline, the community clearly wanted to increase control of students, not decrease it.

Community Services

Community residents were also concerned with the district's direct impact on community life through the entertainment the schools provided the general public, the ability of the district to transport students to school and to generally provide schooling in ways convenient to adults, and the contribution of educational institutions to local community integration. National professionals rarely consider these matters in their assessment of public educational systems.

The schools provided a major source of entertainment for the two towns. The most popular activities were the major sports programs, particularly football and basketball. These activities were well attended by both students and adults, many of whom had no other connection with school programs. Much of the small talk among men in the community centered on the fate of the high school teams; the quality of coaching and refereeing; the better players, some of whom became local celebrities; the prospects of winning the following week; and, during basketball season, the likelihood of attending the state tournament.

Many other extracurricular activities involved cultural events or performances. Beginning early in the elementary grades, students put on numerous plays, Christmas programs, and vocal and instrumental concerts. Although attendance varied, performances at the high school level usually drew audiences as large as those attending the local movie theater, and received extensive news coverage. The bulk of the articles the district placed in the local newspaper were human interest stories previewing or reporting on various student activities.

In addition the district ran an adult education program that served about 185 people a year. It provided an opportunity for high school dropouts to work toward a General Education Diploma (GED), as well as a variety of courses like typing, welding, and adult physical education.

Another important service the district provided was transportation so children in outlying areas could easily attend school in town. Although three-quarters of the district's population was concentrated in the two towns, families were scattered throughout its 430-square-mile area. Even for town residents, the closing of a school was inconvenient. Between 1971 and 1976 attempts to close one school in Butte and another serving 15 children in a rural area were strongly resisted by residents of those attendance areas. On other occasions, small delegations would appear at school board meetings to request that a bus route be altered so one or more families could be better served.

The schools also promoted integration of the local community by reinforcing the ties among its members and providing symbols for common identification, but professional educators rarely attended to this latent function they helped perform. Every day almost a quarter of the district's population (the students) found a field for sustained social interaction within school walls, and public functions offered a setting for adults to interact as well. Moreover, the district was one of the few important institutions over which the local community still had the right to exercise some control through the election of the school board. Finally, as school districts were consolidated, high schools in particular became rarer, and the very existence of such an institution became a status symbol (Alford 1960).

As in other rural areas, attempts to bring together the Butte and Angels Camp districts in the 1960s acted as a litmus test of the importance of these integrating functions to local residents. Fearing that their schools would be attached to Butte, Angels Camp residents rejected two attempts by their school board to dissolve their district, including one that specified that attachment should be to a small elementary school nearby with an unusually large tax base. Tensions between the two towns were very high. Angels Camp residents argued:

> The average family of Angels Camp is higher class than the one in Butte, regardless of income. There are more transients and roughnecks in Butte.

Nor was all resentment found in Angels Camp, as the following excerpts from a letter to the local paper indicates:

> The Angels Camp District attached itself to the Butte District voluntarily. We didn't vote it in or refuse to accept it. But what was the first thing the Angels Camp Board did after voting the attachment? They drew up a list of

recommendations to the Butte Board. . . . The first and
foremost thought in the minds of the Angels Camp Board
was their name. [That recommendation had been to call
the newly formed district the Butte-Angels Camp Independent School District—author]. . . Why should Butte be
recognized, you asked? Well, in the first place, by attaching itself to Butte, Angels Camp is now just a part
of the Butte District, which has been operating for some
time. In the second place, the Butte School Board is the
governing body of the district and were [sic] needed by
patrons of the Butte district. . . . No change is needed
in the name of the BUTTE INDEPENDENT SCHOOL
DISTRICT.

Once community residents stopped fighting the state-mandated
reorganization, attention shifted to matters affecting the distribution
of community status: the district's name and its high school organization. A proposal that originated in Angels Camp to maintain a
separate high school there was ultimately rejected, since economy
and technical improvements could only be attained by reducing the administrative cadre to one superintendent and one business manager
and by using the larger Butte High building for grades 9 through 12
and the one in Angels Camp as a junior high for grades 7 and 8. In
other areas, attempts were made to mollify community sentiments.
"Angels Camp" was added to the district name, and basketball games,
which were more frequent than football contests, were played in
Angels Camp.

PROFESSIONAL INTERESTS IN EDUCATION

In contrast to the local community, professionals found that university education departments, educational research and development
agencies, and federal agencies, such as the Office of Education and
the National Institute of Education, stressed educational functions to
the exclusion of other issues. These national educators were influenced by two factors that had minimal impact locally. The first was
the culture of educators and historical developments within the occupational group. Where the community tended to be conservative,
professionals were more liberal, and they developed a view of the individual learner that was at odds with the local outlook. The second
factor was a series of national trends from which Butte and Angels
Camp were isolated. Many innovations, especially the ideas behind
the ES project, that were adopted and implemented locally were designed by professional educators. Without conducting an exhaustive

survey of the national educational system, this section examines some factors that increased the costs of education locally, the background to some new educational ideas in the district, and the views of national professionals toward community services.

Increased Educational Costs

Although deeply concerned with ensuring adequate income for local schools, national professional educators have not developed an outlook comparable to the community's low-tax ideology. Since the late 1950s, two national educational trends—collective bargaining and an increased interest in implementing a variety of innovations—have increased the costs of schooling.

The effects of the movement toward collective bargaining that received major impetus from the New York teachers' strikes of 1960 and 1962 were felt much later in this state than in other parts of the country. In the early 1960s, the State Education Association (SEA) had very little interest in negotiations. Its primary activity was lobbying in the state for increased aid to education and teacher pension plans, and its small staff did not maintain effective liaison with local organizations. At that time, school administrators were very active at both the state and local levels. In Butte, for instance, the superintendent required that all teachers join the local association.

The impetus for negotiations came primarily from the national level. The major push came from the National Education Association (NEA), which was involved in a national membership competition with the American Federation of Teachers (AFT). In 1962 the NEA took a much more aggressive stand than it had previously and launched a program to initiate collective bargaining. Most local associations showed very little interest in negotiations. The Butte association, which was one of the more aggressive, confined its activities to working to institute a formal grievance procedure.

At first, progress was very slow. SEA sent its field staff to various local associations, promoting the ideal of negotiations and, at the same time, directed its state lobbying activities toward getting a collective bargaining statute through the legislature. The bill that was passed in 1969 required boards to "meet and confer" with teachers and specified a voluntary arbitration process, but it did not allow strikes.

After 1969 SEA continued to work for stronger state legislation by advocating the right to strike and, later, compulsory arbitration. Locally, it sought to strengthen each district association's ability to negotiate. The field staff was increased again through a combination of NEA subsidies and a special levy on most participating locals.

Membership drives began to highlight support for collective bargaining as a major service provided by SEA, rather than relying on administrators' authority.

These changes at the state level had their impact locally. In
Butte and Angels Camp, member attention shifted from earlier emphasis on social and quasi-in-service activities to collective bargaining. The best-attended meetings were those called to vote on the
salary package that had been worked out by teachers' representatives
and the school board. Shortly after the negotiations law was passed,
administrators dropped out of the association. A few years later, as
the tensions surrounding collective bargaining increased, the superintendent also ceased to be a member of the school board negotiating
team.

Collective bargaining had considerable impact on district budgeting procedures. Besides teachers, custodians and bus drivers
were also organized, and the salaries of these three groups constituted 60 percent of the district's operating budget. Other salaries ac-
counted for another 12 percent, and unorganized groups tried to maintain some parity with those that were organized. Hence, almost
three-quarters of the district's expenses were determined through
salary negotiations.

A second pressure from the professional community that raised
the costs of education was the national call for educational reform and
innovation. For instance, the 1950s saw a growing need for more
highly trained manpower in the labor force. This demand was translated into a concern to improve the quality of education, especially in
the sciences, by nationally visible individuals, foundations, and government agencies, a concern that became increasingly urgent with
the Russians' launching of Sputnik. Educators responded with the development of the "New Math" and "New Science" curricula, which
were quickly adopted by almost half the nation's schools (Clark 1966).

The civil rights movement added a new set of national priorities
in education. The Elementary and Secondary Education Act was
passed in 1965 primarily to increase equality of educational opportunity, and it also eliminated most previous barriers to federal aid to
education (Halperin 1975). Henceforth, the federal government would
stress the promotion of innovation in local schools and improvements
in classroom practices while giving special attention to deprived children. Change was supported through the financing of numerous research and development (R&D) projects that generated new ideas for
educational practice (in 1973, the government spent an estimated
$1.9 billion for educational R&D) and categorical aid grants to schools
(Kirst 1974). Presently, a wide variety of university centers, private companies, government agencies, and other organizations are
promoting a host of innovations. These include new curricula, the

use of behavioral objectives, teaming, career education, vocational education, and open classrooms, to name only a few.

Such pressures to innovate added to the costs of running the Butte-Angels Camp district. For instance, in the aftermath of Sputnik, the Butte elementary schools moved to a departmental organization and added specialist teachers to increase instructional competencies in different subject matter areas. Newly developed textbooks were also adopted. More recently, changes designed to increase the diversity of offerings and the range of student choice in the high school through mini-courses helped develop what the school board saw as an uneconomical faculty-student ratio, while special programs like a preschool for disadvantaged children and a work-study vocational program further increased the need for additional staff.

These national pressures to innovate ran directly counter to the low-tax ideology. Because of local pressures to decrease expenditures, few if any costly innovations could be supported through the district's general budget. Therefore, school personnel interested in implementing various nationally advocated innovations began canvassing the professional community in the form of federal and state agencies for the financial support they sought.

Approaches to Instruction

Because it is their livelihood, educators have much more detailed ideas about what should be taught and how than do community residents. These ideas reflect both current events and past work within the occupational group. While such ideas are numerous and vary specialty to specialty, two important trends in educational thought have affected program development in Butte-Angels Camp—individualized education and the profusion of curriculum offerings.

Individualized Education

The idea of child-centered or individualized education dates back at least to Rousseau. In the 1920s, the Progressive Education Movement included several innovations geared toward individualized instruction. By the end of World War II, the idea had entered the mainstream of professional educational thought, and phrases like "recognizing individual differences," "the whole child," "creative self-expression," and "adjusting the school to the child" had become part of the standard jargon of educators (Cremin 1961).

Since then, this theme has had considerable vitality and endurance. It flourishes in spite of the persistence of contradictory trends among professionals and a full-scale counterattack in the name of "rigor" during the 1950s and early 1960s. The Association for Super-

vision and Curriculum Development (ASCD) and the National Society
for the Study of Education (NSSE) both published yearbooks in the
early 1960s with titles like Freeing Capacity to Learn, Human Vari-
ability and Learning, and Individualizing Instruction. More recently,
interest has been heightened in the idea of the open classroom, first
used in England, and the Alternative Education Movement in the United
States. The federal government has also been interested in individualizing education. Besides the Butte-Angels Camp project, the ES Program funded several other projects organized around that idea.

The idea is buttressed in part by scientific evidence on individual human variation. The NSSE Yearbook (1961), for instance, re-
views the biological and psychological evidence that points to important variation with respect to intelligence, maturation rates, and interests—variation, it is argued, that cannot be accommodated by a
standardized instructional system. This scientific evidence is reinforced by a generally optimistic outlook regarding children, who are
viewed as both eager and able to learn naturally in many ways both in
and out of school. A diverse array of authorities is cited to show that
children actively try to make sense and create patterns out of their
experience, but such spontaneous approaches to learning are not believed to be automatic or necessarily effective. What is constant is
the potential to learn:

> The chief object of individualization is the release of po-
> tential in the individual learner. . . . By human potential
> we mean those nascent powers of unpredictable proportions
> which are within the person; powers which can be dimin-
> ished or expanded through educative (and other) processes.
> [ASCD Yearbook 1964, p. 13]

Most treatments of individualized education emphasize that the student
has value in-and-of-himself and that educational processes must be
judged in terms of both skills development and improved self-concept.

According to this outlook, the educator's search is for ways to
release the student's untapped potential. This cannot be done by standardized treatment of large batches of students, and educational reformers within the professional community periodically advocate
structural changes like the introduction of ungraded schools and team-
teaching, which are believed to facilitate frequent, flexible grouping
and regrouping of students. Within the classroom, teachers are
urged, insofar as is possible, to tailor treatment of each child to his
or her own specific needs. Teachers are counseled to diagnose the
special problems of each student and find ways to meet and resolve
each one. The only constant factor in individualized treatment of
children is a warm, supportive relationship based on the teacher's

positive regard for the student. If the teacher shows concern for each student, alienation from school will be reduced.

According to Carl Rogers and other humanistic psychologists, positive regard for the child is valued in itself and defined as:

> Having a positive attitude toward the pupil . . . prizing him as a thinking, valuing person beyond his immediate actions. When a pupil is positively regarded, he is freed in his feelings to be what he is at the moment, thus opening up his own reality to himself. [ASCD Yearbook 1964, p. 46]

This view of children suggests a soft approach to discipline. Harsh treatment of students is to be avoided. Arbitrary discipline that rests on acceptance of a teacher's position and is geared to classroom performance, either deportment or achievement, is believed to reduce the student's sense of his own worth and thereby increase anxiety. At the same time, emphasis on order and neatness as important ends in their own right is often decried because, it is held, significant learning can take place in a jumble of noise and confusion.

Most educational professionals do not deny that teachers should direct or control student behavior in some way; but they do counsel reasonableness, restraint, and a demonstration of concern for the child. Often their recommendations are indirect and too general to provide effective guidance in the classroom. The word discipline is never actually used in either the ASCD or the NSSE Yearbooks on "Individualized Education." In fact, this emphasis on the individual as a willing learner directs attention away from many of the other problems faced in the classroom, most notably, the need to work with groups of 20 to 40 or more children at a time. It is not clear how to balance the needs of individual children against standards of fair treatment and equity to the whole group or how to keep track of the work of many students. Occasional caveats that "complete individualization is not possible" implicitly acknowledge these problems, but they do not help resolve them.

In the Butte-Angels Camp district, interest in individualized education was fostered by an interest in treating learning disabilities. Although research on specific learning disabilities dates back to work with brain-injured children before World War II, these problems only generated widespread interest in the last 1960s. Work in this area strengthens the individualizing trend by elaborating a technical apparatus for diagnosing and treating student problems. Labels such as perseveration, dyslexia, hyperactivity, and those referring to a variety of perceptual problems help delineate a number of barriers to learning, and research on these problems suggests a number of possible ways to alleviate them.

An emphasis on learning disabilities also contributes to an optimistic view of students by providing special explanations for many kinds of "bad" behavior. There is less need to view students as recalcitrant, for instance, when many deportment problems can be interpreted as "hypertension," an uncontrollable response due to a neurological impairment. Moreover, among the many schools of treatment of learning disabilities, some specifically endorse an individualized approach to teaching children, emphasizing that many barriers to learning are caused by poor self-concept and counseling educators to create supportive learning environments for students (Gearhart 1973).

Learning disabilities research continues to direct attention away from group-related issues. This approach is a clinical one; the best-known institutes work with students individually or in small classes of seven or eight, thus reducing the problems of group management. The techniques developed for alleviating learning disabilities have been worked out in these settings while less attention has been given to their use in full-sized classrooms.

Broadening the Curriculum

The Progressive Education Movement, which introduced the ideal of individualized education, also popularized extracurricular activities and such subject areas as vocational education, home economics, physical education, and the arts. Numerous recent national developments have reinforced the broadening of the curriculum, although not all of them have been limited to the efforts of the professional community. For instance, in the early 1970s the push for racial equality and, later, various ethnic-group-power movements created interest in programs focusing on various cultural groups (for example, black studies, Chicano studies), especially at the college level, while concern with middle-class alienation brought a search for relevance that deemphasized some traditional fields of study and broadened the scope of the curriculum. Within the educational community, methods like modular scheduling allowed school systems to develop relevant curricula without making major commitments to new courses or sacrificing more traditional offerings.

In the early 1970s the Butte high school responded to these pressures by rearranging its schedule to allow for the development of minicourses (nine-week courses), primarily in the English and social science departments. "In the 1960s," said one of the teachers involved, "when there was more demand for information on social changes, we introduced quarter courses on relevant topics." These courses dealt with a variety of topics including black studies, Indian history, frontier literature, science fiction, marriage and sex education, and the Bible. At about the same time, the high school physical education department converted its program to emphasize carry-over activities like Ping-Pong and skiing that could be continued after graduation from high school.

Community Services

The local community's interest in the noneducational impact of the school district on the community is an area largely foreign to national educators. Many community services have now become such a routine part of school functioning that they rarely stimulate discussion among professionals. The rationale for introducing most of them focuses on students, not the community. For instance, the introduction of extracurricular activities was justified for its contribution to making school more enjoyable and providing citizenship training; now these activities are part of the standard U.S. high school. Universities and colleges provide preparation for coaches, band directors, and drama teachers without inquiring into the ancillary purposes or latent functions being served. Similarly, there is an attempt to justify adult education more in educational terms than in terms of community service. Such attempts have often been unsuccessful, however (Clark 1956).

The contribution of rural schools to community integration has been consistently misunderstood by educators. Since World War I, when educators were still self-consciously using industry as a model, they emphasized the greater efficiency of large schools. Economies of scale and the possibility of reducing the tax burden have all been offered as justifications for consolidation (Alford 1960). Even modern arguments in support of smaller schools emphasize the alienating atmosphere of large schools and the difficulty of acquiring large blocs of land rather than the noneducational consequences of integrating the local community.

THE EDUCATOR'S LICENSE

The local and professional communities created contradictory pressures for the Butte-Angels Camp district. The local community was most concerned with minimizing costs, but it was also interested in strengthening education in the basics, while national educators promoted individualized instruction and a variety of changes that increased costs. If both groups pressed hard for their interests, there would be an impasse. The strengthening of one group and weakening of another could affect the rate and direction of change in the district. School districts tend to receive the most direct pressure from the local community. District governance patterns, including the locally elected school board and heavy reliance on local property taxes, promote community control as do the frequent opportunities for direct observation based on propinquity. In contrast, national experts use professional status structures and communication networks (Clark 1966). The strongest sanctions available, such as removal of accreditation or state funding, are rarely employed. In Butte-Angels Camp, strong community ties could be expected to have the greatest impact on change projects.

The phenomenon of occupational license tends to weaken community pressures, however. Hughes (1958) says that each occupational group has its own license, a form of socially acknowledged permission to carry out certain activities in exchange for a living. These activities are not permitted of other groups, and, within this area of license, the occupational group has considerable leeway to carry out its work as it sees fit.

License is based on two factors. First, it is reflected in procedures for overseeing the group's work. The less the school board and the community oversee of budgetary personnel and program matters, the greater the professional staff is licensed. Such procedures did not provide great protection in Butte-Angels Camp. Community residents did not question the district's governance system, nor was there public demand for more participation in policy making. Neither the Taxpayers' Association nor the opponents of consolidation argued that they could not get a hearing or that they were excluded from deliberation. Nor did the public complain that its ideas were not incorporated in the district's ES project.

If any group feared its position was in jeopardy, it was the school staff, which on occasion made comments like the following:

> We're professionals, and we should be allowed to run the schools. It's fine to have input from people, but teachers should run the schools. Last year I told [another teacher] I thought it was important to get people's ideas. He said to me, "Would you let somebody come in and run your basketball practice?" That really set me up short. . . . If somebody's going to decide that a basketball practice has layups, I'm going to be the one, and gradually I've come to feel the same way about community involvement in the schools in general.

The school staff disliked formal public meets, which it feared would turn into gripe sessions. One teacher described the gripes she heard as follows:

A lot of them were mickey-mouse: Why can't they chew
gum or wear this or that when there was still a dress
code. Others dealt with the hot lunch program and
crowded buses. They were personal, not for the benefit of the community or the teachers' benefit or interest.

The public was also seen as capricious and having no consistent views
on education. Principals reported a story about how, during planning
for consolidation, a Deep Down engineer from Butte asked at a public
meeting why the Angels Camp students were downtown on Main Street
so much, "cause they seemed to have too much [free] time." Shortly
afterward, a woman from Angels Camp demanded that children get
more free time. "How can we stay in the middle of a situation like
that?" asked the principals. District personnel were generally more
concerned than the general public about the current pattern of school
governance and felt susceptible to harassment.

The second part of the occupational group's license involves the
willingness of the public to grant educators a mandate to perform their
tasks. As public trust weakens, so does the educator's license. In
effect, license is based on the logic of confidence—the willingness of
others to grant that educators are doing what they are supposed to do in
in a competent manner (Meyer and Rowan 1978).

The logic of confidence is most powerful when lay people acknowledge that they do not have the background to assess the competence of practitioners. The practice of medicine is a key example of
an occupation that has won the right to judge member performance.
The public accepts the assertion advanced by leaders of the occupational group that it lacks the background needed to tell legitimate
practitioners from quacks. Educators seek a similar right to monitor their own performance and determine what should be taught, but
such control is usually granted begrudgingly and only on certain conditions (Dreeben 1970; Hughes 1958).

In Butte-Angels Camp, the public felt competent to judge the
work done in school. Thus, a member of the Taxpayers' Association
asked the school board:

What happens if John Raleigh [the superintendent] doesn't
catch the faults of a teacher as he should? . . . Do you
file a complaint with John? If you hear complaints about
a teacher sitting in a room when he should be teaching,
do you go through John?

Residents felt they could assess the work of teachers because the educators' expertise was not believed to be special, nor the most im-

portant characteristic affecting their performance. Local people acknowledged that the staff was well-trained and competent, * but speakers at public meetings assumed they could pick out unqualified teachers. Numerous questions were related to teacher evaluation procedures and the ways the public could initiate action against teachers believed to be poor. Moreover, more concern and complaints centered on teacher "dedication"—their willingness to work and interest in students—than on the question of training. † Poor teachers were referred to as "time-servers" who "only care about their paychecks. " In addition, the idea that teaching is easy work was expressed frequently in public meetings through questions and complaints about the number of hours of student contact teachers have, the length of the school day, and the use of teachers' lounges. These comments suggest a view of teaching as a job that anyone can do if he puts his mind to it and that anyone can assess as well.

Residents of the Butte-Angels Camp area did not lack confidence in personnel of the school district, but confidence depended on the educator's ability to avoid actions to which the public objected. In the Resident Survey, respondents expressed much more confidence in teachers than administrators. Of the 97 comments on teachers in the open-ended questions, 53 were positive, which was only true of 14 of the 35 statements about the administration and 1 of the 18 about the superintendent. Residents were more critical of the administration because of its responsibility for financial management, and many of the problematic conditions in the school were attributed directly to the administration.

While governance arrangements and public confidence are the sources of license for most occupational groups, there is a third element that is especially important in the field of education—license by default (Hughes 1958). That is, while public confidence in educators is not high, laymen find it difficult to know what actually goes on in schools. Moreover, other issues are deemed more important, so education tends to be ignored.

There are two key examples of such license by default in the recent history of the Butte-Angels Camp School District. The first concerns the ES project. Its emphasis on individualized education, the use of learning techniques, and a somewhat liberated pedagogy put it out of step with the local community's interest in the basics and

---

*Eighteen of 22 comments on teachers' training in the Resident Survey were positive.

† Comments concerning teachers in the Resident Survey included 73 referring to dedication (15 negative) and 22 on training (14 negative).

firm discipline. Moreover, although the project was well publicized, it was pretty much ignored by community residents, as will become clear later (see Chapter 6). The second example is the taxpayers' revolt. Although the school board took some actions to mollify the Taxpayers' Association (it refused to build the all-purpose room at one school that district staff wanted), the issue was never really resolved; it simply died out as the public lost interest. Unable to find a tax-conscious candidate for the school board or to get people to continue to attend board meetings, the group simply disintegrated.

These examples indicate that anyone can participate in most school issues. Access is open; however, energy is limited. Community residents enter and leave in ways that are unpredictable to school staff. Residents can have a great impact, but they rarely remain involved. In fact, if there is one guide to prediction, it is that residents rarely become involved. Hence, school staff have license to operate, not because the public is confident in a positive sense, but because it does not care to intervene.

SPECIAL FUNDING

Another factor that can decrease community pressure while strengthening professional influence is the provision of special funds. This factor is also much easier to control than the various components of occupational license. Such funding can be especially powerful in cost-conscious districts like Butte-Angels Camp or during periods of economic scarcity. In more affluent times, these schools innovated on their own. For instance, in the 1950s the well-to-do Butte district departmentalized its elementary schools and added specialists without outside support. In the 1960s financing became more problematic. After the passage of the Elementary and Secondary Education Act in 1965, the federal government provided a major impetus to innovate through its categorical aid programs. Before then, according to one principal, "schools didn't change that much. You ordered books every so often." Afterward, the Butte schools used ESEA Title I funds to run a summer school that experimented with team teaching for disadvantaged high school students and, later, a preschool program. Before consolidation, the Angels Camp schools used Title III funds to expand their very small libraries. Other federal funds were used in the consolidated district to design an environmental education program for the junior high and operate small vocational programs.

By 1971 educators within the district who sought to implement professionally sanctioned activities looked for external support to cope with locally imposed financial limitations. The earliest proposals to the ES Program in 1971 indicated financial constraints on attempts to change:

> The greatest handicap to the successful culmination of the
> [consolidation] program will be due to lack of sufficient
> funds to guarantee implementation without being forced to
> cut back.

This same concern with monetary constraints on program expansion
was apparent in the district's successful application to the ES Program for rural schools, where the first system weakness mentioned
was lack of funds.

The district did include community residents in planning for its
project. However, the interest in vocational education expressed in
those meetings was not reflected in the final plan. The central theme
of the project—personalized education—was consonant with the professionally approved idea of individualized education, but it precluded
acting on locals' concerns to increase discipline, and its contribution
to an increased emphasis on the basics was not clear.

It is ironic that ES/Washington was so strongly committed to
community participation in program development, while its funds provided a means for local educators to develop a program consonant with
nationally approved ideas that lacked local support. Although the community preferred ideas about education that conflicted with the project's main theme, it did not impede implementation. In fact, the community's major concern—cost control—was met.

CONCLUSION

This chapter illustrates the complexity of the environment of a
school district. In Butte-Angels Camp, district staff must reconcile
the contradictory interests of the local and national professional communities. The local community applies the same outlook to the schools
that it does to other institutions. The locally held, low-tax ideology
emphasizes the wasteful nature of governments and their tendency to
misappropriate money or to provide unwanted services. It also highlights the pressures that governmental spending practices place on
individual citizens through increased taxes. Residents apply this
ideology to schools just as they do to agencies that collect garbage,
treat sewage, and maintain roads. At the same time, local residents
are interested in the entertainment and contributions to community
integration the district provides.

National professionals increase the costs of education through
teacher unionization and ideas about innovations, but they have not
developed an ideology relevant to money comparable to the local low-
tax ideology. Instead, they develop and disseminate ideas like individualized education and ways to expand the curriculum. These ideas

are neither completely understood nor strongly supported by the local community. Still, as long as the costs of education do not rise, children receive an education in the basics, and they are kept under control, the local community is tolerant of professional ideas.

This discussion highlights a problem of achieving a fundamental prerequisite for rational project design—consensus on goals. It also indicates that the problem is more complex than was suggested before. The district requires external consensus as well as internal agreement on its goals—a condition that is difficult to achieve.

There are at least four ways to cope with contradictory external pressures. First, a district can attempt to protect itself from the local community be designing procedures and administrative behaviors that drive the community away. This tactic was used by urban school districts, especially in the middle of the 1960s (Rogers 1968). Not only is it inimical to those who believe in local control of education; but in most districts, including this one, school employees lack the power or authority to make that approach effective in the face of any strong community initiative. Second, a district can use public relations techniques to build support for its ideas and a willingness to offer assistance. That approach certainly did not work in Butte-Angels Camp. Most of the time individual residents faced too many demands and had personal beliefs that were too strong for public relations to make a major impact.

A third tactic is to lie low and hope to be ignored. Many changes in public schools take place not because they are supported, but because they are not opposed. The Butte-Angels Camp ES project falls into that category. The problem with this approach is that it is difficult to know what will arouse public opposition.

Finally, it may be possible to play one community off against another. This tactic is most effective when one of those communities is willing to provide what another wants. In Butte-Angels Camp, federal funds alleviated the local community's major concern and allowed educators to pursue ideas that interested them and to which residents were somewhat opposed. These approaches are not rational at all. Instead, they are political means for one group to achieve its ends when it cannot obtain consensus from all parties. The following chapters will show that such dissension was typical in Butte-Angels Camp.

3

INTERNAL ORGANIZATION
OF THE DISTRICT

This chapter sets the stage for the Butte-Angels Camp ES project by describing the district's internal organization. At the same time it explores the assumptions about change indirectly. These assumptions require the existence of certain prerequisite conditions within a district. For instance, rational project design requires that a school district have clear goals. Decision makers must have the capacity to distinguish between important and unimportant goals as well as agreement on which ones are most important. Rational design also assumes that the district has sufficient control and means of coordinating its staff to ensure that plans will be carried out or adjusted during implementation in a way that is faithful to the original project intent.

The assumptions about resistance and participation include the idea that administrators' control of central staff is only mildly problematic. Resistance is usually assumed to be passive, and administrative control, while not complete, is taken to be substantial. Moreover, resistance is usually described in a way that assumes that it is a response to the project in question, not to some exogenous conflict that preceded the project. The extent of conflict in the district is assumed to be low most of the time. Finally, the use of comprehensive change assumes that school districts are so interdependent that organizational inertia will overcome attempts at piecemeal change, that is, change in numerous components of the district that can be reinforcing and is necessary to overcome inertia.

After briefly describing the district, prerequisite conditions for change are examined in sections on the district's goals, its internal control structure, integration and coordination, and conflict based on issues preceding the ES project.

THE BUTTE-ANGELS CAMP SCHOOLS

Although a small system by national standards, the Butte-Angels Camp School District was one of the largest in a state that, until the early 1960s, was made up primarily of one-room, one-school systems. During that time, Butte and Angels Camp each had separate districts with a high school and several local elementary schools. Through the 1950s, these systems were relatively wealthy for the region because of the mine, and were considered to be progressive and of high quality. Just after the turn of the century, the Butte and Angels Camp schools were among the first in the state to be certified by the North Central Accrediting Association. At that time, local teachers earned twice as much as those working in one of the few other comparably sized systems elsewhere in the state, and considerably more than they would in a one-room school. Positions in these districts continued to be highly desirable to state teachers until the 1960s when school consolidation and the equalization of property values between the mining area and other parts of the state closed the salary gap between local and surrounding schools. Many staff members continue to refer to the period when the Butte and Angels Camp schools were considered among the best in the state.

During the 1960s these two districts absorbed most of the rural school districts in the county, and in 1971 they were combined. In 1973 the consolidated district included 135 teachers and counselors in seven buildings. The high school (grades 9 through 12) in Butte was administered by a principal and assistant principal. In Butte the Central Elementary School had one principal, and another was in charge of the West Butte and Lincoln buildings. The latter was closed in 1974 because of declining enrollments. The Angels Camp schools, which served the whole district, were divided into a seventh-and-eighth-grade junior high school with one principal and an elementary school. The Angels Camp elementary principal also supervised three teachers in two rural buildings. The central office staff consisted of the superintendent, a business manager, and several secretaries. The staff would shrink throughout the project.

The 2,300 students in the district were, for the most part, neither high nor low achievers. Mean composite scores for grades 5, 7, 9, and 11 on the Iowa Test of Educational Development in the fall of 1973 ranged between the forty-seventh and fifty-second percentile. There was, however, a declining interest in college attendance—the proportion of seniors entering college dropped from 45 percent in 1968 to 29 percent in 1973. Counselors attributed this drop to the end of the Vietnam War and the draft; nonetheless, this change indicated that the community's interest in vocational education was justified.

Unlike some other rural districts where teacher turnover is high (Vidich and Bensman 1968), the Butte-Angels Camp staff was relatively permanent. Many teachers were born in the district, and still more had received their education there and had gone to college

at the state teachers' college 20 miles away. The 34 teachers interviewed in 1974/75 reported they had lived in the district for 15 years
on the average, and many of them had relatives in one of the two
towns. Some had small businesses like hamburger stands, invest-
ments in ski resorts, and door-to-door cosmetics sales routes. Stability was further increased by the tendency to hire new teachers from
among those who had taught in the district previously or were regular
substitutes or teachers' aides.

Ties to the community can become a condition for conflict,
since the likelihood of open opposition is increased when leaving an
organization is not a viable option (Hirschman 1970). Even if teaching positions were not scarce, the staff would be unwilling to leave because of its ties to the community. Within the district, employment
alternatives were limited primarily to hard and dangerous labor in
the Deep Down Mine.

John Raleigh, the district superintendent, was among the staff
members with deep roots in the community. He had gone to the now
defunct Catholic elementary school in Butte and then to Butte High
School. Such ties can help or hurt an innovative superintendent, and
they hurt Raleigh. Informants suggest that his boyhood peers also
working in the system were jealous of his success. Moreover, before
becoming superintendent, he had been assistant principal of the Butte
High School and assistant superintendent of the Butte system. In those
positions, he developed antagonisms with the staff, especially in the
junior high and the high school, where his office was located. When
the superintendency came open in 1967, teachers opposed his selection. Although they took no formal step to block him, board members
were aware of this opposition, but his lack of experience in financial
matters was a more important consideration. An older man who had
been superintendent in an adjoining district was appointed, with the
understanding that he would serve only for a short term and groom
Raleigh for the position. Within two years, the older superintendent
stepped down. Some teachers informally conveyed their dislike of
Raleigh to the board and the vote was close, but he was at last appointed to the position.

GOALS AND INTERESTS

Information on district goals can be found in the results of the
staff survey conducted in the fall of 1973 and in the documentation of
the planning for district consolidation in the fall of 1970. This planning activity was especially important for the ES project because a
number of issues first raised then resurfaced during ES project planning.

One of the problems the district faced was the diffuseness of its goals. In effect, everything was important and nothing was ruled out. The absence of selectivity was apparent in responses to a staff survey by Abt Associates in 1973. Teachers and administrators were asked to rate the importance of 12 possible outcomes of schooling, including development of basic skills, respect for authority, the ability to lead moral lives, the tolerance to get along with people of different races and occupations, and the ability to think for oneself. Goals could be rated from zero for unimportant to three for very important. Not surprisingly, basic skills instruction received the highest rating—2.9. However, the lowest score, that for understanding a philosophy of life, was 2.2. Hence, none of these items were less than moderately important. Of the 12 items, 10 received the highest possible rating from more than half the staff.

During the planning for reorganization, a centrally devised statement of goals for the new district was widely circulated and influenced the staff in their thinking about new programs. This statement exhibited the same diffuseness found in the survey responses. It identified 16 goals, including reducing the number of drop-outs, developing student interest in the "universe and the balanced ecology which must be maintained for survival," providing academic courses for those planning to go to college and vocational courses for students heading directly to work, and ensuring an extracurricular program that appealed to all students. In light of community and staff interests, a specific goal for basic skills instruction was conspicuously absent.

What drove the district was not these general goals but an array of special interests of individuals and groups within the system. (Interests related to personal gain, higher salaries, will be discussed later.) These personal interests were accompanied by a number of interests in implementing specific approaches to instruction or in adding courses. These educational interests are apparent in the documentation of the planning effort.

John Raleigh's views were outlined in the statement of the district philosophy. The preamble stated that "the objectives of the Butte Public Schools are to attain the cooperative development of the physical and mental processes so that each child may appreciate his total worth and grow in poise and self-esteem." More specific endorsement of an individualized approach to students was found in an example of how to write a curriculum objective appended to the philosophy that stated:

> Each child must have the opportunity to pursue a topic to the utmost of his ability.
> Definitions: Individualized Study—Planning so that the teacher spends less time in formal "oration" and

more time with smaller groups, and on many occasions,
with individual problems. Individualized programs are
not tracking processes. . . .
    Establishing a program of accelerated classes . . .
and slow classes is not a method of individualizing,
but is an abominable process of discrimination.

Teachers also had an opportunity to express their own professional interests during planning for reorganization. They were divided into 22 curriculum or grade-level groups and asked to develop
five-year plans for program improvement. These plans reflected
lukewarm support for John Raleigh's ideas and preference for a number of changes of their own choosing, most of which were minor modifications of existing programs to help them do their work more efficiently. Of the 22 groups, 12 discussed means to individualize education. Although the topic was more widely mentioned than any other,
there was no agreement on what the term meant. One group emphasized helping teachers recognize the needs of different students, another referred to individualization as a way of structuring courses,
and a third suggested buying individualized texts. One group took an
approach opposed by the superintendent that equated individualized
education with tracking.
    There was even some opposition to the general idea. A North
Central Association accreditation report on the high school in 1971
notes that, while working relations between students and teachers
were good, the school was characterized by regimentation not consonant with an individualized philosophy. Moreover, it suggested that
the ideas of some departments were not in harmony with the district
philosophy and should be revised.
    Most teachers did not oppose individualized education, but they
were more interested in other ideas. Nine groups, for instance, recommended developing a vocational education program. This idea
later became many teachers' preferred alternative to individualized
education as an organizing theme for the ES project. Nine others
wanted to eliminate letter grades, but two opposed the idea. A number of suggestions were made by only one group, including recommendations to:

    1. Offer Home Economics courses in the seventh grade and to
high school boys;
    2. Create a mathematics curriculum coordinator with the time
and authority to enforce uniform instruction in that area;
    3. Develop a unit on drugs for the elementary grades; and
    4. Shorten the length of the junior high day.

The range of ideas indicates that teachers thought primarily in terms of their own subject areas and grade levels; the kind of systemwide planning implied by the ES Program's requirement of comprehensive change was foreign to them. While these interests may seem mundane, some of them were deeply held. The consolidation effort did not result in the appointment of a mathematics curriculum coordinator or a shortened junior high school day. These issues were later raised during planning for the ES project in the fall of 1972 and again in the winter of 1974.

CONTROL OF STAFF

Research on educational organizations suggests that one important prerequisite for rational planning—sufficient control over staff to ensure that plans are implemented—is significantly absent. Lortie's (1969) seminal work suggests that elementary schools at least have a steep, centralized formal hierarchy of authority, but that in actuality teachers have considerable autonomy. There seems to be a zoning of control that permits administrators considerable influence over questions of finance and record keeping, while teachers maintain discretion over in-class affairs that interest innovators, those related to instruction. More recent research indicating that teachers have considerable autonomy in the instructional realm prompted the notion that schools and districts be viewed as "loosely coupled systems" (Meyer and Rowan 1978; Weick 1976).

Yet, studies of organizations frequently note that administrators' formal authority does not give them sufficient influence to accomplish their normal tasks, much less the implementation of planned change. It is suggested that informal exchanges between administrators and staff take place in a way that allows superiors to develop influence over their subordinates in exchange for a variety of different kinds of favors and assistance (Blau 1964; Homans 1961). Differences in administrators' abilities to manage such interal exchange may explain why some principals are much more able than others to exercise leadership that contributes to positive instruction (Gross and Herriott 1965).

A pattern of zoned control that gives teachers considerable discretion over instructional decisions could be a substantial barrier to a centralized, comprehensive program for individualized instruction. To find out how much control district administrators had at the project's outset, the everyday administration of the district is examined. The survey of staff conducted in the fall of 1973 is used to examine the zoning of authority in the districts and the limits placed on administrators. Then several areas where administrators and teachers interact are examined to see what exchanges take place and how they affect the distribution of control.

The Zoning of Control

Table 3.1 shows how the staff perceived influence to be distributed among the school board, the superintendent, principals, and teachers. Ten different decisions are examined, and a four-point rating scale is used, with zero indicating "no authority" and three meaning "decisive control."

Teachers had much more discretion over the organization of instruction (items 1 through 5) than over personnel and plant decisions. Instructional decisions were made either by teachers alone or by teachers and principals jointly. Influence of the superintendent, and especially the board, was limited. The superintendent was the most influential person for personnel decisions, although this influence was shared with the board, the principals, or both. Collective bargaining gave teachers minor influence in salary decisions, but that was all. The superintendent and board were perceived to make building decisions jointly, and principals also had some influence in that area.

In the instructional area, teachers' influence was greatest over short-term, single class issues (items 1 and 2). Principals had greater influence over decisions that affected the work of several teachers or had long-term consequences, such as the design of courses, textbook selection, and decisions on what courses to teach (items 3, 4, and 5). In the last area, the principals had more influence than teachers.

To find out how widely the distribution of control was accepted, the amount of influence respondents believed they had over these decisions was compared with the amount they felt they should have. People usually wanted more influence than they had, but the magnitude of the difference indicated how legitimate the existing arrangement was. Table 3.2 compares perceived and desired influence. Differences on this five-point scale range from 0.06 on the determination of daily lesson plans (item 2) to 2.19 on salaries (item 9), an issue that caused overt conflict.

For the most part, teachers were satisfied with their influence over instructional matters, although dissatisfaction rose as one moved from short-term, single-teacher issues to those affecting longer time spans and more staff, the ones where administrators played a larger role. Teachers were moderately unhappy with their influence over what courses would be given (item 5). Moderate discontent also characterized teachers' feelings about how all personnel decisions were made, except that responses to the salary issue revealed serious op-

TABLE 3.1

Distribution of Influence over Selected Issue Areas in the Butte-Angels Camp District

Issue Area	Mean Influence by Position			
	School Board	Superin-tendent	Principals	Teachers
1. Determining concepts taught on a particular day	0.04	0.30	0.63	2.92
2. Determining daily lesson plans and activities	0.01	0.27	0.83	2.91
3. Establishing objectives for each course	0.21	1.05	1.63	2.82
4. Selecting required texts and other materials	0.44	1.65	2.16	2.39
5. Adding or dropping courses	0.80	1.76	2.60	1.87
6. Hiring new teachers	1.87	2.89	2.06	0.22
7. Deciding whether to renew a teacher's contract	2.03	2.88	2.29	0.15
8. Making specific faculty assignments	0.69	2.36	2.73	0.67
9. Establishing salary schedules	2.64	2.76	0.79	1.13
10. Planning new buildings	2.78	2.80	1.73	0.56

Key: 0 = none, 1 = minor influence, 2 = moderate influence, 3 = decisive influence.

Source: Material was taken from a survey of all staff conducted by Abt Associates in the fall of 1973. This survey included all teachers and administrators. Response rate = 92 percent. The number of responses to particular items in this question ranged from 82 to 115.

TABLE 3.2

Perceived and Desired Influence over Selected Issue Areas in the Butte–Angels Camp District

Issue Area	Mean Influence Respondents Feel They:		
	Do Have	Should Have	Difference
1. Determining concepts taught on a particular day	3.52	3.70	0.18
2. Determining daily lesson plans and activities	3.82	3.88	0.06
3. Establishing objectives for each course	3.38	3.69	0.31
4. Selecting required texts and other materials	3.02	3.64	0.62
5. Adding or dropping courses	1.64	2.72	1.08
6. Hiring new teachers	0.23	1.35	1.12
7. Deciding whether to renew a teacher's contract	0.15	1.21	1.06
8. Making specific faculty assignments	0.40	1.44	1.04
9. Establishing salary schedules	0.88	3.07	2.19
10. Planning new buildings	0.44	2.29	1.85

Key: 0 = none, 1 = very little, 2 = some, 3 = moderate, 4 = great deal.

Source: Material was taken from a survey of all staff conducted by Abt Associates in the fall of 1973. This survey included all teachers and administrators, but since the 134 respondents included only eight administrators, responses can be taken as indicative of faculty sentiment. Response rate = 92 percent. The number of responses to particular items in this question ranged from 110 to 122.

TABLE 3.3

Perceived and Desired Influence of Elementary and Secondary Teachers in the Butte–Angels Camp District

| | Mean Influence Respondents Feel They: | | | |
| | Do Have | | Should Have | |
Issue Area	Elementary	Secondary	Elementary	Secondary
1. Determining concepts taught on a particular day	3.30	3.85[a]	3.55	3.91[a]
2. Determining daily lesson plans and activities	3.82	3.81	3.89	3.87
3. Establishing objectives for each course	3.22	3.62[b]	3.56	3.89[a]
4. Selecting required texts and other materials	2.72	3.48[a]	3.49	3.86[a]
5. Adding or dropping courses	1.41	2.00[b]	2.49	3.11[a]
6. Hiring new teachers	0.15	0.35	0.95	1.91[a]
7. Deciding whether to renew a teacher's contract	0.16	0.13	0.89	1.69[a]
8. Making specific faculty assignments	0.41	0.41	1.24	1.78[b]
9. Establishing salary schedules	1.01	0.68	2.87	3.42[a]
10. Planning new buildings	0.38	0.50	2.20	2.45

[a] T-test. p = 0.01.
[b] T-test. p = 0.05.

Key: 0 = none, 1 = very little, 2 = some, 3 = moderate, 4 = great deal.

Source: Material was taken from a survey of all staff conducted by Abt Associates in the fall of 1973. Response rate = 92 percent. Administrators' responses were eliminated. The number of responses to particular items ranged from 109 to 121.

position to the prevailing system. Somewhat surprisingly, teachers wanted a great deal more influence over decisions on the planning of buildings than they have, although that kind of issue rarely arose in the financially constrained district. Overall, however, in Butte-Angels Camp, authority was zoned as anticipated by the loose coupling perspective.

Existing studies of the zoning of influence focus on the elementary grades (Lortie 1969; Cohen et al. 1976). Direct observation indicated that secondary teachers in Butte-Angels Camp were much less willing to accept the prevailing distribution of influence than were their peers in the lower grades.* Table 3.3 compares the perceptions of how influence is distributed and the amount desired by the teachers who worked in the district's lower and upper grades. It shows that the differences between the amount of influence desired by secondary and elementary teachers is significant in eight of ten cases. Secondary teachers consistently wanted more influence than lower grade teachers did.

However, the reasons for this difference vary. Specifically, the first two columns of Table 3.3 show that secondary teachers felt they already had more influence over all instructional decisions, with the exception of item 2, than did their elementary peers. This pattern reflects secondary teachers' competence in special subject matters. Most upper-level instructors taught fields in which their principal had no special knowledge; they believed he did not have the background to supervise them or to select courses and texts. In contrast, elementary teachers were subject matter generalists, like their principals. The differences in desired influence in the instructional area reflect greater initial influence rather than greater demand.

There was no such initial difference in the influence of primary and secondary teachers over personnel matters. Here, secondary teachers showed much greater interest in gaining influence than did primary teachers. This pattern suggests that upper-grade administrators will encounter more opposition to their attempts to impose their authority than will elementary principals. One would expect greater resistance to innovations initiated by administrators in the secondary grades than in the lower grades because of this initial opposition to the prevailing distribution of influence.

---

*Throughout this volume the term secondary will be used to refer to grades 7 through 12 and elementary to grades kindergarten through 6.

Converting Authority to Influence

District personnel spoke of a "chain of command," but, because of limitations to administrative control, the hierarchy functioned more as an appeals and support system. This section examines subordinate expectations and superior performance in four areas of school administration: classroom organization, budgets, discipline, and conditions of employment. *

Classroom Organization

Table 3.2 shows that teachers expected great autonomy in decisions regarding day-to-day classroom activities. Principals accepted this view and said:

> Teachers should be somewhat free to exercise their own teaching style in the classroom. The mother hen [principal] with little chicks in identical boxes has no appeal to me. I admire people with their own styles. The principal should offer leadership and encouragement to carry (the teacher's) own ideas forth because they are more experts in their areas than I. All I can do is sit on the sidelines and look at them from my viewpoint.

This does not mean that principals relinquish veto power over what takes place in the classroom. As one explained, "If a teacher picks up an idea on open classrooms and wants to make a commitment, I'd want to know what that teacher means. Before getting into something, I'd want some goals and objectives and justifications." Nevertheless, the tendency is to grant teachers considerable autonomy.

The idea of teacher autonomy and classroom variation was reflected in practice. Consider descriptions taken from field notes of two social studies classes in the same elementary school. The first

---

*Analysis is limited to the activities of principals in four schools: the high school, the junior high, the Butte Elementary School, and the Angels Camp Elementary School. Two smaller elementary schools in Butte that were administered by one principal are not discussed because of the small number of teachers (of nine, only two were interviewed). Furthermore, one was closed in the fall of 1974. The role of the assistant principal in the high school is not addressed because this person was not responsible for teacher supervision.

is a fifth grade U.S. history course organized in a fairly conventional way:

> The teacher is a tall, thin woman approaching retirement. She introduces me and explains how the class will make land form maps out of salt clay, but they are having trouble finding the right size boxes for the bases. Then she begins a review of the chapter they have been reading.
>
> The teacher says, "We were talking yesterday about why people moved into the Midwest." A girl raises her hand. "Who can tell me why they came to the Midwest?" The teacher waits until all children get their hands up and then calls on the first girl who gives a short answer on which the teacher elaborates. The girl gives a second short answer which the teacher expands on again and then a third which is also commented on. Someone else raises a hand and suggests something which is apparently not in the book so the teacher tells the kids, "No, not exactly." Only those three.
>
> The teacher asks, "Who made the Wilderness Road?" When called on, a boy says, "Daniel Boone." As the questions continue, I pick up the text being used and discover that although she is not holding the book, the questions are designed to check for recall of a specific chapter. The order of the questions asked follows the paragraph structure of the chapter.

The second class is a teacher-programmed course in European history for sixth graders:

> The teacher is a young man approaching thirty who was a principal in a smaller district before coming to this system. He has organized his curriculum to follow the standard Western Civilization format going from Egypt to Greece to Rome and so forth. The lectures he used to give are taped, and he has three cassette recorders in the back of the room where at each one, eight children can listen to a lecture at once. The children also have a textbook, and there are several sets of encyclopedias in the room, as well as library books and filmstrips with individual viewers pertaining to the geographic areas being studied. These materials are orchestrated into a set of units. A child working on one unit will have a sheet of paper indicating the sections of the text to read, a lecture number to listen to, and some exercises to do. These might include drawing a map, looking up some things, and writing a short

essay on a famous person. If he has trouble, the student comes to the teacher's desk and asks for help. As he finishes an exercise, he also brings it up to show the teacher, and before going on to the next unit, he must take a test given by the teacher.

The observer has an impression of quiet bustle. Most children are working at their desks, but a few are moving around looking for reference books, and some are in the back listening to tapes. Occasionally, the teacher has to ask a few children to stop visiting. There are usually two or three children at his desk waiting for help or to get a test. Children are spread out among a set of units. A few are still working on Egypt, but most have gone on to Greece. One girl comes up three or four times. She is tracing a map of Alexander's empire. She has put in the shadings indicating the various peoples included in the empire, but she has not put in the boundary itself. She wants to know if the map is "right." The teacher says no and asks her questions trying to get her to see the point of the map.

Although each teacher worked in a system in which students rotated from specialist to specialist and each taught the expected curriculum for that age level in the district, different classroom organizations were used to impart the same type of information to children of about the same age.

Teachers did not expect complete autonomy over classroom organization. They acknowledged a need to keep their principal informed, especially under two conditions. The first involves the need for supplies. The teacher using the programmed approach just described needed special equipment, so he asked his principal for permission to use the equipment. He had no problem getting it. The other concern is external opposition, an issue mentioned by both principals and teachers. An upper-grade principal said:

If Dr. X comes up to the family course and displays six kinds of prophylactics, I want to know in advance and know why so I can say no or question doing that. When someone calls me about it, then I can say I know about it.

Teachers who depend on administrative support to cope with external opposition accept a principal's veto over material he will not back. As one said:

> I don't want to get burned. If I do a unit on evolution,
> [the principal] should know so he'll know how to defend
> it. If he says no, that's fine. I've got an out.

While teachers expected their in-class autonomy to be protected,
they did not want to be isolated from their principal. They saw him
as a source of advice with difficult problems and wanted to know he
was concerned about what they did. Superiors, however, often have
problems giving advice in a form that is not construed as an order
(Blau 1955; Goss 1961). The problem was compounded here because
teachers' expectations varied. Some expected him to observe and offer suggestions:

> I prefer supervision where someone evaluates what you do
> and comments. . . . If there is a way to improve, I want
> to know. The administrator has a responsibility to the
> kids to do that.

> Teachers should get supervision. Their teaching day
> should be evaluated and remarks made . . . so the
> teacher will know how to improve if she needs to and her
> good points will be reinforced.

Other teachers only wanted to know they can look to their principal
when a problem arises:

> Principals should be in an advisory capacity to help with
> teaching techniques.

> I'd be lost without my principal. He helps with any little
> thing that comes up. This morning I talked to him about
> . . . what to do when I am going through my programmed
> reading faster than usual. How far into second grade ma-
> terial should I go? He said to keep them in the first grade.
> I should spend one [reading] period on programmed read-
> ing and in the other do reading other than the programmed
> text.

Teachers' expectations about who should initiate depended on
their experience and teaching areas. Generally, the newest teachers
preferred to have principals observe and make suggestions, and principals reported that they concentrate on helping first- and second-year
instructors. Older hands preferred to ask for help when a problem
arose. Especially in the upper grades, specialist teachers felt that
the principal could offer very little help with instructional problems
unless he had a background in the subject area in question. While they

would like to have access to useful advice, they felt it was not available except in cases where the principal taught that area previously.

Beyond the advice teachers thought their principal could offer, they also wanted to know he was interested in what they were doing:

> There should be a personalized approach. The principal should show an interest in a teacher as an individual and what his concerns are. . . . I'd like to see more classroom visitation, a greater awareness of what is or isn't going on, without the checklist that shows he's there to determine if you're a good teacher or not. A personal concern rather than a cold, evaluative attitude.

These observations suggest that teachers do not insist on privacy in the classroom as consistently as is often believed. If properly handled, visits by the principal indicate his concern for the teacher. They also inform the principal so he can more effectively offer advice and keep major problems from arising:

> The principal should visit classes enough to know what's going on . . . [He] should have more time to spend with teachers other than nasty meetings. . . . I don't know how they can support us if they don't know what we're doing.

> Too often the administrator goes in only when he suspects a problem. Observation should be ongoing and organized. . . . If a teacher has a problem or question and there is good supervision, the administrator should know about it and help the teacher by knowing about it before there is consultation.

Principals were so concerned not to infringe on the teachers' in-class autonomy, however, that they generally passed up the opportunity to gain influence by visiting the classroom and offering help when the teacher had problems. In interviews they described how, instead, they contributed indirectly to the teachers' work through "general school administration," providing an environment that facilitates instruction. When they did discuss helping teachers, indirect means were described:

> In areas a group of teachers is weak in, we should provide some inservice. Maybe not ourselves, but we should know how to get it for them.

In their attempts to respect the teachers' in-class autonomy, principals did not systematically visit teachers' classes. Their observations were limited to what they saw when they dropped in to deliver a message or ask a question about nonclassroom business. An exception was the Angels Camp principal who said he tried to observe each teacher each year and discuss his observations with her afterward. Elsewhere, teachers with difficulties often received no help. One of the board members, who had become an expert in Indian studies, discussed the problem one teacher was having:

> [The board member] was especially down on [a principal] who ordered a teacher to take the Indians course and then gave him no help at all. There are going to be 90 kids in the class and only 60 books. The board member has been pushing for several changes, and the teacher is not getting any support. The board member says the way the courses went last year was a disaster.

Nor did teachers feel that principals were concerned about their problems:

> We're on our own. . . . I don't want continual pats on the back, but once in a while. They come in only when something is wrong. They never talk to us that much.

> I got (help) in student teaching and the first year from my buddy teacher. . . . Not from administrators, though they've watched and let me work out my problems and said if it had gotten real bad, they would have stepped in. But some days I could have used a hand around the shoulder.

The Angels Camp principal provided the only exception to this pattern. His teachers felt he knew what they were doing, and offered help when needed, although some of the younger ones felt he did not take their ideas seriously and too frequently gave direct orders. This directiveness reduced somewhat the value of any interest or help he offered to those teachers.

Materials and Budgets

Administrators can use discretionary funds to increase their influence, but this resource has limited impact in school districts. In Butte-Angels Camp the only discretionary fund to facilitate instruction was the materials and supplies budget, which was only 2 to 3 percent of the district's budget prior to the district's involvement in ES. Moreover, expenditures were carefully controlled. Supply requests were made to the principal, who forwarded them to the central office, and whose approval was necessary, but not sufficient.

Even the superintendent's discretion was limited in this district
where the school board spent several hours in three board meetings
debating a decision to spend $2,000 on wrestling mats.

Teachers expected funding decisions to be made collaboratively,
but that they would have a great deal of leeway and only need to be
able to justify their requests:

> He should know what we order, and we should justify our
> orders to him. If we can justify it, he should order it.

> You should be given an opportunity to order what you
> need.

> If something is too expensive he'll let us know. . . .
> We discuss before we order something.

Materials ordering was a source of continuing friction in the upper
grades. There, teachers sometimes felt the need for expensive equipment. The high school mathematics department repeatedly ordered
a sophisticated calculating machine so it could offer a computer pro-
gramming course, while the art department sought the equipment to
extend its ceramics program. Staff and community interest in start-
ing an extensive vocational education program would have required a
major capital outlay beyond the range of a regular supplies budget.

Teachers also felt that orders were handled capriciously. Final
decisions, especially negative ones, were frequently not communicated
to the person ordering, so the reasons for rejection were not made
clear. In addition, teachers felt that money was improperly and ir-
rationally distributed:

> There should be a more definite departmental budget.
> What you have now is a "cream-can budget." Whoever
> talks best gets the most is how it works.

> They've gotta establish a reasonable basis for who gets
> what, when, and why [in the areas of] supplies and facili-
> ties. I think of supplies 'cause sometimes they say, . . .
> 'cut all orders in half,' and the teachers who over-order
> get what they need. The others don't get enough.

Discontent with the distribution of materials funds was most extreme
in the upper grades.

Discipline

One of the most important areas where teachers expected administrative backing was that of discipline. While one of the teachers'

most important tasks was maintaining order; serious challenges could not always be mastered alone. Some parents questioned assignments or the use of corporal punishment. Moreover, teachers feared that injury to a child under their supervision would lead to action against them in the district or in court.

The administrative chain of command functioned as a judicial system handling appeals of parents and teachers. Teachers expected firm backing from their superiors in such instances; corrective action was expected only after the threat from child or parent had been disposed of:*

> Total [support]! On the student issue, the teacher should be defended. If the teacher must be reprimanded, it should be in private.
>
> If a kid falls down and cracks his head open, the principal shouldn't say to parents, "I told the teacher not to let the kid fall on the ice." Maybe the teacher has 200 kids to watch.

There was a division of labor in the handling of discipline. One principal reported his major responsibility as being

> discipline. Not in the classroom. The overall tone for the school.
>
> Q. Is that set by the principal?
>
> A. In this school it is! . . . In other schools the principal may have a different attitude and won't care about dirty words on the latrine walls. I do. That's my responsibility, not the teachers'.

The principal had primary responsibility for the nonclassroom areas of the school: bathrooms, halls, and playgrounds. In these areas, though, he could legitimately seek teacher assistance, for instance, by asking teachers to patrol halls between periods. Within the classroom, however, as another principal put it, "Teachers should skin their own skunks when possible." Principals expected teachers to be able to handle the normal range of classroom discipline problems alone. If a new teacher could not maintain order in the room by the end of the first year of work, termination was not unlikely. On the other hand, they expected to help teachers in extreme cases.

----

*This discussion of discipline has been influenced by Becker (1953).

Teachers felt that the way the principal handled extreme cases and policed nonclassroom areas affected their ability to maintain control of students. Moreover, in his handling of extreme cases, the principal determined what means the teacher could use to maintain discipline. Inconsistency on his part increased the teachers' difficulties:

> We don't know how far we can go with kids. One time we do something and it's right. The next time it's wrong. For a while the sixth grade was spanked. Then we were told we couldn't. If we sent kids to the office, it finally got to the point where he wouldn't take them anymore. Teachers shouldn't have to take the guff they do from some kids.

The superintendent's role was similar to that of the principal, but on a districtwide basis. He was only involved in the most extreme cases, such as a decision to expel.

Especially in the secondary schools, teachers felt that discipline was a major problem. In the junior high school there were complaints of frequent fights in and around the building. At one time the principal had to leave a meeting early to deal with a girl who came to a gym course drunk. In the spring of 1975, a teacher resigned after being hit by a student. These extreme behaviors highlighted junior high teachers' continuing problems in maintaining order.

Attention in the high school focused primarily on nonclassroom behavior. In 1971/72, the Butte High School abolished study halls and went to an open-campus organization. Students were provided with a lounge, furnished with games and pop and candy machines and a resource center/study area in addition to the already-existing library. When not in class, they were expected to be in one of those areas or out of the building. Teachers complained that control problems increased as a result of this arrangement. Notes from a conversation with a teacher after a particularly bad period indicate that "Kids were complaining that their lockers were broken into. Kids were writing dirty words in the bathroom as well as knocking holes in the wall and smearing 'filth' [feces] on the walls." About the same time, the problems of getting students to do assignments were increasing, according to the teachers.

Problems in the elementary schools were less severe. Occasionally, students would skip classes, and individuals or groups of students who could not be controlled did emerge; but there was less of a sense that staff control of the situation was being regularly challenged.

Especially in the upper grades, teachers felt that some kind of crackdown was in order, but that necessary support for a more punitive disciplinary policy was lacking. John Raleigh opposed an aggressive approach to discipline and refused to become involved. He told principals:

> Discipline is a problem of the classroom. The administration is only involved when the teacher can't handle it; then there are prescribed pathways to follow. Generally, discipline problems are a reflection of poor teaching.

The superintendent's outlook was apparent to teachers in buildings where discipline problems were severe. Said one, "There is no support from the superintendent. [He] makes it clear that kids aren't to be handled in ways that put pressure on him. That means discipline but no hitting or suspensions."

His position constrained principals to take a less punitive approach to student management than they had in the past. Principals were not always happy with this new approach. A high school principal reflected:

> I've changed in the way I handle discipline. It may not be too good. If a girl comes in and says she's living with her boyfriend, I don't treat her absence like if she were living at home. . . . I try to think about what's best for the situation and pay less attention to consistency.

In the elementary schools, too, teachers noticed changes in the principal's handling of discipline problems. Said one, "[He] has had to change. People told him he was too brusque and physical."

In most buildings, teachers complained about a lack of support on disciplinary matters. These were strongest in the junior high. After an incident in which a student struck a teacher, the staff initiated the formation of a discipline committee consisting of three teachers, a counselor, and the principal. At the start of the fall of 1974, it formulated an extensive set of rules for student conduct and began policing all teachers to ensure that they would help maintain order in the halls. In extreme cases, it urged the principal to mete out strong punishment and tried to back him when he did. In this case school leadership was effectively captured by the teachers.

In the high school, teachers complained that use of the student lounge was supposed to be continued only if no problem resulted. Yet the lounge stayed open until the spring of 1976, five years after it was opened.

Similarly, teachers in the Butte Central School, after noticing their principal's declining use of extreme sanctions, wondered what kind of support they would receive in a different situation. Only in the Angels Camp School were teachers confident that when parents complained about student treatment or when extreme discipline problems occurred, "Our principal stands behind us." In this regard, the Angels Camp principal clearly stood out from his peers.

Conditions of Employment

Administrators share control over conditions of employment with the school board, but they can use their access to the board to gain influence with their teachers. Carlson (1972) describes how an innovative superintendent pushed through a fringe benefit program and an improved sick leave policy as part of a conscious attempt to gain the approval of his teachers. Examination of a number of salary and fringe benefit decisions shows that the Butte-Angels Camp administration did not follow this course of action.

When collective bargaining was initiated in 1969, before consolidation, the Butte superintendent became part of the school board bargaining team. Teachers attributed their failure to achieve greater salary increases in large part to John Raleigh. In fact, teachers did worse in the first four years after collective bargaining began than they had in the previous nine years. The average annual increase of the base salary between 1960 and 1969 was $267. Between 1969 and 1973 it was only $200. During that period, the school board was most sensitive to the low-tax ideology and the district's financial constraints, and small increases created a great deal of tension between teachers and the school board negotiating team. The tension culminated during the negotiations for 1973, which began bitterly when the teachers' negotiators asked for a $1,300 increase and the board was unwilling to grant any increases at all. When an impasse was reached, a non-binding arbitration panel was convened, which recommended that teachers be granted a 6 percent cost of living increase, which was considerably smaller than they demanded. The board rejected the panel's recommendation, and granted no raises at all. This action enraged teachers. Shortly afterward, John Raleigh asked to be removed from the bargaining team.

Even after his removal from the team, Raleigh continued to advise the board to minimize all concessions made to teachers through negotiations. Two issues that most concerned administrators were proposals to reduce the number of student-teacher contact days from 180 to 175 (the state minimum) and to allow teachers to leave the building at 3:30 P.M. when school closed instead of at 4:00 P.M. Regarding the first issue, one of the board members reported in the spring of 1974 that "We discussed [with teachers] as an alternative to more money that we allow them a 3:30 release time and 175 contact days. We've asked this before of John, and he feels that when the education of kids is at stake, there should be no negotiation."

When negotiations did not lead to a shortened school year and teachers petitioned later to reduce the number of contact days, he argued against the change on grounds that district policy did not allow for it; the following year he continued to press for a long school year.

As the chief interpreter of school board policies affecting employment conditions, the superintendent had an opportunity to apply relatively lenient or harsh interpretations, and he consistently chose the latter. For instance, during 1973/74, he interpreted the district's policy of a teacher's receiving 15 sick leave days per year to mean that those days would be earned at the rate of 1.66 days per month while the teacher was working, rather than that they were granted as a block at the beginning of school. This interpretation led to a reduction in benefits to a new teacher who was sick early in the year, and to an older teacher who was injured and could not work for over a month in the winter. When the teachers' association filed a grievance, the board overruled the superintendent in favor of the more lenient interpretation. Similarly, earlier in the same year, Raleigh interpreted a district policy that teachers would only receive credit on the salary scale for courses in their primary area to mean that teachers taking an in-service course on supervision of student teachers could not receive credit; he thus countermanded a contradictory interpretation by the principal supervising the workshop.

Lack of support on conditions of employment was a greater concern to secondary than elementary teachers. Eventually, the upper-grade teachers took countermeasures, which will be discussed below. Their orientation to John Raleigh was quite clear. As one of them said:

> The attitude is very bad up the line. It's impossible to
> talk to the [superintendent]. He lives in the ivory tower.
> He's always right and he's got everything decided in ad-
> vance. He doesn't support us with the community or the
> board.

The Superintendent and the Principals

The superintendent needed the compliance of principals as well as of teachers. Principals felt much more dependent on the superintendent than teachers did on principals. Still, they felt that the superintendent's contact with individual buildings was so limited that they needed considerable freedom to efficiently operate their schools. When asked about the areas in which he had discretion, one principal said:

> It's up to the superintendent. Most superintendents are
> willing to let you make the day-to-day decisions about

your place unless it's against his philosophy. Decisions
affecting the whole district have to be the superintendent's
prerogative. Expenditures of funds in even one school have
to be made by the superintendent.

According to principals, superintendents also predominate on transportation matters, school closings, and hiring and firing teachers.
To operate independently, however, principals believed they had to
have the superintendent's support. As one pointed out, "The superintendent has to support his lieutenants or they can't function. If I
have to check all decisions with him, the process becomes too involved."

John Raleigh's actions left principals in doubt about the support
they could expect. When thinking about his administrators consciously,
he indicated his reliance on them and support for them:

> The superintendent has to support his administrators. . . .
> Even though the responsibility and blame fall on the su-
> perintendent, we have a horizontal administrative team.

> There are some people on one's staff that are dispensable
> if you get into political problems in the community. Good
> principals are hard to find and should be protected no mat-
> ter what, but teachers are relatively dispensable, and
> coaches are a dime a dozen.

Yet, he would scold principals at administrators' meetings and, on
occasion, before teachers. Nor did he always support their decisions.
For instance, he countermanded the principal's ruling that a workshop
on supervising student teachers would count as credit for advancement
on the salary scale. Similarly, although he was anxious to promote
democratic administration, he blamed rather than encouraged his
principals when he did not get the participation from them that he expected. At one meeting, he asked:

> Do we have a true team? A team is what its members
> are! . . . If you don't react, the team won't work. My
> anger can't stifle discussion and reaction. I don't feel
> you haven't had the opportunities to react to total programs
> and situations. I'm not saying you've reacted fully, but the
> opportunity was there.

As a result, principals doubted that they had the support they
needed. They avoided taking stands until they knew how the superintendent felt. As one said, "When something nitty-gritty came up,

we'd say, 'You're the boss. This is our input, but it's your decision.'
We weren't willing because we might be overridden and voted down
by the superintendent.'' At administrators' meetings they would pref-
ace their remarks with long qualifications like ''This is a glittering
generalization, and I may be way off base, but—.'' Within their buildings, principals would often check with the superintendent on seem-
ingly minor matters like whether or not a group of high school students, as part of an activity, could stay overnight in a nearby town.

In summary, there was a zoning of control between teachers and
administrators in the Butte-Angels Camp School District that worked
differently at the elementary and secondary levels. Secondary teachers had more influence, but they were less satisfied with the influence
they did have. Closer examination of relations between teachers and
administrators shows that superiors at each level had a variety of
ways to increase their influence informally. However, whether the
issue was offering advice on how to organize a classroom or obtaining
salary increases and benefits, the superintendent and principals did
not use their positions to increase their influence with staff.

INTERDEPENDENCE AND COORDINATION

One prerequisite for rational program design is the capacity to
coordinate implementation. A prerequisite for comprehensive change
is substantial interdependence among system parts. Where coordination takes place through standardization—for example, advanced scheduling, detailed policy specification, and extensive curriculum guides—
there is little flexibility. The mechanisms to monitor activity and
make midcourse corrections required for planned change are not already in place. However, when coordination takes place through mutual feedback, for instance, through frequent meetings permitting discussion of instructional activities, such mechanisms are already in
place, and staff are used to using them. Coordination and interdependence are related. When interdependence is low or sequential because
one person's work provides the raw material for the work of the next,
standardization will often prevail. When interdependence is higher
and more immediate, mutual feedback will occur (Thompson 1967).

Interdependence is least in the old-fashioned ''egg carton'' school
where each teacher works in a self-contained classroom without help
from other professionals. Even in Butte-Angels Camp, however, this
idea is something of a myth because the district's professional staff
specializes. Teachers specialize by age level in the elementary
schools and by subject matter in the secondary schools. Moreover,
specialization by subject matter is spreading in the elementary grades.
In 1973/74 the district employed one full-time physical education

teacher just to work with students in grades 1 to 3. The equivalent of two more full-time physical education teachers and three art and music instructors also worked in the elementary grades. In addition, all fifth- and sixth-grade teachers in the system specialize in subject areas like reading, language arts, arithmetic, science, and social studies.

As specialization increases, student contact time becomes a scarce commodity. Specialists usually seek to increase their share of the student's day. During discussion of possible introduction of a swimming program for primary grades, for example, a first-grade teacher argued that, "You're taking away a lot of time when they should be doing schoolwork. . . . We're wasting time that they should be using for reading, writing, and arithmetic." Past reduction of time for instruction in those areas was attributed to the introduction of art, music, and physical education specialists. In addition, at various times, high school fine arts teachers have argued that the number of required solid or academic courses should be reduced so students would have the opportunity to take music, drama, and art, while the mathematics teachers sought to increase their enrollments by reducing the number of required social studies courses.

One way to coordinate time use is to institute mutual feedback procedures to allow teachers to negotiate schedules. Such procedures have the added advantage of allowing teachers to tailor time use to short-term instructional needs. The Angels Camp school experimented with this approach in 1973/74 when its fifth- and sixth-grade teachers first began specializing. Teachers would meet after school each day to schedule another day. After one-and-a-half years, the group became extremely versatile; they could organize a day to allow one student to work alone with two or three students or to bring all students together for a movie or lecture, and they could readjust schedules on short notice. However, they voluntarily dropped the procedure because of internal conflict. The three reading and mathematics teachers wanted to ensure that their subjects would be taught daily, a guarantee that could not be made with the earlier, flexible scheduling system. A set schedule guaranteed a fair distribution of student contact time, and it only had to be negotiated once.

This example indicates that a school with specialists requires tighter coordination than a school with only general classroom teachers. However, mutual feedback may still not be necessary. In fact, it will be avoided because it promotes conflict. Standardization through a fixed schedule provides adequate coordination without conflict.

Curriculum content also requires coordination so students can move from one grade to another. However, precise coordination is not usually necessary because it is difficult to show that variation in instruction at one level affects the work of teachers in another. For

instance, teachers in the upper grades attributed poor student performance in their courses to poor instruction and lack of coordination
at lower levels, but only one attempt was made to prove the assertion.
The high school mathematics teachers developed a testing program
that indicated that students coming out of the Butte Central Elementary School were less able to recall basic mathematics facts than
were students from Angels Camp. While these differences were
small, they persisted over several years. However, junior high
school mathematics teachers did not report difficulty in coping with
a wide range of student readiness for seventh-grade mathematics.
Moreover, administrators reviewed the test results but did not change
the elementary curriculum as a result.

Standardization in general terms provided adequate coordination
of curriculum content. One such form was required curriculum guides.
However, these were rarely referred to and were quite general. The
days when such guides were "our Bible," as one teacher put it, or
included detailed specifications of the time required for each area under a subject had long passed. Common textbooks provided another
form of standardization. Each first- second-, and third-grade teacher, for example, used the same reading series. Coordination was
less problematic in upper grades where only one teacher would teach
a course like physics, creative writing, or business typing. Then
the teacher had considerable leeway to determine what was taught.
For instance, when asked how he would handle a new geography course,
one high school teacher replied, "I don't know yet. I haven't taught
it." He did not have to specify the course content to administrators,
only its title.

Curriculum standardization served both internal and external
functions. As one teacher suggested, "It's not as scary for the teacher
if she knows what is really important for the child to learn." In addition, teachers reasoned that the guides proved to the public that the
district had worked out a curriculum while removing some of the responsibility for what was taught from the individual instructor's
shoulders.

Another prerequisite for rational planning is effective means for
collecting information. Without such means, it is difficult to know
what goals are not being met so planning will be haphazard. Centralized information collection techniques were limited in Butte-Angels
Camp. There was a budgeting and financial reporting system, a set
of records for tracking student attendance, and the annual testing
program including both nationally designed tests and the tests developed by the mathematics teachers. These were supplemented by occasional direct observation of teachers by principals—there was no
formal teacher evaluation system during the project's first two years
—and by discussion in committees during planning activities. All

teachers in the district were organized into groups for major planning activities like preparation for consolidation of the two districts. Smaller groups would be formed for more specific tasks like redesigning the high school social studies curriculum or developing a new elementary report card. These meetings were usually chaired or visited by a principal who reported findings and progress to the superintendent.

These information sources provided very little data for rational program planning, however. Administrators were most concerned about budgetary problems and declining enrollments. These problems were identified in proposals submitted to the ES Program. However, administrators had very little control over either area. District income was determined primarily by the county commissioners, and most costs were fixed. Three-quarters of all expenditures were for salaries. Enrollments were determined by birthrates and migration. Test scores did not indicate any areas that required special attention to administrators. As the superintendent described the situations, all tests were at about the mean. The only attempt to use detailed analysis of test scores to pinpoint program problems was the one by the mathematics teachers mentioned earlier.

In sum, interdependence of staff in the district was low, although the proliferation of specialists made it higher than would be expected in an egg carton school. Coordination was managed through standardization that employed division by broad categories. That is, schedules and curriculum guides specified when courses would be taught, but not their contents. Information sources were too limited for detailed central coordination. This pattern of interdependence and coordination demonstrated to the public that the right things were being done while maintaining staff autonomy and minimizing internal conflict over time allocations. However, it did not promote rational planning or coordinated implementation of change, nor was it conducive to comprehensive change.

INTERNAL DIVISIONS

Differing staff interests, administrative styles, and teachers' responses combined to divide the Butte-Angels Camp School District into four groups: two sets of teachers, the superintendent, and the board. A review of the two years of history preceding project implementation helps to clarify the pattern of cleavages.

In the early 1970s teachers were concerned about the balance of rewards that they were getting for their work. Attention focused on collective bargaining, but the collective bargaining procedure required by the state was not producing salary increases that teachers thought were adequate. The slow rise in salaries was accompanied by heavy demands from the superintendent that many teachers thought were beyond the bounds of what he could legitimately ask for. Although various programs, such as the competition for the American Flag Award granted each year to one school system of distinction, the North Central Evaluation in the high school, and another evaluation in the Butte Central Elementary School designed by the Association for the Evaluation of Elementary Schools, were often centered in a single school, the superintendent was usually associated with it. But the number of programs generated a kind of cynicism that was directed at the ES project and the superintendent:

> Teacher 1: This is the thing Mr. Raleigh has sort of made himself famous for: He's brought lots of federal money into the system and nobody can deny this. . . . Last year when I was working on [ES project planning], a group of people said, "Well, what's this latest fiasco you're indulged in?" And they said Mr. Raleigh must have a big file cabinet in his office that he walks to proudly and he says, "Now, here's the file when we piloted this, and there's the file when we piloted that. . . . And they think a lot of these things are just spurts and will die of natural causes and he'll find something else to take the place of it.

> Teacher 2: I'm in my fifth year here and each year we've had a special emphasis. . . .

> Teacher 1: And things, through all the changes, go on about the same.

These various projects helped the superintendent develop his ideas for what became the ES project, but they also had a discouraging effect on all teachers.

While the superintendent supported some change programs of his own, he vetoed a number of others that had been suggested during preparation for consolidation. Those most talked about came from teachers, and included requests to create a mathematics coordinator position, to shorten instruction time in the junior high, and to create an environmental education program in the high school, all ideas that would be revived during implementation of the Experimental Schools project. Not all requests were denied. Between 1972 and 1974 a new bioethics course was developed and implemented in the junior high, but the pattern of rejection created the impression that teacher requests for change were unlikely to be accepted.

Not all teachers joined the opposition to the superintendent. In fact, the faculty was divided into two distinct groups. As in large urban systems, the more militant teachers were primarily males in the high or junior high schools, while the more conservative ones tended to be female elementary teachers (Rosenthal 1969). All but four or five elementary teachers were women, while 59 percent of the junior high and high school staff was male. Moreover, within the high and junior high school staffs, a smaller core of extreme militants had been most active in securing better salaries and more authority for teachers and also in opposing the superintendent.

The militant and conservative teachers were clearly polarized in the fall of 1973 by an action of the National Education Association (NEA) that would have more than doubled the dues required to join the Butte-Angels Camp Education Association (BACEA) by requiring membership in the state and national organizations as well. During a meeting held then to discuss whether teachers should continue affiliation with the NEA or start an independent bargaining organization, a new teacher who was a long-time local resident commented to the whole faculty on how the divisions among them were so strong that they had become reflected in seating patterns: "The boys have got to stop sitting away from the girls, and the Butte teachers separate from the Angels Camp teachers, and the high school teachers separate from the junior high school teachers." While open conflict within the staff was fairly rare, the divisions among the levels and sexes were fairly permanent and regularly registered through seating patterns at systemwide faculty meetings where most women sat in front and to one side while the men and some female high school teachers sat toward the back and on the other side.

The militant and conservative teachers were divided in their perceptions of the nature of administrative authority and in their concerns about the balance of rewards to work. Field notes indicate that disagreements about relations with administrators became especially apparent during the debates about continued relations with the NEA:

> Jane Doe started talking about what it means to be a professional. Dennis Clark asked Jane, "What do you mean professional?" She likened professionalism to democracy because in both you have to respect authority. In the latter you have to respect the Constitution, in the former you respect your superiors. In addition, a professional is "willing to go that extra mile." Dennis objected to having obedience in the definition, and Jane said, "It's not obedience, it's respect."

The militants were also more concerned about John Raleigh's tendency to press his own programs without supporting theirs, largely because they were in the upper grades where teachers developed their own program ideas. However innovative individual elementary teachers were in their classrooms, they did not propose any changes that required decisions at the building or the system levels. Those changes that did take place in the lower grades were spearheaded by principals. The change proposals the superintendent vetoed came from the secondary teachers.

The split between the militant and conservative teachers helped to determine the tactics that the militants could use. The most bitter teachers were the small group who did the salary negotiating in the early 1970s. These groups conducted some discussions with an AFL-CIO representative, and when negotiations were the least productive they considered a strike-like action, refusing to sign contracts for the next year. The majority of teachers would not follow their lead, so they sought a tactic that would be effective regardless of internal divisions. The approach they chose was to run their own candidates for the school board.

Teachers and the Board

School board elections are usually characterized by low public interest, low conflict, and low turnout; incumbents routinely beat candidates who are not already board members. The failure of an incumbent to win is usually taken as a sign of a significant internal crisis (Iannaconne and Lutz 1970; Zeigler and Jennings 1974). This pattern characterized the Butte and Angels Camp schools before consolidation. Only 6 of the 16 elections through 1970 were contested, and only 1 was lost by an incumbent, as a result of disagreements over consolidation. Incumbents won the first election in the combined Butte-Angels Camp district as well. Teachers were not a factor in board elections during this period.

This pattern changed in 1972. That year Mike Randall, a seven-year school board veteran and a Deep Down Mine department head, was defeated by Jack Ianetti. Although Randall was reappointed to fill a vacancy, he lost again to Bill Bunyan in 1973.

A school board campaign was an ideal tactic for the divided Butte-Angels Camp teachers, and Jack Ianetti was an ideal candidate. Such a campaign was unlikely to be opposed by conservative teachers. As long as opposition was not active, the militants had a chance to affect the election, since fewer than 1,500 votes were being cast. All that was required was a crew of volunteers to telephone people and remind them to vote and a small fund to pay for advertising.

Two factors increased the teachers' effectiveness. First, since many of them were long-time residents, they had numerous friends and relatives whom they could call on for support. Second, many residents opposed John Raleigh's administration because they felt he was spending too much money and was dominating the board. As one put it:

> I wanted Jack Ianetti in there. . . . I wanted someone on the board that Raleigh couldn't wrap around his finger. Jack could keep his head up with finances, prevent us from going too far into debt. Deficit spending has never been a fear of Raleigh's.

Jack Ianetti was not the first person the militant teachers approached, but he was closely tied to them. A former teacher himself, he had served on the teachers' negotiating team previously. He had recently quit teaching to start a business in a nearby town, but he still lived in Butte. He was also a friend of many militants. He was a member of a teachers' bowling team and was invited to semiannual stag dinners held at the cabin of a high school teacher.

Teachers made their largest campaign effort in 1972, but the following year they interviewed candidates for two board positions. While they endorsed both Bunyan and the Reverend Rick Maslow, the organizer of the campaign said, "We gave our money to Bunyan because Maslow implied that he had enough." Only half as many people worked on the teachers' telephone canvasing in 1973 as in 1972, but Bunyan and Maslow organized their own campaigns. Observers of the elections agree that teachers were a force both years, but that they had their greatest impact in 1972.

The Reverend Maslow's erudition and liberal social conscience (he has a divinity degree from Harvard) made him an anomoly in the area. His pastoral work and training in social work gave him some ability to assess the quality of the district's program, and his professional responsibilities gave him a great deal of discretion in how to use his time. Bill Bunyan was a logger from one of the more isolated parts of the district. Although not tied to John Raleigh, he felt more loyalty to his neighbors than to teachers.

On the eve of project implementation, these three members and two others comprised the board. Euell Douglas, a highly trained professional who headed one of the more technical departments in the Deep Down Mine, was appointed to the board in the spring of 1973. Ella Smith had only served on the board for two years, but she was the senior member. As an Angels Camp housewife who was very popular in both towns, she was close to a number of teachers. This board's orientation to teachers was very different from its predecessor's. One indication of this difference is that in November 1973, only a few months after the previous board had refused to grant teachers any raise through collective bargaining, the new board voluntarily gave all teachers a $400 bonus.

As project implementation began, then, the district was divided into four groups. The superintendent and militant teachers were at odds with each other. The superintendent had lost the support of the board, which had formed new ties with teachers, but the militants and conservative teachers were still divided.

Internal Divisions and Views of the ES Project

Internal divisions affected initial orientations to the Butte-Angels Camp ES project. The project was initially seen as the superintendent's possession, and teachers made the connection between his role in determining conditions of employment and his role as an innovator, as the following letter to him from a high school teacher, written shortly after the board vetoed all salary increases in the spring of 1973, indicates:

> Dear Mr. Raleigh,
>
> [The ES project consultant] will never be able to come up with an inservice workshop that will undo the damage done to . . . the ES project by the Board's firm action on Tuesday night. . . .
> The law demanded that teachers turn in contracts May 15, which they did. However, these contracts do not buy the things that the school district needs to personalize education—vigor, dedication, and goodwill of its teachers. Money does not necessarily buy those things either, but it helps, particularly when it is an indication of a positive attitude toward the people upon whom the district depends for the implementation of the ES project. . . . The alienation of the teachers is too high a price to pay for the money saved by rejecting the Advisory Board's recommendation for the 6 percent cost of living increase. . . .
> Do you remember the elation we felt when word was received that the project was funded? Can you imagine how disheartened we would have been if, after all our work, the letter had said, "We will not fund you; however, we will allow you to keep the $40,000 that you have already been granted, and we do want to keep lines of communication open. If you have any ideas about the ES budget, let

us know." You know the depression that would have followed such a note. Our teachers have not been funded.

Opposition to the project was concentrated where opposition to the superintendent was strongest. On the staff survey from the fall of 1973, 82 percent of the elementary teachers (42 of 49) responded that they thought the decision to have an ES project was a good idea; only 57 percent of the secondary teachers (24 out of 42) took the same position.

CONCLUSION

On the eve of implementation of its ES project, the Butte-Angels Camp School District was torn by internal conflict. On one side was John Raleigh, the superintendent, with his administration. He was committed to economizing to respond to external pressures, but he also pressed for his own view of personalized education. Raleigh was opposed by a core of militant teachers in the upper grades who sought larger salary increases and wanted to make innovations in their own content areas, but who did not share his interest in personalized education. A significant portion of the teaching staff, however, was neutral, opposing aggressive tactics of the more militant teachers, but not inclined toward economizing either. In pressing its view of good educational practice, the administration's influence was limited in two ways. First, there was a zoning of control, which is typical of American schools but which constrained administrative attempts to mandate new modes of instruction. Second, the impact of this zoning was intensified by the failure of most administrators to carry out their responsibilities in ways that would enhance their influence.

This depiction indicates that several of the prerequisites for successful change were missing in the district. For instance, goal consensus, a prerequisite for rational planning, was quite low. Both formal goal statements written in the district and survey responses reveal that teachers and administrators believed a large number of possible goals were important; so many goals were important that there was little basis for making choices. What really motivated people were personal interests that were often based on their work. These include individualized education, shortening the junior high school day, obtaining a mathematics coordinator position, and a host of others.

Interdependence of workers and assignments, an apparent prerequisite for comprehensive change, was also limited. The growing number of specialists in the district was increasing such interdependence slightly, but coordination was still better achieved through standardization in scheduling than mutual feedback. There seemed to be enough slippage among various parts of the system that changing several of them would not be mutually reinforcing.

Finally, as project implementation approached, there was clearly opposition to the leading innovator, the superintendent, but this opposition did not take the form of classical resistance to change. Several earlier issues divided the staff, including salary negotiations and the selection of innovations for adoption by the district. Moreover, with the militants' school board campaigns, opposition had already passed beyond the passive forms most often considered in discussions of resistance. There was a strong possibility that the ES project would become embroiled in this preexisting conflict. The extent to which staff participation in planning for change could or would be used to reduce opposition is the subject of the next chapter.

4

PLANNING IN THE DISTRICT
AND IN WASHINGTON

The Butte-Angels Camp ES project grew out of the interaction between the ES Program in Washington and numerous factors in the district. Once under way, district activities, particularly planning and interaction with the funding agency, were controlled largely by the superintendent and his staff. In this and the next two chapters, planning and implementation of the district's project are described. The focus is on the interplay of teachers, administrators, the funding agency, and others who became involved, especially the school board.

Description of planning activities throws light on all four assumptions about how to promote planned change, those concerned with rational planning, participation, comprehensive change, and the role of the federal government. Rational planning requires that goals be identified and that possible innovations be compared with those goals so those innovations that best help reduce discrepancies between goals and performance are selected. Although staff participation is generally recommended as an ingredient for building support for a project, writers disagree on the extent to which planners should share decision making with staff and about the consequences of doing so. ES assumed that comprehensive change was a useful way to unfreeze a school district and reinforce reform of its separate elements. Otherwise, it was argued, organizational inertia would overcome the change effort. Finally, federal initiatives are often assumed to be beneficial for local schools, but the conditions under which benefits are forthcoming have not been well specified.

Examination of these issues focuses on the conditions that led to and shaped ES/Washington's rural schools competition: planning activities in the district, including the problems raised by the federal agency and the nature of staff participation; the resulting plan; the impact of final contract negotiations between ES/Washington and the district; and the effects of staff participation on initial attitudes toward the district's project.

GENESIS OF THE EXPERIMENTAL
SCHOOLS RURAL PROGRAM

The ES Program* was first announced in President Nixon's budget message to Congress in January 1969. The president's Message
on Education Reform and Renewal in March 1970 described the program as "a bridge between educational research and practice."
This same presidential message proposed the creation of the National
Institute of Education (NIE), and the ES Program was seen by some
as a prototype of the research initiative that the NIE would carry out.
Further detail on the ES Program was provided in the president's
budget request for the fiscal year (FY) 1971, where it was described
as an effort to

> test, develop, and demonstrate comprehensive new ap-
> proaches to increasing the achievement of students in ac-
> tual school situations. The most promising research re-
> sults already available—including for example, curriculum
> materials, different types of scheduling and new patterns
> of staffing—will be integrated and used in one school set-
> ting. [Doyle et al. 1976, p. 28]

A variety of people within the White House; the top levels of the
Department of Health, Education and Welfare; and the Office of Education—all contributed to thinking about the ES Program. Unfortunately, this multitude of sponsors did not signify a solid consensus for a
single item. Rather, it indicated that the ES idea meant different
things to different people, that even before it began, the program was
part of various power struggles within these agencies.

The president's FY 1971 budget request included $25 million for
experimental schools, but the program did not do well in Congress.
That year the president's education budget was cut from $118 million
to $90 million. The ES Program was authorized but not given an ap-
propriation, whereupon Office of Education officials allocated $12
million of discretionary funds for program start-up (Doyle et al.
1976). Their long-term plans for the program called for the expenditure of $190 million over eight fiscal years.

---

*Because I was located in Butte-Angels Camp, information on
the events in Washington described in this and succeeding chapters
comes primarily from secondary sources, including the reports of
Corwin (1977); Doyle et al. (1976); Herriott (1979); and Sproull, Weiner, and Wolf (1978); although these are supplemented with other reports
and documents.

Nevertheless, the ES Program got off to an aggressive start. Four months after the budget was passed, Sidney Marland began his term as commissioner of education. He seized on the program as one of the few new ideas available for implementation at the time. On December 28, 1970, eleven days after he took office, the ES Program sent out announcements of its first grants competition.

The announcement of the first competition seeking "Comprehensive Combinations of Promising Practice" was sent to 20,000 schools; about 500 Letters of Interest were received and reviewed. In February 1971, one-month planning grants of $10,000 each were made to eight school districts. Three of these districts were chosen as ES sites in April 1971 and given long-term grants for the implementation of the plans that they had prepared during March. A second competition was announced on March 31, 1971, resulting in four-month planning grants of approximately $35,000 each to eleven organizations, three of which subsequently received long-term grants. However, program staff were concerned that the previous competitions had discriminated against small, rural school districts, both because of the lower limit of 2,500 pupils and the necessity to prepare a sophisticated response rapidly. Therefore, a third competition, one exclusively for small, rural schools, was announced in March 1972.

The rural ES competition was publicized through an "Announcement of a Competition for Small Rural Schools." Hereafter, this document will be referred to as The Announcement.* As described in The Announcement, the rural program had a number of special features:

- Funded projects had to be comprehensive.
- Projects had to be developed locally. In requiring local development, ES/Washington believed it was breaking with the pattern of the 1960s in which a federal agency persuaded school districts to accept a federally endorsed innovation. It believed that the problems of small districts required special approaches and had to capitalize on unique community strengths, so federal direction was inappropriate.
- Extensive participation in project planning was required, but the importance of lay participation was stressed more than that of teachers and other lower-level professional staff.
- Some constraints on local initiative were specified. Funds could not be employed to subsidize activities already under way in the district or to pay for routine capital improvements and operating

---

*The Announcement has been reproduced in its entirety in Herriott and Gross (1979).

costs. Moreover, at the end of five years, each district was expected to provide continuing support for the new activities developed with ES funds.

- Funded projects had to include an internal formative evaluation component, and the districts had to agree to cooperate with a separate research project conducted by Abt Associates.

The Announcement was sent out in late March 1972. Districts interested in developing ES projects were asked to submit 15-page Letters of Interest by April 15. In asking districts to prepare the letters, ES/Washington sought a rational basis for judging the readiness of applicant districts to undertake a comprehensive project. The agency was particularly interested in the districts' current programs, their strengths and weaknesses, and their ideas for change.

Of the 7,000 eligible districts, 320 submitted Letters of Interest. The letters were written hurriedly, no doubt because of the four-week deadline for submission. They were also written to respond to the perceived priorities of ES/Washington to obtain funding. The letters were subjected to a complex review process: each was read and rated by at least two ES/Washington staff members. In addition, five panels, each consisting of about ten members, were convened to review and rate regional groupings of letters. From those ratings, 25 finalists were selected and their letters subjected to further review and rating by a committee of consultants assembled for two days in Washington. Afterward, three-member teams visited 13 applicant districts to obtain firsthand knowledge considered helpful in the site-selection process.

Two groups of districts were selected for some participation in the rural schools program. Six were awarded one-year grants of $90,000 or more to plan a five-year comprehensive change project, with a moral commitment that they would subsequently be funded for four more years. Six others, including the Butte-Angels Camp district, received one-year grants of $46,500, but with the understanding that long-term funding would be conditional on the outcome of the planning process (Rosenblum and Louis 1979).

THE DISTRICT'S SEARCH FOR A SPONSOR

Because of the Butte-Angels Camp district's growing financial problems in the early 1970s, implementing any ideas for educational change on a very extensive basis required outside support. The district did, however, have a built-in capacity to seek out such resources in the form of a number of somewhat hidden positions held by school personnel. For instance, Jane Doe, the district's journalism teacher, had a greatly reduced course load so she could act as district public relations director and as a liaison with local media and community groups. Although not a skilled writer, she had the time to write and follow up on proposals for new programs. Her position was a legacy from earlier, more affluent times in Butte and had never been eliminated from the budget. In addition, one counselor with a certain entrepreneurial ability had been assigned the task of developing and publicizing a number of smaller special programs in previous years and had some experience with proposal writing. Moreover, since the district had a reputation within the state as being interested in developing new programs, information on new funding sources was frequently related to local personnel.

In late December 1970, the Butte district received a copy of ES/Washington's first announcements of a funding competition from the state superintendent of education shortly after it was released. This announcement was aimed at larger school systems. A small team—including Doe and the counselor-program writer, but no teachers—wrote the proposal that was submitted in January and again in May 1971. Although this application was highly descriptive and gave relatively little room to explaining proposed new developments, it identified the district's financial constraints and gave some indication of the direction the superintendent would take in applying additional funds to educational programs. These ideas were unclear and not yet well developed; the only concrete suggestion related to the use of minicourses. Still, some of the language was already surprisingly similar to what was later submitted as the final project plan:

> The basic objective [of the project is] to develop a comprehensive child-centered educational system to serve the needs of each individual child for which the two districts are responsible.

> Restating the goals for the new district, they include primarily a child-centered curriculum; individual instruction to meet individual needs.

The 1971 attempts failed, but when the announcement of the rural ES Program was distributed from Washington the following year, the same small group wrote a new proposal. Changes in this second proposal focused on curriculum and teaching practices. There was some suggestion that available money would be used to expand vocational education offerings and the partly developed television facility, but the main thrust was toward developing an approach to individualized instruction. The primary new development that the Experimental Schools grant would promote was described as follows:

The major change envisioned would be by completely developing a program which would be <u>diagnostic and prescriptive</u>
in nature for each child, in which children would never have
to experience frustration through being forced to do work
which is beyond their capabilities. . . .

In order to implement such a program, prescriptive educators would be needed as well as diagnosticians on a pilot
level. If this program could be implemented system-wide,
individualized programs could be prescribed for each child
with measurable success because of pre and post testing
procedures. [Emphasis added]

On June 30, 1972, the district received formal notification that
it had been awarded a one-year planning grant. The superintendent
interpreted the award as endorsement of the individualized education
theme, but ES/Washington ensured for itself an important continuing
role in planning by withholding further funding until the formal plan
was submitted. Since individualized education was only partly understood by district staff and not uniformly supported, and since the program's requirements for comprehensiveness were largely foreign to
them, during the 1972/73 school year the superintendent had to devise
a clear, workable plan and simultaneously gain support for it from
his staff and from ES/Washington.

INSTABILITY AND AMBIGUOUS GUIDELINES

Preparation for planning in Butte-Angels Camp began in July
1972 when John Raleigh and the counselor-program writer attended
a meeting in Washington at which representatives of all funded rural
districts met the ES Program director to learn about planning procedures. At about the same time, the ES Program was moved to the
new NIE. Program staff quickly perceived that the NIE was a more
precarious environment in which to administer their program than
the Office of Education had been (Herriott 1979). After describing
the problems faced by program staff in Washington, the impact of the
new instability will be presented from the viewpoint of district staff.

The NIE's initial leadership was skeptical of all inherited programs (Sproull, Weiner, and Wolf 1978). The agency hoped to have
an extended period to plan and implement a new form of educational
research before being held accountable for the results. Having to assume ES and other ongoing programs left the new agency vulnerable;
it was responsible for the problems (and possible failure) of those
programs, thus drastically reducing its honeymoon period as a new
agency. Its FY 1973 budget, appropriated by the Congress in October

1972, was much lower than anticipated, as was the FY 1974 budget being prepared at that time by the executive. The continuation costs of the inherited programs (only $25.6 million of the $190 million originally anticipated for the ES Program had been appropriated prior to the move into the NIE) were thus quickly recognized as a major threat to the ability of the NIE to obtain funding for its new initiatives. The ES Program was a source of special concern because it was one of the largest, single inherited programs.

Later there was also concern about the specific methods of the ES Program. Although inaugurated as a "bridge between educational research and actual practice" (a goal very much in harmony with that of the NIE), the way in which that bridge was being built seemed to the leadership of the NIE to be earmarking too many dollars for practice (Herriott 1979). From its inception, ES spent $3 supporting improved practice through awards to local school districts for every $1 that it devoted to research on those practices. The NIE's leaders believed they were getting too little research leverage from the funds allocated to this program. The program also brought into the NIE a group of project officers who seemed committed primarily to facilitating practice rather than studying it.

Thus, during the period when the program was working with the rural districts to develop their long-range plans, the foundations of its approach to educational change were under attack within its parent organization. Unwilling to change its basic approach, the program became convinced that its work would have to be well executed to ensure survival. Moreover, the program director believed that short-term survival depended in part on making sure that the local districts produced strong plans. Strong plans were all the more necessary because the program contemplated making substantial awards to each district. Yet, program staff doubted that these small, rural districts had the experience with comprehensive planning necessary to develop plans with the level of sophistication that would be acceptable within the NIE. To make up the difference, ES Program staff would have to intervene.

The ES Program had one advantage in its efforts to help local projects develop strong plans—its size. At one point in time, as many as five projects officers were assigned responsibility for monitoring the ten rural projects that were finally selected. In general, the project officers' loads ranged from two projects to seven, but the typical load was more like three or four, a very light load. Throughout the Department of Health, Education and Welfare project officers were generally assigned as many as 10 to 15 contracts or 20 to 30 grants (Corwin 1977).

The large staff for project monitoring touched the Butte-Angels Camp district directly. While the district was writing its project plan, ES/Washington maintained contact with the district through a regular project officer and a consultant hired by the federal agency. The consultant's special concern was to support program development.

To this advantage must be added two disadvantages: the staff's lack of experience with education and federal program management, and an ambiguous program mission. The first ES Program director was not a career bureaucrat; he had been a professor of education at an elite university before accepting his government position. Most project officers hired were also from outside the government. Moreover, their direct experience in schools was limited: only five of the ten for whom Corwin (1977) reports information had taught. Three reported over six years' teaching experience and two reported over five years' work in school administration, but only two of the five had previous experience with innovative programs. On the other hand, they were well educated. Two of the ten project officers had bachelors' degrees, six had masters' degrees, and two had doctorates.

Perhaps because of the program's rapid start-up, a number of the key concepts of its mission were never defined in ways that staff could operationalize when working with districts in developing plans. In particular, the idea of comprehensive change proved elusive. This difficulty is apparent in the comments of project officers (Corwin 1977, pp. 16-17).

> We didn't necessarily think through, as a group, and come to some sort of consensus on what the behavioral manifestations would be of what we expected. I mean, what did it actually mean to expect a comprehensive plan or expect community involvement, and how would that translate into our behavior on site?

> I was responsible for going over their drafts and criticizing them from some basis, which really wasn't specified— something to do with "feasibility," and whatever "comprehensiveness" was. . . . I really couldn't explain to a local community why things in their plan weren't acceptable. I found that the most difficult, because I didn't think there was a firm guideline to give them.

Nevertheless, the ES Program developed a set of expectations for the results of the planning period that were communicated to the districts in three forms: a set of guidelines sent out to the districts in November 1972 for preparation of formal project plans, the formal grant documents for the planning activity that were accepted by the local school boards, and communications with project officers during site visits and by telephone, letters, and memoranda.

Through these media, ES sought to communicate a limited number of expectations to their counterparts in the districts. Besides an emphasis on comprehensive education, these included the following:

- A required formal plan: these were to be no more than 100 pages long and organized in a format specified by ES/Washington, but they would be local statements of comprehensive goals for the district, and of procedures and resources necessary to accomplish those goals.
- Broad participation of affected groups: the agency emphasized in the announcement, grant document, and phone calls, that leaders of the planning process must obtain broad participation from teachers, students, parents, and other citizens while identifying goals. Each district was asked to form an "advisory council" to the local ES project director with representatives from each group.
- Prior approval by ES/Washington of budget and staff: the grant document required that all professional staff being considered for major roles in the project be "acceptable to the federal government," and that all anticipated expenditure for equipment of over $200 receive prior approval.
- Contracting for implementation: the NIE required ES/Washington to contract with the school districts for the implementation of formal project plans to maintain a greater measure of control.

A number of characteristics of ES/Washington's approach to the district created confusion in the district. For instance, the program's staffing pattern was unclear to people in the district. They were not sure what decisions could be made by the project officer, which were being made by the program director, or where the consultant fit in at all, although the superintendent found the consultant the most amenable of the three to his approach to individualized education. Hence, it was difficult to know which ideas coming from Washington were suggestions, which were orders, and where the district had room to bargain and negotiate. While the district plan was being written, contact between Washington and the district was maintained by weekly telephone calls between the consultant and various school personnel. The consultant visited the district in August 1972 and again with the project officer in November of the same year.

Moreover, ES/Washington was supportive but vague in its advice and direction to the district during the fall. During the November visit, ES personnel met with 45 local staff members to discuss the project. The concluding comments in minutes to that meeting indicate that

the meeting did turn out to be a rather general meeting, and that had not been the intention when letters of invita-

tion were sent. . . . No specific action was an outgrowth
of the meeting. Comments of evaluation concerning the
Washington consultant were overwhelmingly positive. The
congeniality and knowledge of our visitors were much appreciated.

Initial guidance from Washington was low for three reasons.
First, the program believed local participation would benefit its projects. It was committed to local development of project plans and did
not want to prejudice the outcomes of the planning work. Second, support for the program was eroding in Washington so it felt the need to
keep its options open. Third, the program had not adequately defined
a number of key concepts such as comprehensive change. In addition,
district staff perceived that the program used procedures and held expectations that were standard and so ingrained in Washington that they
could not be specified, and thus remained foreign to district personnel.
For instance, later on when the plans were written, writers found that
their documents were not acceptable in Washington until they stumbled
on proposal formats of other federal grant programs to use as guidelines in shaping their own efforts.

Nonetheless, ES/Washington staff did specify some criteria for
a successful project, the most important of which was comprehensiveness. Special documents and the advice of the consultant and the
project officer provided during the planning activities were intended
to help define that idea. Still, district personnel felt that ES/Wash-
ington never clarified the term enough to facilitate program design.
When asked if he knew what was meant by comprehensiveness, John
Raleigh, the superintendent, replied:

No, because I don't think they knew either. I think none
of us knew. We were all feeling for a definition. . . . So
many times we would get into our meetings and visiting
with people from Washington, D. C. , and also our project
officers; and comprehensiveness to them was not comprehensiveness to us and vice versa.

A few less complicated criteria were adequately clarified for
the district. These included stipulations that federal money not be
used for the renovation or construction of facilities or for major pur-
chases of capital equipment, that the plan include provision for local
documentation and evaluation, that community residents be involved
in the planning process, and that the planning activities be documented.
Beyond those expectations, the district felt that ES/Washington had
other criteria that were somehow being kept secret. The superintendent recalls dealing with Washington as

a very frustrating thing to say that we have no guidelines and yet to be evaluated on a sub rosa-type set of guidelines that, you know, that we didn't know but we found out later they were evaluating on. . . . If they'd just told us that to begin with, it would have been a lot easier than to try to outguess them all the time and wondering if we were getting the right things in. So what was supposed to be a proposal based on our ideas was based upon what they wanted. . . . We were playing games with each other. Rather than just having them say we've got to have this because Congress has said this, why not just tell us that.

PLANNING IN THE DISTRICT

The federal project monitors stressed from the beginning the need for extensive participation, especially from the community, in designing its ES project. To demonstrate that there was participation and also to meet ES/Washington requirements for documentation of the planning process, nine teachers, chosen from among the staff's informal leaders, were assigned the task of recording the meetings that took place and collecting information from them for use in writing the plan. They also played an informal liaison role between teachers and the district leaders. Besides contributing written records, they took advantage of their position to put forth teachers' ideas wherever they could, and they were used by the leaders in turn as a sounding board for teachers' reactions to their ideas. Through attendance at planning meetings and especially administrative meetings, these nine teachers were among the school personnel who were best informed about the planning process and may also have served as an informal channel for other teachers.

Community and staff participation took place primarily during two sets of large meetings held during the fall of 1972. These meetings were confusing and disappointing to staff because of ambiguous description of the project's central theme and lack of specification of the participants' role in planning.

The planning grant enabled the district to add Mark Morand to its central staff as a consultant on individualized education. Morand had a Ph.D. in education psychology and ran a center for children with learning disabilities in a small city nearby. He and John Raleigh had met at workshops in the area and shared similar educational philosophies. It was hoped that the procedures Morand had developed for working with children in a clinical situation at his center could be adopted for use with normal students in a school context through the ES project.

Ambiguous description of the project theme stemmed partly from attempts to anticipate demands from Washington, but it also resulted from continuing flux in the project leaders' ideas about what it should be. One indication of the flux that leaders' ideas about the project theme went through is the shift from using the phrase indi-vidualized education, a term developed during the planning for consoli-dation two years before, to personalized education. With this change, the leaders adopted a phrase used by teachers and parents and, at the same time, tried to remove the idea held by some people that students should be isolated from their peers to receive effective treatment. The change, however, created cynicism about the leaders' motivation. One teacher observed that "every couple of years we get new jargon, a word for the year. Every year something new comes up."

Ambiguity about the nature of the program was more than a mat-ter of terminology, however. According to John Raleigh,

> Individualized education that you use in, let's say an Eng-lish class, is merely one way of meeting the needs of spe-cific children. But the d/p process (the basic means speci-fied in the project proposal for achieving program goals) doesn't work and doesn't work properly until such time that you're able to incorporate all these types of innovations in trying to meet the needs of children. For example, indi-vidualized education is one way of going at it. . . . You can take programmed materials as (another) way of going at it to meet the specific needs of a special child.

Whatever the educational consequences of the open-ended approach to the district's program, it created confusion about its central thrust and about the limits of what was allowable by ES/Washington standards.

Confusion about the role of nonadministrative participants in the planning process is hinted at by frequent but contradictory complaints from teachers that this stage was characterized by both manipulation and lack of leadership. The following dialogue, recorded in the offi-cial minutes of an administrators' meeting during the fall of 1972, shows the ambiguity of the district leaders' position:

> Prin. When we do recognize a trend in the documentation, who makes the decision about what our program will be?
>
> Supt. We have to change attitudes, individualize.
>
> Prin. Who makes the decision?
>
> Supt. Our faculty does this.

Prin.　How are we going to do this?

Supt.　We must all come to the same conclusion. We have some idea about where we should end up.

Cons.　We've gotten bogged down in trying to answer problems traditionally. Hopefully we can show parents that we can operate prescriptively with success. I think we are going to find answers in prescription . . .

Prin.　Who has determined that we will have prescription and attitude change?

Supt.　I have decided. We hope the facts are so well grounded that we can come to no other decision.

This dialogue suggests that administrators did not clearly distinguish between the influence and the social control approaches to participation (Gamson 1968, chap. 1) during planning, but rather that the superintendent was trying to share influence with his staff while maintaining control over the outcome of deliberation. As a result, the roles of various participants remained vague.

Militant secondary teachers were especially sensitive to any hints that influence would be shared, as well as to attempts to limit their impact on planning. These teachers' initial orientations were shaped by planning activities and previous change projects. Morand, who was still new to the district, reported that from a quarter to a half of the teachers, mostly in the high school and junior high, "didn't enter into the full spirit of planning." As one teacher described it,

> Things sort of started out with a kind of defeatist attitude since all of these departments had come up with this five-year plan for [district consolidation] in which they totally reworked the things they were doing. . . . It seemed that if teachers themselves didn't just go ahead and really take action . . . , they just didn't get done. And some of them had a very black attitude.

During planning for consolidation two years before, the district had developed a five-year plan that served as a basis for developing the plan for ES/Washington as well as for the procedures for participatory planning that could be used with some modifications in this effort. Procedures for community participation were changed only slightly. For instance, instead of holding districtwide public meetings, separate sessions were held at each school. Frequently, meetings were divided into smaller groups to facilitate discussion and collection of ideas by the documentors. Between October 4 and December 12, 1972, three sets of meetings were held. The program was explained to the public, interspersed with many of the superintendent's ideas. However, there was no sense that those ideas were being aggressively sold. According to one mother, the meetings were about

> mostly the things John Raleigh wanted to do. And I just have a notion that he was setting his program before us before he even called it that. I think he didn't want to turn us off completely by giving us a government program, because government program has a bad sound to me once in a while too . . . but he was also asking [for] opinions, and opinions he got by the bushel.

These meetings became a forum for airing general complaints about the school system, many of which were about matters of detail such as the selection of fifth-grade cheerleaders or the advisability of continuing the operation of a student lounge at the high school. Other questions such as whether there should be year-round schooling or more discipline were also discussed.

There was considerable discussion of vocational education at these sessions. There was a consensus that the high school curriculum was imbalanced in the direction of preparing students for college, and that a vocational program with more courses directed toward manual and shop-type skills would meet an important need, especially in Butte, which has a large blue-collar population. This issue received considerable support at the high school meetings and some attention as well at the junior high meetings.

Three sets of meetings were also held with teachers. The agendas for these meetings and the guiding ideas for consideration were established by administrators in advance, which reinforced militant teachers' perceptions that a promise to share influence was being made and not kept. According to one,

> At each of the curriculum meetings there was a new word. . . . Regardless of what had been done up to this time now, you had to change all your plans and go this way. So it got to be that a lot of the curriculum work just kind of was a matter of sitting down and waiting 'til somebody made up their mind which way they wanted to go.

At the first meeting on October 19, teachers were introduced to the program, and the importance of comprehensive planning was stressed. They were then broken into groups similar to those used for curriculum planning during the year of preparation for consolida-

tion. These groups were asked to assess progress made in implementing the five-year plan and to suggest what directions should be emphasized and how ES/Washington money could best be used. Working
from the five-year plan ensured that there would be some consideration of individualized education.

At the second meeting on November 27, the rephrased project
theme—personalized education—was presented, along with a new
statement of the district's philosophy. This statement included a list
of 18 goals, the first 4 of which were directly related to the major
emphasis of the project:

1. Comprehensive planning.
2. The development of diagnostic procedures and prescriptive programs. [These became the means for achieving
   personalized education. The finalized procedures will
   be described in the following chapter.]
3. Allowing students to grow as individuals but not in iso-
   lation.
4. The development of a variety of educational approaches.

Other goals made reference to differentiated staffing; aide programs;
and evaluation of teaching methods, programs, and staff; but not to
vocational education. Small group sessions at that meeting were devoted to discussion and clarification of these goals.

At the final planning meeting on January 15, 1973, teachers were
asked to make their recommendations as to the content of the project.
The small group reports gave considerable attention to individualized
or personalized education and to diagnostic and/or prescriptive teaching, but these ideas were not yet well understood. At least four
groups requested workshops to clarify the nature of this teaching approach, and three requested that special personnel be hired to diagnose
students and prescribe for them.

Many of the recommendations were at best loosely related to
the project theme, but they reflected some recurring concerns of
teachers. There were occasional requests throughout the system
that teachers be given time to work and plan together. While this request was often justified as a way of developing better diagnoses, it
was also defended on curriculum-centered grounds as a means of developing stronger programs. The report of the Butte Central Schools
fifth and sixth grades focused on the problems of scheduling specialist
teachers in that building, while that of the fifth and sixth grades in
Angels Camp was a proposal for team teaching, an innovation that the
principal had been trying to accomplish since before the two districts
were combined. The justification for the development of teaming,
however, was argued in terms of its usefulness for personalized edu-

cation. Two other items mentioned in the five-year plan, the mathematics department's request for a curriculum coordinator and the junior high's request for a shorter day, were also repeated.

A few recommendations actually clashed with the project leaders' orientation. Three groups recommended some form of grouping as a way to achieve individualized instruction. Although most requests for materials to be purchased through ES/Washington were submitted separately, those that were included indicate that many teachers were seeking ways to enhance their current educational approaches. Such requests included teaching carrels, cassette recorders, projectors and dark shades, and new physical education equipment.

Once the staff meetings were completed, a small group was formed to write the district's plan, with the responsibility of balancing the interests of the various collectivities. It is important to note that it was made up largely of the district's central staff—Jane Doe, the counselor-program writer, and Mark Morand—and that its work was carefully followed by John Raleigh. The only teacher representative was the chief documentor, and there was no representation of community residents.

THE DISTRICT'S PLAN

The plan the district submitted to ES/Washington in the winter of 1973 was 96 pages long. It was repetitiously written and did not clearly distinguish between presentation of proposed innovative activities to be started the following year and description of the existing program, although it was filled primarily with the latter. It was organized around five components of comprehensiveness defined by ES/Washington, but its central theme was that of personalized education. According to the plan,

> Personalized education . . . considers the academic, social, emotional, and physical needs of children and then provides for these in a way best-suited to the child. A determination is made as to the needs, readiness . . . and interests of the child. A personalized program is then designed for the child with due consideration to the best utilization of the staff, the community, and its resources.

The central means proposed for achieving personalized education was a procedure called diagnosis and prescription (d/p) to be followed by the teacher in the regular classroom. The plan describes d/p as follows:

Diagnosis is derived from the information or observations
the individual teacher has at her disposal. This would include some information about the child's background and
family, plus classroom observations relating to academic
prowess, interests and aptitudes and the quality of the
child's relationships with peers, teachers and other
adults. . . .

The classroom teacher knows that Johnny is the youngest
in a family of six; she observes that he gets along well with
his peers and it is a matter of record that he is behind in
reading. From this information, the teacher concerned
with personalized education can prescribe techniques,
strategies and alternatives which will most benefit this
child.

The discussion of d/p described staff training and administrative procedures such as team teaching, as means to facilitate its use. This
process would be implemented in a common form at all grade levels
from kindergarten through high school.

Another major component of the plan was a governance system
that had been added in order to meet ES/Washington's interest in community involvement and changes in administration and governance.
Three new related kinds of committees were described in some detail.

Staff suggestions received a mixed treatment in the plan. The
vocational program was seen as a crucial indicator to secondary
teachers of their ability to influence the planning process, and was
also supported by the community. According to one documentor,

The emphasis was really there for a vocational alternative
for students, or something of that kind: job training or life
study, work study. . . . We got to the point where the decision was announced, and it seemed to be that that was not
considered a major emphasis.

Project leaders said that ES/Washington's refusal to allow the purchase
of capital equipment did not permit the district to start the kind of program the staff and community wanted, yet no attempt was made to
start the kind of smaller program that Washington might have supported.* Apparently, this step was never considered. Nor were the
mathematics coordinator idea or the proposal to shorten the junior
high school day included. The most important items included were

---

*Vocational education programs were supported in other rural
ES projects.

an aide program (which interested elementary teachers), the Angels Camp principal's teaming project, and a plan suggested by counselors to revise their program. All these activities could be justified in terms of personalized education.

Despite the plan's length, it did not provide useful guidance for the activities that would be initiated in the coming year. In fact, although the revised plan was widely distributed, it was rarely referred to.

CONTRACT NEGOTIATIONS

As the district's planning activity drew to a close, the threats to the continued existence of the Experimental Schools Program were intensified. In November 1972, the NIE undertook its first formal review of the program. This review led to a decision to hold no further competitions. A subsequent review by the ES Program of its research contractors, conducted at the request of the NIE, was basically supportive, but a later review by the General Accounting Office was highly critical of the performance of one of the evaluation contractors. This caused some embarrassment to the NIE in its interactions with congressional appropriations committees considering the FY 1974 budget.

During the spring of 1973, there was considerable discussion within the NIE regarding whether the director of ES had had the authority in 1972 to make moral commitments for long-term funding, whether these commitments should be honored with all 12 districts, and for how long funding should be given. Late that spring the decision was made to honor the commitment to the districts that showed a willingness to continue their relationship with ES/Washington. However, the districts would receive three-year contracts with an opportunity to renew for one more, instead of the four-year grants ES/Washington had intended to offer.

In the face of attacks within the NIE and the lack of external support, the first ES Program director felt trapped by changing requirements for his program. He described his predicament to Corwin (1977, p. 47) as follows:

> The early arguments were . . . give the money to the communities. That's it. And if they burn it, or blow it, have a big party, or whatever they do, it's their money. However, I think it's fair to say that in 1970 the emphasis of the federal bureaucracy was on carrying out some explicit program . . . not being creative. . . . The experiment was only that by the time [the community] got through all the

hurdles to get the money, the experiment was going to be
successful; that was the last criteria.

In response to these pressures from the NIE, program staff became
extremely abrasive in dealing with local districts during negotiations
of plans and contracts in the spring of 1975 (Corwin 1977). However,
the local projects did not understand that the director's hands were
tied; his options were limited to making contract awards to the 12
rural projects that had received planning grants or allowing the funds
to be used elswhere within the NIE. In the end, awards were made
to 10 of the 12 rural districts.

Meanwhile, on May 31, 1973, a small group from the district
consisting of John Raleigh, Mark Morand, an elementary teacher,
and Mrs. Smith from the school board were flown to Washington to
negotiate the district's contract. Unfamiliar with federal contract
negotiations procedures and unaware of the special problems that
ES/Washington faced, they expected the meeting to be a routine matter of clarifying details and fixing the final dollar amount. Instead,
it was a harrowing experience that left the district personnel with the
temporary impression that they would receive no money at all and a
fear of ES personnel that lasted until after a new director was appointed almost two years later. One incident, often retold afterward,
sums up local impressions of what happened. At one point, the ES
Program director entered the room where negotiations were going on
and abruptly asked Mrs. Smith, the board member, to explain some
of the technical jargon buried in the proposal. His questioning sur-
prised her and was so abrasive in tone that it quickly reduced her to
tears. The following year when she had to return to Washington, she
did so with the greatest trepidation. After the first day's session, it
is reported that the superintendent and the counselor sat up most of
the night trying to revise the plan.

Part of this harshness stemmed from ES/Washington's standard
procedures at the time and reflected pressures from their parent
agency requiring the development of strong planning documents. But,
in addition, the agency felt that the district's program was unsound
and distrusted its reporting. ES/Washington felt that the district was
too large for the rural competition. In 1971 the district had a few
more than the prescribed 2,500-student maximum, but the student
population dropped the following year. When implementation was begun in 1973, enrollment was down to 2,300.

Still, the agency basically approved the district's plan and
granted it a three-year, $734,000 contract. In approving the plan,
ES/Washington did not tamper with the parts dealing with individualized
education, but changes were required in the sections on supplies ordering, staffing, and evaluation. Teachers had hurriedly put together a

long list of materials they wanted to buy with the new money that would be coming to the district, but the list was never collated and edited before being sent to Washington. The superintendent did not realize that his teachers had ordered about 17 overhead projectors until he was so informed by the ES/Washington program director. The director insisted that materials be reordered the following fall, but not until a complete list of equipment already available had been compiled in a form that would facilitate sharing among buildings. In addition, the purchase of each item had to be justified in terms of the item's contribution to the new diagnosis and prescription process, although the criteria for an adequate justification were never clarified within the district. An elaborate series of budget constraints that were apparently unique to the district were also developed to help ES/Washington keep better track of how the district used its funds.

The district's program writers originally requested a special project director who would be subordinate to the superintendent and would coordinate ES-related activities. Such a position, they argued, was needed because the administrative staff was already overburdened. ES/Washington adamantly refused to allow such a position because it feared that hiring expensive personnel would reduce the amount of program funds available for use in the classroom, and the Washington project officer felt that the request represented the superintendent's interest in increasing his own prestige more than actual district needs. Final agreement on this point was not reached until the spring of the first year of implementation; but, by the beginning of that year, the basic arrangement—with the superintendent holding the title of director and the local consultant working in the district several days a month for the duration of the project—had been approved verbally. Because the plan's specifications for evaluation were unclear and the district did not have any staff with expertise in that area, Washington insisted that a position for part-time evaluator be created and filled from within the staff. In addition, the district was required to hire a consultant chosen by ES/Washington to draw up a detailed evaluation plan that an untrained person could follow.

TEACHER ORIENTATIONS ON
THE EVE OF IMPLEMENTATION

When the project actually began operation, resistance to it had not yet crystallized. In fact, the staff survey conducted early in the fall of 1973 shows that 72 percent of the teachers and principals thought that having an ES project was a good idea, 12 percent had no opinion, and only 15 percent thought it was not a good idea. If acceptance of the project was pervasive, it was not particularly strong, however. One young elementary teacher reports:

I was really excited about the [ES project]. I thought the others here were too, but some elderly teachers get so established. They were willing to cooperate, but not excited about it.

In offering explanations of project procedures, some teachers informally referred to notices requiring attendance at paid, summer workshops as draft notices and commented that, "Here we are, supposedly personalizing education, but we are getting mass indoctrination." If teachers viewed receiving three-quarters of a million dollars favorably, their support for the project activities was neither wholehearted nor lasting.

The planning process itself had actually reduced potential support for the ES project. The elaborate structure of meetings seemed to offer to the staff the promise of substantial participation in deciding what the project would accomplish and how, a promise that was accentuated by the rhetoric about participation coming from ES/Washington and the district office. In spite of these formal opportunities to participate, teachers argued that they had little or no influence over project plans, citing as evidence the planning document submitted to Washington:

> We were never involved. What seemed to take place was
> that the documentation was there; and at some point last
> fall during the planning stage, the administration—namely,
> Mr. Raleigh—presumed that enough documentation had
> taken place to solidify the project and state what it's going
> to be. And from that point on, the project assumed his di-
> rection and overall control.

In response, John Raleigh and Mark Morand argued that teachers did have a major influence on the content of the project plan. According to Morand,

> When I look at what [the teachers] had in mind, not the par-
> ticular things but the philosophy of what they proposed from
> all levels, they wanted more personalized education. It's in
> the five-year plan [from consolidation]. I assume the five-
> year plan came from teachers. It looked to me like that
> when I looked at it.

The arguments that teachers did have an impact on the plan stemmed partly from the diversity of ideas and the need for a more narrow focus. On the one hand, project leaders argued, the general theme running through all of them was the idea of personalized education. On the other, the problems of integrating the diversity of ideas into a "comprehensive" program was stressed, and diagnosis and prescription was presented as a vehicle through which everyone could be satisfied.

These arguments were not convincing to the staff, however. The 1973 survey shows that teachers felt that the planning process was unfairly dominated by the superintendent and that they had too little to say. Of the respondents, 94 percent felt that the superintendent had "a great deal of influence" over the project planning, 45 percent thought the local consultant did, 26 percent thought ES/Washington did, but only 15 percent thought teachers did. When asked how influence should be distributed, only 42 percent thought that the superintendent should have a great deal of influence; 16 percent thought the consultant should have that much; and 24 percent thought ES/Washington should have that much. Those that felt that teachers should have a great deal of influence totaled 63 percent.

Teachers' perceptions of their influence during the planning process affected their initial orientations toward ES/Washington. Table 4.1 shows that those who did not think it was a good idea for the district to have a project were primarily the ones who felt that they had not had much influence in the planning process.

TABLE 4.1

Teachers' Perceived Influence in Planning and Acceptance
of the ES Project

Perceived Influence	Becoming an ES Project Is a Good Idea	No Opinion	Becoming an ES Project Is Not a Good Idea	Total
Very little or less	16	8	15	39
Some	38	5	1	44
A great deal	16	1	0	17
Total	70	14	16	100

Note: $X^2 = 27.31$; df = 4; p > .001.

CONCLUSION

The early history of the Butte-Angels Camp ES project illustrates many of the difficulties that school districts face when they attempt to plan rationally and comprehensively, implement participatory planning procedures, and develop federally funded projects. For instance, the district did not develop its plan rationally. Goals were not identified and seriously discussed, and consequently, no consensus on them could be reached. No analyses of test scores, teacher performance, budget trends, or other data was conducted during planning. Change ideas were not generated through a systematic search of the environment. Instead, all of the old, but unimplemented, change ideas valued by staff were revived. To these were added the ideas generated by the superintendent and his personal contacts, especially the project consultant. The final plan reflected the interests of the dominant parties during planning: the superintendent who advocated personalized education and ES/Washington, which required a comprehensive effort.

John Raleigh's confusion of the social control and influence approaches to participation exacerbated the problems caused by the lack of a rational approach. The actual writing of the plan was done by those who had been traditionally involved in such activities under the close supervision of the superintendent, and did little to incorporate the ideas of teachers and community members into the overall theme as prescribed by the superintendent. Teachers' influence was particularly limited by their lack of time to work on proposal writing. As a result they were constrained from negotiating their differences with the superintendent over the direction the project should take. Under these conditions, the ambiguous invitation to participate raised teachers' hopes and increased their opposition when those hopes were not met. As one teacher explained, "If they had simply said to us . . . 'This is going to be it,' it would have been easier to swallow than saying, 'You people suggested this. Now, this is it.'"

The militant teachers in particular judged their impact by examining the project plan, and from that they deduced that their influence had been minimal. Those who felt the absence of influence were the least supportive of the project. Although opposition to the project was not widespread, support for it was weak and tentative. It would be reduced still further by the events of implementation.

Although the district's plan met some criteria for comprehensiveness—it included all grades from kindergarten through high school—it did not meet others. Many of the program components were only loosely justified in terms of their contribution to personalized education. Some, like the committee system, could not be justified in those terms, and no alternative explanation for their inclusion was offered. It should be pointed out that the district faced a major obstacle in developing a comprehensive project using participatory methods. The staff was not trained to think comprehensively. Teachers were interested in their own local concerns: vocational education, schedules, curriculum coordination. Their orientations were a strong indication that the sort of system interdependence that ES/ Washington sought to overcome did not really exist.

To plan comprehensively, some distance from the staff's specific interests was required. If those interests were to be taken seriously, either the plan had to include something for everyone or else it had to be based on some integrating principle that cut across the interests of all staff. Personalized education seemed like such a principle to the project consultant, but it was not so viewed by the staff. Hence, ES/Washington's concern for comprehensiveness and the staff's more specific interests seemed to be in conflict, a conflict that was exacerbated by the federal requirement for participation as it was locally interpreted.

In fact, the district's planning effort was shaped substantially by guidance from Washington. Since the promise of future funding was withheld, the district's planning effort was in large measure a proposal writing and negotiation activity. The possibility of carrying out the ideas developed was contingent on receiving approval from ES/Washington. Hence, whatever the goals or needs of the district or individual staff members, those issues had to be addressed within guidelines established by the program. That task would have been easier if the program's guidelines were clear and if a climate conducive to negotiating differences were established. However, the program did not clarify a number of critical points, especially the key concept of comprehensiveness. Moreover, the program's organizational structure created difficulties in knowing with whom it was appropriate to negotiate, and its inconsistent behavior toward the district, especially its increased hostility during final negotiations, precluded effective negotiations.

A major contributor to the program's behavior toward the district was the hostility of its Washington environment. The program never was supported by a powerful constituency with a clear sense of what it should accomplish. After the move to the NIE, it came under severe fire for a number of reasons, some having to do with its approach to change and some related more to the NIE's own problems. Hence, the program devoted a great deal of attention to its survival as a unit, and many of the pressures it faced were passed on to the districts negotiating for funding.

The involvement of a federal agency significantly changes the dynamics of the planning process. Most previous writers on educational change have assumed that, except insofar as innovations are imported from the outside, planning for change is essentially an internal process.* Only one organization's goals must be considered if efforts are made to plan rationally. Administrators have more discretion to share influence with staff because there is less need to comply with external guidelines. When innovation is synonymous with the management of a federally funded project, however, planning must be viewed as an interorganizational process. Such a view helps to explain many of the apparent irrationalities of educational change efforts.

---

*This assumption has generally been unstated. For an exception, see Herriott and Gross (1979).

5

IMPLEMENTATION AND CONFLICT

As has been described in the preceding chapter, the planning process of the Butte-Angels Camp ES project, as managed by the superintendent and his colleagues, did little to integrate the ideas of teachers and residents about the needs of their schools and communities into the overall program design. Consequently, staff enthusiasm for the project was low, and the implementation phase was troubled by opposition and conflict.

Implementation activities took place in three general areas: the educational program (curriculum), governance, and evaluation. In each area, barriers were encountered.* Each of the three areas will be examined in terms of program activities as they were initially conceived, the barriers to implementation that developed, and initial staff reactions and eventual progress toward implementation.

EDUCATIONAL PROGRAM

The primary new activity called for by the ES project was the use of the diagnosis and prescription (d/p) process in the regular classroom, an activity that required the cooperation of all teachers if it was to succeed. The d/p process was a codified procedure for working with students individually. The tasks of developing the procedure and showing staff how it was to be carried out fell to Mark Morand, the district consultant, who codified the process as a five-step procedure. Teachers were instructed to (1) pick a student for the d/p process and summarize quantitative and observational information on that person, (2) formulate a diagnosis of the student's needs

---

*Gross, Giacquinta, and Bernstein (1971) provide the most important discussion of how barriers to implementation can subvert a change effort.

or problems, (3) identify a set of treatment objectives, (4) specify a plan for treatment, and (5) implement that plan. This sequence was made more concrete several weeks into the fall semester of 1973 when the consultant introduced the d/p sheet, a form for recording the results of each stage. One of these sheets is reproduced as Figure 5.1.

In explaining the d/p process to teachers, Morand said that it had been used clinically in other professions and in education by people like school psychologists who dealt with problem students. The innovative aspect of this district's program would be the adaptation of that process to the classroom for use with any child in the system. The essence of the program was not any particular intervention strategy but, rather, one of fitting the specific treatment to the child's individual needs. As he later explained:

> In the past a school system used method number 1 and got a mean score of 50 'cause it only hit half the kids. Then they switched to method number 2 and they still got a mean score of 50 'cause they hit the other half. D/p is method number 3. You use method number 1 with some and number 2 with others, and you should get a mean of 100.

Project leaders argued further that the successful application of this process would make teaching more satisfying and professional.

The rest of the staff had different ideas. Teachers argued that they had worked with individual children in past years, that in fact individualization was the essence of what the teacher in the one-room school was forced to do, and that the district had worked on developing new curriculum alternatives before the project began. Hence, as one principal told a group of parents, the only thing new about d/p was the write-up. Anticipating the impact of the program, teachers expected "a lot of paper work," which they resented. One comment that drew applause from everyone during a volatile teachers' association meeting that fall was, "I wish they'd give us time to teach."

The threat of even more paper work stemmed from the reordering of materials and curriculum catalogs that ES/Washington required. These were to be more exhaustive than anything previously done in the system, covering a wide range of materials and describing the uses of each item. In addition, the application of each item to d/p was to be indicated so that the catalog would tie in with, and support, that activity. Once completed, the catalogs for each building were to be combined so that there would be one overall catalog for the whole system that would be available to teachers using the d/p process or ordering materials. In fact, materials orders were to be justified

FIGURE 5.1

A Specimen D/p Sheet

Student's Name_____   Teacher's Name_____

Area of Diagnosis_____   Grade Level_____

Date of Birth_____   Date of D/p_____

STUDENT SUMMARY

DIAGNOSIS AND PRESCRIPTION

A) Summary of Data Collected (i.e., test scores, grades, etc.):

B) Diagnosis (statement of need or direction):

C) Objectives (short- and long-range):

D) Prescription and Plan:

E) Progress Report:

in part by using the catalog to show that the requested item was not already owned by the system.

Barriers to Implementation

Implementation of the educational program was impeded by four major obstacles: additional work, confusion, incompatibilities of of scheduling and staff competence, and threats to teacher autonomy.*

Additional Work

The added work teachers expected quickly materialized. The following problems with the project are taken from the minutes of an all-staff meeting in one school in January 1974:

> D/p takes too much time from actual teaching. . . .
> There isn't enough time for the special teachers, with
> a large number of students, to do what is asked.

Two elementary teachers described the ways the project took additional time as follows:

> She says she is doing d/p sheets on six kids and she says,
> "I have responsibilities to all other kids in my class too."
> She sees a potential conflict between the time she has to put
> in on d/p and the time she has to put in for the other kids.
> She says she arrives at 7:00 in the morning and works till
> 4:00 in the afternoon planning her lessons and working on
> this, that, and the other thing; and she has very little time
> to get around to working on the d/p sheets. [Field notes]

> The idea is good, but it requires time, and I don't like that.
> It takes time from preparation. . . . I try not to pack stuff
> home. I like to get my work done at school. I refuse to
> take sheets home and work on them for two hours. [Quote
> from interview]

Administrators' arguments that it should not take too much time to fill out a few sheets, especially in the upper grades where teachers had two preparation periods, did little to convince teachers.

---

*The barriers identified by Gross, Giacquinta, and Bernstein (1971) are quite similar. They include role overload or added work, confusion about what is required by the innovation, inadequate training in new techniques, and incompatibilities between work arrangements and the innovation. These are similar to those identified here except for the addition of threats to teacher autonomy. The Gross barriers are technical and can be overcome by managers who plan well or who obtain sufficient feedback to identify the problems. Threats to autonomy are more political, involving differences of opinion over the "rights of office" of teacher and administrators.

One point of confusion concerning the amount of work involved was the question of how many sheets each teacher had to fill out. The district's evaluation design stated explicitly that one quarter of the students in the system would be processed through d/p by the end of the first year. Teachers in the upper grades, who often had over 100 students, feared that they would be required to fill out 25 sheets or more. Official clarification that no teacher would have to fill out more than six or eight did not reduce anxieties because rumors continued to spread that many more would actually be expected.

In discussing how they used their time, teachers emphasized the importance of their regular work and continued to put that first in spite of what they saw as a new emphasis from the administration:

> I consider my regular work first and the project work second, but Mr. Raleigh wants me to put the project first and everything else second. When I work on the project, I work on it just as hard as I work on everything else, but I just don't get to it very often.

> It takes time from preparation, and they've all but said that's OK. . . . I'm here to teach kids. I spend more time with them instead of spending time with the sheets. . . . I feel that with classroom time, it's very important that it is planned right for children. I may neglect the sheets for the kids.

To keep up their regular work, some teachers did work longer hours, although others sought ways to reduce the new demands made of them. Even so, they believed that the additional work was decreasing the effectiveness of their regular teaching. Said one, "We've been personalizing so much in our classes that we're a month behind."

Confusion

Both the d/p process and the curriculum catalogs created confusion among the staff. The project consultant conducted workshops during the summer of 1973 to help teachers understand how to implement d/p. During the 1973/74 school year, he spent three days a week in the district working with teachers and principals individually and attending administrative meetings. In the paid, mandatory summer workshops, the consultant explained to all staff the diagnostic procedures to be used and emphasized the importance of concern for individual students. The primary activity of these workshops was the discussion of a series of cases of students with problems that were presented by various participants. Although there was some variation from session to session in the workshop format and the means of presenting cases, three stages in dealing with the target student were always mentioned. Participants were encouraged to (1) decide what data were relevant, (2) reduce those data to a short summary statement of the student's problem or problems, and (3) suggest a treatment for the problem under consideration.

In spite of these workshops, teachers initially did not understand how to diagnose and prescribe. They reported reading and rereading instructions several times without understanding the mechanics of filling out the sheets and, as a result, they put off doing the paper work even though they may have picked out students to work with. At a series of meetings in late October, teachers asked detailed questions about how many sheets they had to do, whether they had to do d/p work every day, and whether they had to fill out several sheets if the student had several problems. The kinds of data to be included and the amount of detail recorded also caused concern.

Besides being distressing, this confusion increased teachers' work. One teacher, for example, said her impression had been that all relevant information should be recorded on a child's d/p sheet under the data heading, but her principal thought that only test scores should be put there, so he made her rewrite her sheets. Later, when he found that a variety of data should be recorded, he made her do them again to get them back into the correct form.

The curriculum catalogs added to this confusion. During the summer of 1973, one of the high school departments thought that there was money available for curriculum development and set about listing and rearranging all the materials it had on hand and preparing for a new program it was designing. Later, they found that there was only money for cataloging, which, according to the department chairman, had to "follow some kind of format—no one knew what," and that they had already spent its budget for that purpose. Because the format for the catalogs had not yet been determined, this department was allowed to present its work to the district administration to see if it would meet districtwide requirements for a catalog. It became apparent at that meeting that the department had spent more time considering problems of cataloging than the administration had, so the department's catalog was approved, and various administrators began calling the department head for advice on catalog development.

Confusion surrounding the catalogs was all the more frustrating because teachers did not see the value of their work. In fact, catalogs were never fused into a single systemwide mechanism for finding materials, and after they were completed, they were almost never used.

Incompatabilities

Diagnosis and prescription was found to be more incompatible with the organization of the secondary schools than with any others.

It was difficult to implement because of scheduling, and it forced subject matter specialists to expand their roles in ways they felt untrained and unwilling to do. Throughout the district, however, the process increased problems of classroom management.

In the upper elementary grades, d/p had to be accommodated to the teachers' multiclass schedule, which not only increased the number of students each instructor saw but also reduced the time available for each student. The d/p process required, it was said, long-term contact with students in order to be effective. This contact was difficult to maintain throughout the upper grades and almost impossible in those high school departments where quarter courses required that students change teachers each nine weeks.

High school teachers also argued that their special competence was in instruction in their particular subject areas, but they felt that d/p required them to address a range of personal problems that they were uncomfortable with and lacked the expertise to handle:

> A lot of us felt that . . . we had no business, with our training, playing around in the personal lives of children and making diagnoses that involved complex psychological understandings that we didn't have, and took us out of our subject matter area. Subject matter was kind of dismissed as, well, as inconsequential. . . . If you know your subject matter, you ought to be able to address each child as he needs it. But without content, what's the point?

> I've got a girl who's never dated. The problem is bothering her, but I wouldn't touch that with d/p with a ten-foot pole. I look at my job as a _____ teacher. I don't believe I know how to handle that problem with a 16-year-old girl.

Moreover, many felt that the psychological emphasis they saw was undercutting standards and not allowing them to teach as they saw fit:

> A lot of them feel that this is nothing more than a watering down of standards and requirements for kids to the point where teaching means almost nothing anymore. You might as well get someone in off the street to do this.

Although teachers found it difficult to condemn any program that "helps kids," the secondary staff's focus on subject matter expertise and standards provided a basis for arguing that the specific tasks required by d/p were beyond their competence. This outlook was not shared by elementary teachers.

All teachers found that the d/p process accentuated the ever-present tension between attending to individual students and to the whole class without suggesting ways to solve it. One indication of this problem surfaced during the last workshop during which a teacher presented a case where the problem was not an individual student but a whole class that was being disrupted by a clique of five or six students. After some discussion, the consultant indicated that the teacher had two choices. She could try to use the d/p process on several of the problem students at once, but he recommended that she use some other approach in that class and only try applying d/p in other classes where discipline was not a problem. This example suggests that d/p could not be effectively applied to group problems except where these can be reduced to those of individuals, and that it was only useful where order had already been established.

Threats of Autonomy

Teachers also feared that new program activities would be used as a means to institute staff evaluation procedures. At first, Morand met some resistance because teachers felt that part of his job was reporting to the superintendent on their general ability. Later, the focus shifted to the d/p sheets, and doing d/p became synonymous with filling out sheets since there was no way of telling whether the teacher was actually working with students differently from before unless the paper work was done. The very nature of the d/p sheets facilitated evaluation, since presumably a teacher's ability or compliance with the program could be measured by counting the number of sheets completed and assessing their quality.

The fear of evaluation was not completely ungrounded because, throughout the school year, the board of education was pressing the administration to develop mechanisms for teacher evaluation. The board wanted evaluations to be based on principals' observations in the classroom; but, as the superintendent feared that that effort would compete with the attempt to implement the d/p process, he told the principals that evaluation was to be linked to the teacher's work on the ES project. The major element of the principals' work with the project was to help teachers become better at implementing d/p. Each principal was to meet individually with his teachers, as did the consultant, to review their d/p sheets and discuss with them ways to improve their work. The quality of the teacher's work was to be recorded on teacher visitation forms. In response to board pressure, the superintendent told principals that those visitation sheets would be the major form of teacher evaluation for that year.

Attempts to Overcome Barriers

The project offered two potential incentives to teachers that
might have reduced the work required by the project or at least made
it more palatable: curriculum materials and additional teachers'
aides, on which a significant proportion of federal funding was spent.
During the first year, $63,000 supported 24 of the district's 36 aides,
and another $21,000 was spent on instructional supplies. These items
made up 45 percent of the $186,000 spent by the project in 1973/74.

However, significant problems limited the impact of each of
these items. The arrival of instructional materials was repeatedly
delayed. Teachers had ordered materials once in the spring of 1973
and again that fall. After the second set of orders was submitted to
the administration, teachers heard no more about them. As late as
the end of March 1974, none of the ordered materials had arrived in
the district, which caused considerable distress among the faculty.
As one teacher reported:

> The teachers had requested some things, and there was to
> be some justification for what had been asked for . . . and
> I don't know if anyone knows what became of it, if any of
> these materials were ever ordered. It just seems to me
> that it was all sort of a fakey deal. I mean the various
> teachers want [materials] so they can do this and this and
> this in their program; and it seemed the administration was
> satisfied because it all sounded pretty good when it was
> finished. And they shot it off to Washington, and that was
> kind of that.

A number of problems initially limited the value of aides to
teachers as well. The most pervasive of these concerned allocation.
Because the aide was shared by teachers, that person was frequently
working in one teacher's class, while another teacher was planning
for her next assignment in a different class. As a result, class time
had to be employed for explaining the aide's assignment. Moreover,
aides were frequently used as substitutes, especially early in the
year. Aides had three advantages over substitutes: (1) they were on
hand while regular substitutes were not, (2) they were frequently
familiar with the class that they would be expected to teach, and (3)
their daily salaries were lower than that of substitutes. In February, 63 of the 74 teachers who used aides reported that their aides
were used as substitutes in other classes. Because it was rarely
possible to predict when aides would be used as substitutes, teachers
found planning for their use difficult. After February this practice
was prohibited.

Another problem with the aides was concentrated in the high school, but it stemmed from the fact that the district wanted the project to subsidize the use of aides, while federal regulations prohibited the use of ES money for ongoing programs. In 1972/73 the district employed 26 aides; with the advent of the ES project, 10 positions were added and several were supported by the project budget. In order to comply with federal regulations, a distinction was created between clerical and instructional aides. It was argued that previously aides had been used primarily in a clerical capacity to type stencils, correct tests, and so forth. Instructional aides would now be used in the classroom, usually to help implement the d/p process, but definitely to work directly with students. Although this distinction seemed clear enough, it became a source of friction in practice, especially for teachers who wanted traditional clerical aides. Furthermore, the distinction was not applied consistently in all buildings. In the high school, aides were used as they had been in previous years, until after New Year's when the superintendent intervened. He suggested as a guideline that aides could devote 25 percent of their time to clerical work if the rest was spent in the classroom. This decision upset many high school teachers who really wanted clerical help. Teachers reported cases where they left their classes with aides so they could do necessary typing themselves. The aides also were placed in a difficult position. Many had not objected to doing clerical work, although they would have been happy to work with students if their job were changed. Still, for over a month, they felt trapped between the administration, who wanted them in the classroom, and the teachers, who did not.

Reactions to Problems of Implementation

Reactions to the extra work and uncertainty or ambiguities created by implementation of the d/p process varied according to an individual's commitment to the project. The superintendent and the consultant felt closely associated with d/p and had the best understanding of its basic purpose. Consequently, they were among those least upset by the trial-and-error process involved in getting the project off the ground, and with the initial ambiguity that existed.

Mark Morand had used a less codified version of the diagnosis and prescription process in his clinic, but some experimentation was required to adapt it for use in a school system. As a result, the formats of the different summer workshops varied as he developed both his understanding of the system and his mode of presentation. The actual d/p sheets were not developed until after school started. Similar forms to help structure principal-teacher conferences about the use of d/p forms went through several drafts and were not finished until Christmas. John Raleigh was comfortable leaving the details of catalog development and cross-school coordination of the ordering of materials to the principals.

The rest of the staff felt less committed to the project and less clear about its overall conception and goals and so were constantly seeking specific guidelines and instructions, becoming disconcerted when these were not available. Field notes indicate that the principals, who were supposed to act as leaders in their buildings, shared the teachers' general ignorance about the goals and procedures of d/p:

> One commonality among some of the administrators is their lack of knowledge about the program. [This principal] is unsure about a number of points and doesn't feel any need to defend the administration. . . .
>
> [A teacher] has done her homework by reading much of the project literature. She seems to know more about the project than [a principal] who is willing to admit his ignorance.

Generally, the principals kept some distance between themselves and the project. They suggested in staff meetings and private interviews that implementing the ES project added another task to their jobs, which were already demanding. Field notes of a conversation with a principal at the end of the year showed the following:

> All the principals were at least selective in their acceptance of the ES project. One said that he took a long time to figure out the d/p process. He believes in it now and tries to make it go, but he's not interested in evaluation and has as little to do with it as possible. He thinks some other principals didn't understand d/p or weren't interested in it so they didn't do much with it at all.

The principals' reservations were apparent to teachers, one of whom observed:

> A. [The principals] are well-meaning individuals who happen to be caught in the middle in this situation, having to agree with the faculty's dissent about the project and at the same time, holding to their jobs, which means cooperating with the [superintendent]. They've expressed that themselves in informal conversations with teachers. . . .

Q. So they have some discomfort with this too?

A. Oh, there's no question about it. They feel very uncomfortable.

It was also apparent to the superintendent, who spent a great deal of time in fall administration meetings exhorting principals to vigorously support the project.

The principals' response was to ritualize project activities by seeking out very specific guidelines and then following them to the letter. They spent a great deal of time on the telephone, "sharing each other's ignorance," as one of them put it, and trying to figure out what they were supposed to do. When the superintendent instructed the group to work out ways to coordinate materials ordering across buildings, one of them asked several times for a specific procedure for coordination.

The reaction of teachers to the program was more varied, partly because of the split between the militant and conservative teachers. Most of the conservative teachers responded very much like the principals—by disassociating themselves from the project. Like the principals, they ritualized their activities and were so concerned with correctness that they frequently redefined suggestions that had been offered as directives. The consultant, for instance, saw that some inventive teachers had started attaching samples of student's work to d/p sheets. What he and the initiators of this practice saw as a good idea was quickly transformed into a requirement by some of those who were looking for concrete guidelines. A few days later teachers were telling each other that they were now supposed to include samples of student's work.

Ritualization of activities reduced confusion, and displacement reduced the work that was required. The major form of displacement was to shift emphasis from student treatment to filling out forms. This shift allowed teachers to batch-process d/p sheets by collecting test information on a whole class at once or developing broad gauge diagnoses like handwriting problems or spelling problems to facilitate treatment of a number of students with identical problems. While this solution reduced teachers' time investment, it also replaced individualization with another form of grouping.

Secondary teachers shared in the ritualization and displacement activities evident throughout the district, but their opposition was more open and intense. The militants in the district were concentrated at this level, and implementation problems were more complex there.

Because of problems with the d/p process, Morand, who had expected to spend most of his time helping teachers refine their diagnoses and developing more creative treatment alternatives, concentrated during the first quarter on getting teachers to try the process and helping them understand what the forms called for. His efforts and those of other administrators to get sheets filled out were successful; by the end of the semester, 674 d/p sheets had been started, including about 343 in the secondary grades. Comprehension of how to fill out the sheets evolved more slowly. An assessment in early February of sets of d/p sheets filled out by 25 randomly selected teachers indicated that teachers did not understand the mechanics of filling out the sheets.

GOVERNANCE

A change of governance of the schools was prompted by ES/ Washington's definition of comprehensiveness and the regulations that called for changes in community involvement and administration, organization, and governance. The new development was a system of quasi-legislative committees that was parallel to the existing administrative hierarchy except that it was limited to developing and ratifying proposals for curriculum changes that would be systemwide (that is, involve more than one building). These committees were organized on a hierarchical basis, with the Curriculum Development Councils (CDCs) and Tri-Parties reporting to the Curriculum Cabinet, which in turn reported to the school board (see Figure 5.2). Whereever possible, they were modeled on committees used previously in the district.

The CDCs were the successors to the groups that had been formed to develop the Five-Year Plan and later the district's ES project plan, and their primary function was to be, according to the plan, to "coordinate curriculum proposals with each of the nine areas." Instead of dividing into 20 or more groups, as had been done in the past, however, the faculty would be split into 9 sections. Provision would be made for the groups to meet during half-day, release-time meetings, four times a year, but much of these groups' work would be done during the summer.

The Tri-Parties were to be the major vehicle for community input into district decision making. The name, which refers to students, school personnel, and community people, was taken from the group that had met during planning for district reorganization. The original Tri-Party provided a major forum for the two communities to voice their objections and for school people, especially leaders of the Butte district, to explain the value of consolidation. Unlike their predecessor, however, these Tri-Parties were to be three in number, one for every 800 students. The high school, the Butte elementary schools, and the junior high (located in Angels Camp) and Angels Camp elementary schools were each to have one committee. The

FIGURE 5.2

Organization of the Butte-Angels Camp Governance System

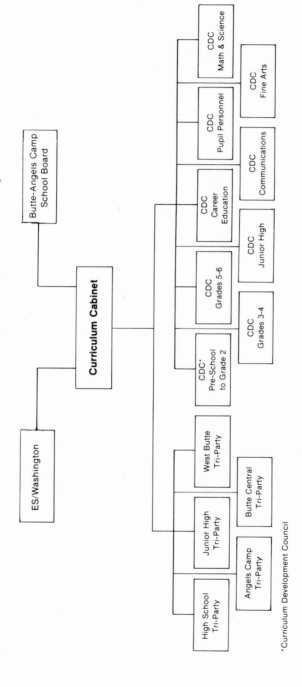

*Curriculum Development Council

plan specified that lay people (including students in the high school) were to outnumber school staff, but it also said that principals would chair the meetings. Just before the groups were first organized, however, the principals and superintendent decided to add two tri-party groups (making a total of five), so that each principal's jurisdiction (the high school, the junior high, Butte Central School, the remaining Butte schools, and Angels Camp Elementary School along with the two outlying schools) would have a tri-party group to represent it.

Curriculum proposals approved by the CDCs or Tri-Parties would go to the Curriculum Cabinet, which consisted of nine teachers (one from each CDC), five parents (one from each Tri-Party), one high school student, all six principals, one school board member, and the superintendent, who was designated as chairman. Although it was assigned some administrative tasks, its primary function was to pass on or veto these curriculum proposals. The project plan specified criteria, including comprehensiveness, and fit with the goals of the ES project that were to be applied to submitted proposals. Approved programs still had to be sent to the board of education for final ratification.

Barriers to Implementation

Implementation of the governance system was impeded primarily by three barriers: threats to administrative authority, confusion, and incompatible arrangements. Administrators had previously maintained the right of ratification of new proposals; at each level they could veto new ideas, approve those within their sphere of responsibility, and pass others on for approval by their superiors. The new committees forced the sharing or even the preempting of this right. One principal argued that this project component created a dual authority system in which the right of ratification rested with the committees, while the responsibility for implementation remained with the old administrative hierarchy.

The dissatisfaction with shared authority was intensified by the inclusion of the general public in the committees. Administrators had recently taken part in a series of bitter meetings in connection with the consolidation of the two districts. Although administrators feared that lay participation would lead to some decisions that they would disapprove, they were especially apprehensive about gripe sessions and discussion of personalities. Gripes were small problems, usually affecting individual families or otherwise of limited concern, and often concerned administrative or procedural matters such as the arrangements of bus routes or the selection of cheerleaders. Discussion of these issues put both principals and teachers on the defensive and took their attention away from what they saw as more important problems. Apparently, earlier meetings had been the stage for attacks on specific individuals and had prompted the only firm ground rule that administrators kept to—no discussion of personalities. Principals were also concerned about how to schedule the agenda with lay people included.

The central points of confusion with these committees were the same that appeared during project planning: how much influence should participants have, and how should such influence be shared? At the same time that administrators were worried that they were losing influence, they did not always accept some of the ramifications of the committee system for their roles, or understand how their actions limited the influence of others. Confusion about how influence was actually distributed is apparent in the superintendent's description of the Curriculum Cabinet's functions at early meetings. He told members that "We're all equal here" and that each person had one vote, which implied equal influence for all, but he also said that the cabinet was where he got his ideas and that he retained veto power. The very name cabinet implied that the body was advisory rather than legislative.

Two widely held preconceptions further limited participant influence: that there was a correct way to make decisions, and that all groups with lay members could serve as publicity channels. As a result, early cabinet meetings were filled with activities providing information on project activities and group progress.

Confusion about participant influence pervaded the CDCs as well. Here the question was whether these committees were work groups or decision-making groups. Since they so closely resembled earlier planning committees, old procedures determined their organizational structure and, following the tradition established the year before, detailed agendas were created before each meeting. For instance, the first meeting in the fall of 1973 was used to explain the newly devised committee structures and evaluation system and to discuss the d/p process, although time was also allotted for the discussion of teachers' concerns. A great deal of time at a second meeting was devoted to discussion of procedural matters like the required format for proposals, the use of the new curriculum catalogs, and reports from various groups. At the high school, discussion time was structured by a set of questions posed by the principal. These agendas increased committee members' confusion about their roles. In a later discussion of the CDCs, at a Curriculum Cabinet meeting, one teacher told the superintendent the following:

> My group was unclear. There was a difference between
> what we wanted to achieve and what we were supposed to

achieve, and we were uncertain about whether to go with what we wanted to do or what we should do.

The committee structure was incompatible with district organization in three ways. First, the establishment of Tri-Parties originally cut across the administrative organization of the district, but this problem was quickly rectified. Second, the CDC groups were artificial and lacked cohesiveness. The nine groups specified in the proposal consisted of combinations of people who had not worked together previously and who sometimes felt that they did not share any interests, as in the case of the unit composed of physical education and counseling personnel. A revised grouping in the second meeting contributed to the discontinuity between it and the first one. Third, meetings were always planned and called by the administration, with no provision for teachers or groups to call their own meetings. Since only four meetings were scheduled and almost three months separated the first two, it was difficult for the CDC units to develop any cohesiveness and to devise proposals.

Committee Activities

The task of organizing the Tri-Parties fell to the principals, and the project plan provided initial guidance. It specified that principals should chair the sessions, that they should invite parents, and that a certain number of parents should attend each group meeting. Discussion at an early administrators' meeting raised questions about the advisability of having principals chair meetings, and whether these meetings were open to the public. The first question was left to the discretion of the principal, and the second was not adequately clarified, since some administrators left the meeting feeling Tri-Party sessions were supposed to be open, while others thought they were to be limited to invitees. The superintendent also responded to principals' concerns about how to fill the time by saying that Tri-Parties provided an excellent opportunity to publicize the school system, including the programs of particular schools, and especially of the ES project.

Ambiguity about whether meetings were open or closed, the procedure of inviting the participants of the previous year's planning session, and lack of adequate premeeting publicity, all contributed to a feeling among interested parents who had not received invitations that the meetings were closed. In response to complaints after the meetings, the superintendent clarified that meetings were open, but the system had to spend the next two years combating the impression left by the first meetings.

After the first meeting, a dual pattern occurred that, with a few exceptions, characterized all future tri-party meetings. First, lay turnout was so low that administrators worried about how to increase attendance. Fortunately, they received help from board members who wanted to encourage lay participation and felt that Tri-Parties were not working. Second, the meetings were used primarily for instructional purposes and came to consist of presentations by staff, sometimes to explain program elements, and sometimes to advocate changes proposed by the staff. After the first meeting, these presentations were rarely related to the ES project, instead they focused on building concerns, usually matters considered important or entertaining by the principal, but about which parents often had questions.

The first two CDC meetings were highly structured by district administrators. Still, the second CDC meeting was the scene of open expressions of opposition to the ES project, so the administration may have feared to have anymore. Those two were the only ones ever called. The only reason given for their discontinuance was that, as the superintendent put it, the administrators did not think the CDCs were "very successful."

The administration developed two procedures that further inhibited the development of the cabinet. First, a five-part format was required for all proposals. This format included sections that defined the need that the new program would meet, the goals of the program, the program's objectives—which were to be more specific than its goals—the actual activities involved, and the means for evaluating the program's success. Parts of two meetings were devoted to explaining this format. This heavy emphasis on proposal form inhibited the frequent submission of new ideas. Second, proposals had to be submitted to the superintendent a week in advance so he could have them duplicated and circulated to members before the meeting. Once proposals began to appear at cabinet meetings, they were rarely presented to the superintendent as required, and his office did not circulate in advance those that did get turned in. The major significance of the requirement was that it complicated the process of developing and presenting new ideas. Moreover, when a proposal of which the superintendent disapproved was presented, these rules gave him procedural grounds on which to attack the idea and thus delay its acceptance without having to discuss its substance.

The cabinet met regularly through January. The agenda was filled with procedural and educational matters. One of these was a set of brainstorming exercises designed by the superintendent to demonstrate "proper decision-making processes"; a cabinet workshop on decision making was conducted by a specialist from the state Department of Public Instruction in April. Other educational activities referred to general questions of curriculum and teaching methods and to the ES project. Among these was a demonstration of how to fill out d/p sheets, a presentation by a book company salesman on new ideas in educational materials, a review of existing programs by building principals, and regular reports from the group evaluating the project. Two or three ideas for changes were discussed and one written proposal was presented, but very little substantive discussion took place. Many members became frustrated.

EVALUATION ACTIVITIES

The third component of the project consisted of the within-district activities necessary to evaluate its progress as required by ES/Washington. Although consultation with Washington program staff in the spring of 1974 indicated that district evaluation was to provide information for ongoing improvement of the project, this activity was always considered by the locals to be primarily an aspect of federal surveillance of the project's progress. In fact, because of its specificity, the evaluation design, a document specifying what parts of the program were to be evaluated and how, proved to be a more effective and demanding guide for action than the project plan itself during the first months of implementation. At an early administrators' meeting, the superintendent referred to it as "your Bible." This design included a series of objectives, time points for measuring success in meeting objectives (deadlines), procedures for measuring progress in meeting objectives, and criteria for success. These criteria included the quota of students to be channeled through the d/p process in the first year (25 percent) and later, an elaborate procedure for rating the quality of d/p sheets, and specifications of acceptable levels of staff support for the program (that is, participation by 80 percent of teachers and aides as indicated on a questionnaire distributed in the spring). It also provided procedures for measuring student outcomes.

Barriers to Implementation

Threats to staff autonomy and confusion were the major barriers to implementation of the evaluation plan. Existence of the plan increased teachers' fears that the ES project would be used as a means to evaluate them, a fear that was increased by creation of the position of teacher evaluator, which was taken to mean that the person would have responsibility for evaluating teachers. The title had actually been chosen to indicate that the person holding the position would be a teacher who had been relieved of part of his or her teaching assignment in order to perform evaluation functions. Fears about the teacher evaluator's job and concern that it might require much work made it very unpopular, and the person first considered for it refused to take it. To overcome these problems, the job was redesigned and assigned to a committee consisting of one representative from each building. Even under these conditions, considerable cajoling was needed to induce people to serve on the committee.

The teacher evaluator committee shared some of the anxieties of their peers and felt a responsibility to help alleviate them. For instance, when a checklist for d/p notebook evaluation was being constructed, the committee felt it should be distributed in advance to teachers so they would know how they were being evaluated. The project consultant opposed this move because he wanted to eliminate teaching to the test. Later on, teacher evaluators became almost fanatical on the subject of confidentiality and frequently would present data only in highly aggregated form to protect individuals and the staff of particular schools. The group felt rewarded for its extreme concern, however, because it was confident that questions concerning attitudes toward the project had been honestly answered. Thus, the teacher evaluators walked a fine line between following the evaluation design and thereby meeting the demands of ES/Washington, on the one hand, and relieving the anxieties of their peers, on the other.

In spite of its importance, the writing and implementation of the evaluation design, which took place after the district's contract was signed, were characterized by great confusion. The consultant that ES/Washington had required the district to hire had no previous knowledge of the district, so he had to rely primarily on impressions gained through a few discussions with project leaders and on information available in the project plan. After initial consultation with the district staff, he drafted a design that was revised and completed by him in cooperation with the superintendent, the district's own project consultant, the public relations director (acting as confidential secretary), and the counselor-program writer during two days of conferences. Throughout these conferences, the evaluation consultant urged the group to be as specific as possible in specifying objectives and to clearly devise measurement procedures. Because he would return to the site only once, and it was anticipated that whoever would carry out the design would have very little background in evaluation methodology, he tried to develop simple procedures that would not require much subsequent elaboration to be understood.

The district staff responded to a variety of local concerns. One was that student outcomes not be tied to achievement tests, partly because most district test scores fell near the national average and the superintendent felt that raising those scores significantly would be difficult but also because project leaders wanted to emphasize affective outcomes wherever possible. Some attention was given to possible effects of the evaluation design on teacher attitudes. Terminology used to define behavioral objectives was avoided for fear that it would scare the staff, who had already had some training in that area.

Still, some decisions that proved to be very important and constraining were made based upon insufficient information, and with little attention paid to their possible side effects. Since no one knew yet what kind of work would go into filling out d/p sheets in a public school context, annual production quotas had to be plucked out of the air. Diagnosis and prescription objective number 8—which specified that "teachers will be able to [develop] appropriate and concise diagnostic need statements . . . [which] will be written so that objectives for individuals can be determined"—was added as an afterthought as a way to ensure that excessively sensitive information on students and their families would not be collected and to help maintain confidentiality. It later became a major quality-control device and a source of great tension.

The six teachers who made up the committee had no background in testing and measurement, and they quickly ran into two problems. First, in spite of efforts made when the evaluation design was written, the document was difficult to understand. Some understanding was required because the evaluators were supposed to translate statements of procedures into questionnaires and checklists, as well as to administer and tabulate them. The project consultant who met with the group frequently was able to clarify some points, but a great deal of ambiguity remained. When the evaluation consultant met with the committee at the end of November 1973, even he could not recall what the intention behind some objectives and measurement procedures had been. Because the committee felt it lacked the expertise and authority to deviate intelligently from the evaluation design, sessions were frequently devoted to long, involved discussions in an attempt to decipher the meaning of objectives and ways to implement them.

FROM TENSION TO CONFLICT

By December the district was in what the superintendent later referred to as the Christmas doldrums. The d/p process created more work and new problems for teachers, but that work was under way, even though the faculty and principals were not sure what was expected of them. The system of teacher visitations and the evaluation component raised the threat of teacher evaluation and consequent loss of autonomy and job security. While the new committee structure offered the promise of more staff participation in decision making with respect to curriculum, it also threatened administrators' authority; and there was no action to indicate that any of the new groups would show any independence. These factors contributed to an overall sense of frustration and depression within the district. The period from January through March 1974 marked the high point of conflict over the ES project. Teachers' fears that the project was being used to evaluate them came to rest on the attempt to measure d/p objective number 8 in the evaluation design, the objective added to reduce collection of sensitive information about students. The procedure called for random selection of 25 d/p notebooks. Some sheets from each notebook would be assessed for their quality according to a checklist devised by the teacher evaluator committee. Each book would be rated by the project consultant and a principal, but the teacher's name would be removed from the sheets to guarantee that the evaluation would be of the "progress of the district, not of specific teachers," to paraphrase a common explanation. Still, many teachers feared that this measurement procedure would be used to identify those who were doing poorly, and several began writing out d/p sheets in January to be sure that they did not get into trouble.

The measurement procedure was explained to teachers at the January CDC meetings. Before the high school staff broke into subgroups that day, a number of administrative matters were explained to the whole faculty, including the notebook evaluation procedure. The high school teacher evaluator who explained the procedure emphasized the elaborate precautions that the committee had taken to ensure that there would be no way for raters to identify individual teachers' notebooks. He also passed out copies of the checklist to be used by raters and explained how it worked. The evaluator, a popular teacher, was uncomfortable about having to speak for the administration on such an unpopular topic, and he drew laughs when he made a joke about how teachers could use the checklist to grade their own d/p sheets. When, in an attempt to encourage teachers to read the evaluation design, he suggested, "If you have 15 minutes to spare and are really bored, you should read this section [of the evaluation design]," he broke up the house. A few minutes later, a teacher pointed out emphatically that, since she was the only person who taught her subject matter to high school students, there was no way to maintain the confidentiality of her d/p notebook; and the whole room broke into laughter again. Her statement was followed by several minutes of nervous comments and questions, and a few derisive ones, as well as some laughter.

When, shortly after this general discussion, John Raleigh got up to speak, he was furious. He castigated the teachers for making light of the teacher evaluators' work and said that they were working very hard and sincerely trying to maintain the confidentiality of individual notebooks. He then said that, because the teachers did not support the ES project, they did not care about students. "Your attitude," he concluded, "is 'damn the children and full speed ahead!'" and he stalked out of the room.

The superintendent's speech put the high school faculty in turmoil. A few were not sure what had triggered it, but many who had spoken out or made loud comments thought it was directed specifically at them. The woman who had spoken up was in tears. A large number were incensed at his outburst, which they felt was inappropriate, and a very few said they were on the verge of quitting during the speech. As word of the event spread through the system in the days that followed, it caused reverberations in the other buildings.

In the weeks that followed, pressure on the staff increased. Raleigh told his principals:

> Teachers see d/p as a cumbersome process that was thrust
> on them. It isn't. They are completely involved. More im-
> portant, it's a new way of teaching. Unless they change
> their attitudes, it will be a cumbersome process. . . . I
> don't buy that the morale of teachers is low. It may be
> because they don't want to get off dead center. I don't
> want you hiding behind tradition. I know it makes your job
> more tenuous.

He also encouraged moving toward the implementation of more advanced elements of the project. At that time, the Angels Camp elementary building was believed to be the most advanced in its understanding of the project and its acceptance of d/p, while the high school was seen as the source of greatest resistance. Because the Angels Camp school had just implemented its team teaching program, getting teachers together to work on d/p and develop educational alternatives was seen as a way of facilitating progress on the project. Various forms of teaming had already been considered as ways to improve d/p later on, but until January 1974 they had not been stressed. At that time, the superintendent indicated that board pressure for staff evaluation would be met through use of the teacher visitation sheets that were being designed to assess teachers' progress on d/p.

Two messages to teachers indicated this increased pressure. First, the number of d/p sheets that teachers were expected to do increased:

> Earlier they said we should have five or six done. Now,
> they don't think that's near enough. The consultant said
> five or six was enough. He now thinks they're trying to

> rush it, is my impression. . . . At the last meeting with
> [my principal], he said to do one a week, and if there are
> any failures over a nine-week period, you will do a d/p
> sheet on them.

Second, teachers' tenure was threatened. The last part of the principal's teacher visitation form asked for an indication of the teacher's attitude toward the project. When high school teachers asked whether their tenure depended on their attitude toward the project, they were told that it did, but that their principal felt that his job was on the line, too. This information also spread to other teachers in the system and was confirmed by less explicit communications from other principals.

Shortly afterward, the committee structure was put to the test as two teacher-initiated ideas, which had been alive in the system since planning for consolidation, were put before the Curriculum Cabinet. Significantly, neither of these ideas was routed through the CDCs. One came from the high school Tri-Party. In response to parents' questions about mathematics instruction, the mathematics teachers indicated they felt that student achievement was low and could be improved through coordination of the curriculum from kindergarten through grade 12. Their report was presented to the high school Tri-Party in March, and shortly afterward the cabinet received a request to create a half-time mathematics coordinator for a one-year trial period.

Progress was made more quickly in the junior high school, which had felt since consolidation that its long school day contributed to discipline problems and detracted from student learning. The staff had concentrated on getting the length of the day reduced, but was faced with technical problems resulting from the district's complicated bus schedule and opposition from the superintendent who felt that the proposed change would weaken the school's program. That fall, the building's new counselor suggested that a form of modular scheduling, with which he was familiar, might offer a solution to the school's problem by breaking up the day for students and making it more interesting. Two proposals were then prepared by the school's staff, one for a shortened day and another for modular scheduling. Both were presented at the cabinet's February meeting, but without following the required procedure of delivering them to the superintendent a week in advance. The superintendent raised a number of difficult questions at the meeting about the relationship of the proposals to the project, and then announced a number of decisions on procedure and agenda for the rest of the year that precluded action on them. The next day, he went to the junior high and castigated both the counselor and the principal for their roles in developing those proposals.

TABLE 5.1

Orientations of Teachers toward the ES Project, Spring 1974
(percentage of positive responses)

	Elementary	Secondary	All Staff
To what extent has the d/p technique resulted in a positive direction of change for the students for whom you have diagnosed and prescribed?[a]	—	46	55
To what extent are you satisfied with your participation in the policy-making procedures of the ES project?[b]	47	21	32
To what extent do you feel that your recommendations for the project have been given adequate attention by the administration?[b]	40	18	28
To what extent do you support the ES project?[a]	—	59	62
To what extent do you desire to continue the project?[a]	—	45	53

[a]Administered in early March; overall response rate is not known. Because of difficulties recovering junior high questionnaires for reanalysis, the response rate for that school is only 71 percent, while that for the high school is 91 percent.
[b]Administered in mid-April; 90 percent response rate.

Note: Based on questionnaires administered by the Butte-Angels Camp School System Teacher Evaluator Committee. Respondents had four choices with numbers 4 and 3 marked positive and numbers 2 and 1 marked negative.

These actions indicated that ideas of which the superintendent disapproved would never receive cabinet ratification.

Under the circumstances, it is not surprising that questionnaires distributed by the teacher evaluators in the early spring indicated limited support for the project. Secondary teachers were consistently more opposed to the project than their peers in the lower grades (see Table 5.1). Almost half the teachers did not believe that d/p was helping their students. Teachers' major objections, however, were that their ideas were not given adequate weight when decisions were made. Most elementary teachers shared this complaint, which was almost universal in the upper grades. Hence, fewer than two-thirds of the teachers said they supported the project, and only a bare majority wanted to continue it for another year.

Enter the Board

It is the loser who calls in outside help and thereby expands the conflict (Schattschneider 1960); and, as pressure intensified, militant teachers in particular felt that they were losing. They had no recourse within the administrative hierarchy, since the man at its apex was the strongest advocate of the project, which was the source of so many grievances. Organized disobedience would have been impossible because of the split between the militants and the conservative teachers. Instead, the militants turned to the new school board they had done so much to help elect. Communication with the board was facilitated by teachers' old friendships with Jack Iannetti, Ella Smith, and the Reverend Mr. Maslow. In fact, the practice of bringing problems to the school board directly, but informally, had developed in the fall before opposition to the project became so intense.

The slowly developing harmony between the board and teachers received a severe setback in January when the board reelected the superintendent and principals for the 1974/75 school year, and a report highly laudatory of the administration was published in the local newspaper just six days after the altercation between the superintendent and the high school staff. This report severely disappointed teachers who had complained about the event to the board and had hoped the board would defend them against future attacks and retribution. In fact, the board had doubts about a number of actions taken by the administration, and a prolonged but inconclusive discussion had preceded the decision to reelect.

In the succeeding weeks, teachers kept the board abreast of events, including the threats that noncooperation with the ES project would lead to loss of jobs, and the way that the junior high proposals were handled by the Curriculum Cabinet. Simultaneously, the board took steps to ensure that it would have greater direct control of the school system, to reduce what it saw as illegitimate threats to the faculty, and to get the administration to accept its own evaluation program. The local newspaper was asked to cover board meetings directly and not to rely on press releases from Jane Doe, who was seen as part of the administration. Informal communications with the superintendent became more frequent, and, as distrust deepened, the board began sending pairs of representatives to meet with him. It also considered having formal fact-finding meetings at each school, but never actually did so.

At the end of January, the board met privately with principals and ordered them to take a more direct role in supervising teachers, but to refrain from threatening to fire them. It also indicated that no principal would lose his job because of nonsupport of the project. Although principals were asked to communicate the board's position to teachers, they never did. In fact, principals considered the meeting a breach of the chain of command that put them in the difficult position of receiving contradictory orders from their superiors, thus adding to their insecurity. Consequently, the board communicated its position to teachers informally.

By the March board meeting, there was considerable speculation within the system about whether John Raleigh would be fired. While this action was not taken, five motions were passed that considerably constrained his freedom of action, including one that endorsed the Curriculum Cabinet, enjoined it to follow all outlined procedures for submitting proposals, and directed it to consider all proposals before it at the next meeting.

Federal Intervention

ES/Washington did not become aware of the problems in the district until they reached crisis proportions. In fact, ES/Washington effectively lost contact with more of its districts after the school year began. Project officers did not answer telephone calls, answer correspondence, or promptly review documents called for by the newly signed contracts because they were often too preoccupied with the continuing struggle to ensure the survival of their program. Communication was further encumbered by a rapid turnover of project officers, which led to the loss of personal contact between agency and district.

In Butte-Angels Camp, serious communications problems began in August 1973, when the first project officer for the district left ES/ Washington. After a lapse of over a month, a second project officer was appointed who served until Christmas. From then until almost the end of the school year, the district dealt sporadically with a number of people and often had no contact person in the Washington office. As a result, money came into the district slowly during the first months of the project, and the board had to borrow from its general fund to pay teachers for summer training workshops. As late as December 11, 1973, Washington was still $22,000 behind in its payments and the district was borrowing to make up the difference. Approval to spend money for specific items as required in the contract also came slowly. By the time the necessary several months passed to get one workshop ratified, the teachers who had requested it no longer felt the need to have one. More important, teachers' requests for curriculum materials that had been made in the fall of 1973 were not processed by Washington for months, resulting in a huge delay in their arrival (as discussed earlier in this chapter).

In late February, after the district had been without a project officer for two months, it was visited for a day by two ES/Washington staff members. Although they spent most of their time visiting with project leaders and observing model project components, they did receive some indication of the district's problems. Shortly after that visit, ES/Washington requested a meeting to discuss the district's "cost underrun" and help it find ways to spend out its budget.

At the board's direction, teachers were included in planning for the trip. These sessions, which were held after the March board meeting, became a stage for a three-way interchange among the superintendent, board members, and representatives of teachers and principals about the progress of the project. Numerous complaints about a variety of topics ranging from the absence of ordered supplies through lack of staff participation in decision making to threats to tenure were aired. It also became apparent that these problems were attributed primarily to John Raleigh. One teacher reported, "I've psyched myself up to say this so I guess I will. At the high school, most people are not against the program, but the superintendent."

As the system's agenda for the trip developed, four issues that needed discussion were isolated: planning for summer in-service, which was behind schedule; the use of aides; the work of the teacher evaluators; and the need for a project director. The more militant teachers originally opposed the idea of a full-time director if it meant that project money would go to outside experts, but when they were assured that the position would be filled from within the faculty, they supported it as a means to gain more control over the project. In addition, the more militant teachers hoped that ES/Washington would somehow resolve the local conflict in their favor.

The group that went to Washington to discuss the problems within the system consisted of the superintendent, two board members, one principal, two teacher evaluators, and one high school teacher.

Although some local concerns, like the teacher aide program, were not discussed, there were two clear outcomes. First, ES/Washington became aware of the magnitude of conflict within the district, and quite pessimistic about the ability of the district to solve its own problems. Second, the district learned that the idea of a project director was still unacceptable, but they were urged to find another solution to its problem. The program director strongly suggested that the governance system outlined in the project plan be revised and that the Curriculum Cabinet, which he felt was too large to be efficient, be reduced in size so that it could act as a steering committee. A deadline for the reorganization of that system was established.

A First Accommodation Is Reached

Even before the trip to Washington, the basis of a new accord within the district was beginning to emerge. Just the weekend before, the board met with John Raleigh for ten hours to discuss their differences. During that meeting, the superintendent indicated his assent with the board's wish that less pressure be employed to achieve staff compliance with the ES project. In the remaining two months of the school year, he made a number of attempts to develop more cordial relations with teachers.

The Curriculum Cabinet also became more responsive to teachers' ideas. At its April meeting, the proposals to shorten the junior high school day and to appoint a mathematics coordinator were passed. The modular scheduling proposal was deemed a building concern that did not require cabinet action, and was referred back to the junior high school, which began preparations to put it into action the following year. A staff proposal to develop a comprehensive environmental education program was also accepted by the Curriculum Cabinet and the school board, subject to approval for funding by ES/Washington. During this period, too, curriculum materials ordered the previous fall began to arrive in the district.

The teachers' success in the Curriculum Cabinet had a direct effect on the attempts to develop a new administrative-governance structure for the project. Two competing alternatives were the old proposal to hire a project director and the ES/Washington directive that the size of the Curriculum Cabinet be reduced so that it could serve as a steering committee. After the Washington trip, a committee consisting of one teacher, a board member, and a principal met to consider these alternatives. It concluded that a project director or a steering committee could not meet the more militant teachers' objectives of reducing administrative control of the project. Most district personnel believed, however, that the Curriculum Cabinet was becoming an effective channel for teacher input. While they acknowledged that the cabinet might be inefficient, they felt that its size permitted more effective representation of a variety of interests in the system and therefore opposed the program director's suggestion that the number of people on the committee be reduced. At a meeting between district representatives and a newly appointed project officer in late May, agreement was reached not to modify the formal structure at all. Instead, a slowly developing practice of appointing ad hoc committees to facilitate the consideration of particular changes was codified in hopes of increasing the cabinet's efficiency.

The appointment of a project officer was in itself appreciated by district personnel, and his suggestion that teachers could contact him directly about major problems was well received.

These changes were all part of a major reallocation of power and authority within the district. Involvement in the ES project was redefined from mandatory to voluntary, and teachers found that they had more opportunity to implement their own ideas. When these changes were recognized, opposition to the project began to evaporate, as these notes of a conversation between two militants in a teachers' lounge indicate:

> The two of them agree that the system has passed the point
> of just being out to get the superintendent. They feel that
> he's "pulled in his horns" and that they have more of a say
> in the project. So Dennis Clark now feels it is up to the
> teachers to go with the program. Otherwise, "We have met
> the enemy and it is us." He says it would be a shame to
> lose the $700,000 that ES was providing the district.

Moreover, end-of-the-year reports show that the district met its d/p objective: by June 29.5 percent of all students had been diagnosed and prescribed for. Of the sheets completed, 54 percent were filled out in the six upper grades, which is not out of line with the proportion of staff (53 percent) or students (41 percent) in school at that level.

CONCLUSION

Early implementation of the Butte-Angels Camp project raises questions about the four assumptions about resistance to change identified in Chapter 1. Contrary to the first assumption that resistance to change is irrational, resistance was highly rational from the individual teacher's or principal's perspective. The project created costs of belonging to the organization in the form of four barriers to implementation: added work, confusion, incompatibilities with existing arrangements, and threats to individual autonomy. It also offered two potential benefits: increased student performance, which would be rewarding to teachers, and added material and help from aides. Unfortunately, neither benefit was adequately provided. Another indication of the rationality of resistance is that it declined as the balance of rewards for teachers increased, when teachers found that they could use the project to initiate and support their own change ideas.

Second, resistance is assumed to be a reaction to the change project. This assumption proved partly true in Butte-Angels Camp. However, another important issue was that of John Raleigh's administration and overall handling of relations with his staff. The increase of opposition after the superintendent threatened to fire noncooperating teachers, and the responses to the teacher evaluator survey, which indicated that teachers were more unhappy with their limited voice in project decision making than with the d/p technique, lend additional credence to this interpretation.

The third assumption is that resistance is generally centered in lower staff. While the most adamant resistance did come from teachers, not all teachers opposed the project. Resistance was concentrated among the militants. Moreover, project support of two other groups, the principals and the school board, was also lacking.

Finally, resistance is assumed to be passive. Project displacement and the principals' distance from the project are evidence of passive resistance. However, resistance became more active when the superintendent took actions that were perceived as illegitimate by threatening to fire noncompliant staff. Then teachers took strong measures by appealing to the school board and ultimately gaining greater control over the project.

The resistance formulation is limiting. It hides some aspects of the change process and masks the similarities between change and other organizational processes. Such resistance is a special case of the opposition that takes place whenever workers are faced with orders that are viewed as not legitimate and that increase the work required without providing additional rewards, whether those rewards are in the form of money, advancement, or the opportunity to help children learn (where that is seen as rewarding). This formulation should be replaced by a broader view that identifies the potential costs to participants in the form of barriers to implementation and competing commitments from ongoing work; the seeds of opposition that stem from other issues, which color participants' perceptions of the specific project; and the different interests and concerns of teachers, principals, and superintendents, among others.

6

THE PROJECT TRANSFORMED

The first year of the Butte-Angels Camp ES project (1973/74) was a watershed for both the district and the project. During project planning and early implementation, John Raleigh was able to dominate events in the district and to establish his innovation, d/p, as the major program component. After the conflict in the spring of 1974, a new balance of power emerged in the district. D/p was never eliminated from the project, but it was deemphasized. Moreover, the project incorporated a number of new elements. This chapter describes the outcome of the project's transformation during the 1974/75 and 1975/76 school years. It first considers the project's new context and then examines changes in actual project activities.

THE NEW PROJECT CONTEXT

After 1973/74, the federal context in which the project operated changed dramatically. The National Institute of Education reassigned the first ES project director in December 1974. His departure was followed by an 18-month period of laissez-faire project administration before the program was finally dismantled. The effort to keep the program intact became an impetus to define almost anything a local project did as a sign of success.

Within the district, the conflict over the project in its first year created a new balance of power. The school board became an integral part of the district's decision-making structure, and its influence increased at the expense of administrators. This influence further increased during the third year of implementation (1975/76), when John Raleigh took a year's leave of absence to continue his doctoral work. In the spring of that year, the board announced that he would not return. One of the principals replaced him as superintendent. This section explores these changes by describing the demise of the federal ES program, the new balance of power in the district, and orientations to the project in Butte-Angels Camp.

Demise of the ES Program

After the contract for the Butte-Angels Camp ES project had been signed, and throughout the first year of implementation, the National Institute of Education (NIE) management continued to pressure the ES program to reevaluate its obligations to the 18 existing projects and related research efforts. The NIE wanted to reassign resources committed to ES activities to its new initiatives. The ES program director tried to resist these pressures as he had previous ones, but the program's support had weakened appreciably. One reason was that the abrasive handling of contract negotiations with local districts prompted a number of complaints to congressmen about the program. Hence, although the program did provide direct support to educational practice, it did not have congressional backing (Corwin 1977). On December 6, 1974, the director was abruptly relieved of his responsibilities and reassigned to a staff position in the Office of Education.

At the time of the reassignment of the original director of ES, the program included 11 additional staff members, several of whom were assigned to it only on a part-time basis. There was a director of programs responsible for the monitoring of the 18 local projects and 7 project officers working under him.

There was also a director of evaluation responsible for the monitoring of the 7 evaluation contractors. He had 2 project officers working under him. The director of evaluation was appointed to serve as acting director of ES and was later made director. The new director could claim as his major expertise the design and implementation of program evaluations, having been an evaluation officer for 5 years with the Office of Economic Opportunity. He had little expertise in the design or implementation of the programs themselves, and readily acknowledged his lack of first-hand knowledge about public schooling. He exhibited little hesitancy to take an active stance vis-à-vis the various evaluation contractors to the ES program, but seemed reluctant to adopt the highly active stance of his predecessor vis-à-vis the 18 local project sites.

When the original director of ES departed, the NIE leadership acted promptly to validate its authority and to make the ES program responsive to the NIE's priorities. An Experimental Schools Review Committee consisting of ten NIE staff members who were not affiliated with ES was appointed and held its first meeting on December 13, 1974, one week after the reassignment of the original director. The acting director of ES was asked to prepare a Mission Statement for review by his immediate superior, who revised it and forwarded it to the review committee on December 23. During January 1975, briefing materials were prepared by ES staff members for the committee. On January 28 a letter was sent to the superintendent of schools in each of the ES project districts informing them of the NIE review of the Experimental Schools Program. During February site visits were made to all eight urban sites and to four of the ten small, rural sites, not including Butte-Angels Camp. Reports were prepared by each site visit team and forwarded to a steering subcommittee of the full committee. The steering subcommittee met several times during March and prepared a draft report, which after review and revision by the full review committee, was forwarded to the acting director of the NIE on March 28, 1975 (Doyle 1975).

One of the major issues addressed by the ES review committee was whether the ES Program should remain intact as an entity within the NIE or have its various contracts assigned to other existing units. The staff of the ES Program argued strongly for the former on the grounds that their ability to deal consistently with the various school districts depended upon the continuation of a single-program office. Although their preference prevailed and the program held together for the moment, it was subsequently assigned to a subordinate status within one of its formerly coequal programs within the NIE.

Although the program was allowed to continue, the review was critical of several aspects of its operation. In particular, the idea of comprehensive change as employed by the program came under attack. The review concluded that the ES Program had failed at its effort to promote comprehensive change. However, it suggested other aspects of the program, or at least its separate projects, did show "genuine promise" (Doyle 1975, p. 8). The final recommendation of the review team was that "the director [of the ES Program] and his staff should be directed to identify the most promising themes emerging from the sites for special attention" (Doyle 1975, p. 22).

In responding to these criticisms, the new director sought a more open definition of the program's mission, one that viewed its local districts as representatives of user groups and allowed them to define their own problems:

> This program provides resources and assistance to school districts to help them organize and attack significant problems that they faced and identified at the time of initial funding: integration . . . inadequate intellectual and vocational preparation; community participation in school affairs. . . . These problems are still relevant today and are being actively addressed by ES schools. . . .
>
> The documentation of these attempts at solving the problems school systems face and the development and implementation of the local plans for change are the major concerns of the Experimental Schools Program. Practitioners concerned with . . . remedies for declining or stagnant

rural systems all will be audiences to which ES findings
will be of great use.

Such a revision of the program's missions allowed it to define any
positive development in one of its districts as a sign of success and
a reason for its own continuation.

The second program director's orientations and the program's
revised mission encouraged a more laissez-faire approach to local
districts than had been employed previously. In conversation with
district leaders in Butte-Angels Camp, the new director contrasted
his role with that of his predecessor, saying that the first program
director tried to rigidly implement a model of how to bring about
change, an approach that he was moving away from. His approach
would give project officers more autonomy in working with local districts. One project officer summarized this difference as follows:

> [The second director] was pretty loose. It was [the proj-
> ect officers'] project; they had to see the thing through and
> they couldn't expect a whole lot of direction from their su-
> perior. [Corwin 1977, p. 48]

During this period, ES/Washington project officers took on more advisory and technical assistance responsibilities. While they challenged
local project personnel to justify their approaches, they avoided the
high-pressure tactics used during contract negotiations in the spring
of 1973.

Even before these changes in Washington, the district's third
ES project officer had begun defining the local project more broadly.
In the process, he took steps that increased teachers' influence. On
his first visit to the district in the spring of 1974, he indicated his
support for teachers. He chastised the superintendent for not informing the staff about deadlines for planning for summer in-service and
curriculum work and indicated that teacher requests should be solici-
ted and honored. He toured two buildings, including the high school,
and met with teachers in the absence of administrators. At that time,
he encouraged some militants, who had change proposals of their own,
to pursue those ideas and to inform him if they met obstacles. A
member of a minority group himself, he became very interested in
the following year in attempts to develop and revise an Indian Education program for white students and apparently suggested that two
courses in the high and junior schools be broadened into a kindergar-
ten-through-grade-12 curriculum.

The project officer's endorsement of new directions for the
project was encouraged by the ES Program's new laissez-faire approach. In 1976 a thumbnail description of all ten rural sites written

in Washington listed three new developments in the Butte-Angels Camp
project: the use of teacher evaluators, the Curriculum Cabinet, and
the environmental education program—but not d/p. Field notes from
a conversation with the ES project officer indicate that new criteria,
not related to comprehensiveness or to the project's original theme,
were being used to evaluate the district:

> [He] recently reread the plan and thinks a lot of important
> things were not tied down in it, but grew out of the project
> over time. One of those is the increasing sophistication of
> the evaluators. . . . Another interesting thing is the Cabi-
> net. . . . He is also interested in the "increase in self-es-
> teem and professionalism or whatever you want to call it
> that comes through d/p." [The consultant] has helped a lot
> of teachers feel their work is more important. . . . When
> I asked how important d/p is, he said, "It's important."
> He's not convinced about how important it is, to the exclu-
> sion of other things. D/p may be one way of bringing about
> renovation of the school system. What happens to teacher
> professionalism is important for change. Maybe the prac-
> tice of teaching will develop because of d/p or the cabinet
> or whatever. Many things can develop and depend on d/p.
> They are by-products, but just as important.

The program's laissez-faire approach did not save it from dis-
solution, however. The eight staff members who left during this period were not replaced. In November 1975 the second director requested and was granted reassignment as a project officer. By December 1975 the program was a shell of its earlier self. The morale
of remaining staff members seems to have been badly shaken by the
reassignment of the first director, and the review and reorganization
that followed. The lifeblood of the relationship between the project
officers and the rural districts was travel funds, for periodic site
visits, which were severely constrained by cuts in the Department of
Health, Education and Welfare, in general, and in the NIE, in particular.

In the spring of 1976, districts were expected to submit requests for their last year of funding. At that time, most project officers lacked the funds to visit sites to verify firsthand the status of
the projects whose continuations they were expected to approve. In
comparison to earlier periods, the program no longer seemed interested in events in the rural districts.

Nevertheless, in April and May of 1976, contract renewals were
offered to all ten of the small rural districts, thus honoring all commitments for long-term funding made by the original program direc-

tor. These were the final awards made by the program. The task of administering them was spread within the NIE, and the program as a distinct entity was finally disbanded.

The New Balance of Power in the District

While the ES Program proceeded to its own demise in Washington, a new balance of power developed in Butte-Angels Camp. This change resulted from the first year's conflict over the district's project and was an important factor shaping later implementation. Central to the change was the enhanced role of the school board in operational decision making.

In the spring and summer of 1974, the board took two actions that set the stage for the second year of implementation. First, in an executive session near the end of the year, the board told the principals that all but one of them, who had been more responsive to its wishes, would receive only token raises; and the board instructed them to make particular efforts to implement an evaluation system in the district and to improve discipline in all buildings. Second, during the summer, the board and John Raleigh took one step toward such an evaluation system by working out an "accountability contract" for Raleigh, which would make his salary increases for the coming year contingent upon satisfactory performance (in the eyes of the board) of a series of mutually agreed on tasks.

These steps were cause for initial optimism within the board as the 1974/75 school year began. Board members reported that the superintendent's "personal relations" with the board, and apparently the staff as well, were improving. Other indications of change were apparent in the superintendent's relations with other administrators. At the first administrators' meeting after school started, John Raleigh reviewed efforts to develop accountability contracts similar to his own for all administrators and pressed them to quit dragging their feet in that area:

> I've scrutinized myself. The board is right. They caught
> us with our pants down. We're not filling the leadership
> role. . . . I'm enthused about performance contracting for
> me. I told you three weeks ago, I want to talk to you about
> your objectives (to be written into such contracts) when
> you're ready. Only one of you has come in. This won't
> go away fellas!

At the same time, he was asking the board for help to get other administrators to support this effort, and another administrator to devise a different kind of evaluation system for teachers. Efforts to develop both new systems continued through lengthy meetings for the rest of the 1974/75 year, and both were ready by the fall of 1975.

Principals were aware of the changed relations between the superintendent and the board and felt it affected their own work. As one reported:

> In the last two years, the superintendent has functioned
> differently, trying to avoid being put in a corner by the
> board. His credibility has been jeopardized. This has
> changed the principals' situation. We still say, "You're
> the boss," but we don't like the way he's handling things
> because he's responding to the board. . . . He's lost some
> of the backbone that a superintendent needs in relation to
> a board. He'd like to make a recommendation that he and
> we support, but we go some other way 'cause that's the
> way the board is going.

For their part, principals felt some need, too, to conform to board wishes. A great deal of time was given to problems of discipline, staff evaluation, and their own new contract; and in setting up the staff evaluation system, they tried to anticipate what the board wanted. Yet, because of their sense of the importance of "the chain of command," they did not deal directly with the board except at its initiative. As one said, "I make a habit of not going to the board. If I bypass the superintendent . . . , I haven't done my job right."

The board was not uniformly successful in its dealings with the administration. Administrators sought ways to maintain as much freedom to operate as possible. In preparing for board meetings, they tried to structure events to minimize board input. When discussing an upcoming presentation on rules for conduct in different buildings, the superintendent warned his principals, "Don't ask the board for suggestions on building rules 'cause they'll give them. Tell the board that they are needed." However, administrators' passive resistance was more effective than their concerted attempts to mobilize. For instance, a board member who worked closely with several teachers in the system in subject areas where he had special competence was convinced that one teacher was incompetent. He worked for two years to get that instructor's principal to submit a formal evalution of him. That objective was never achieved, although the teacher did finally resign after considerable pressure was applied.

The 1974/75 year ended with everyone disappointed. At a May meeting held to discuss a set of curriculum changes the board wanted to discuss that night, one principal said, "We're being asked to play defense. I'd rather do that than nothing." John Raleigh replied:

I don't like playing defense. You can't be a leader and play defense. . . . This process is completely undermining the principle of administrative leadership. They aren't leaving us the dignity of being leaders in this system.

A few days later, one of the board members complained to the project consultant about the administrators as follows:

The principals talk about teachers not cooperating. I wonder how much the administrators are cooperating. Kids have to be in gym even if they are in athletics. . . . We can't change our administrators on this. [The superintendent] looks at us like we're crazy, and he's the initiator of NIE.

The superintendent's departure promised that the situation would improve soon, but not immediately. After apparently looking for another position throughout the year without success, he announced in the late spring of 1975 that during the project's third year he would take a year's leave of absence to pursue his graduate studies. Although it seemed likely that he would seek other employment, he continued to operate publicly as if he would return, which constrained others to act accordingly. During his absence, his seat was always kept vacant at administrators' meetings, for instance. The board, however, clearly indicated in private, at least, that it hoped he would not return. After describing some steps being taken to encourage the superintendent to look elsewhere for work, one member said privately, "I don't necessarily want him to leave mad, but I want him to leave." In the spring of 1976, the board announced that John Raleigh would not return.

The increasing importance of the school board did not necessarily mean that teachers' roles in collective decision making expanded accordingly. In fact, the close working relations that developed during the crisis of the previous year were strained, though not completely sundered during 1974/75. Three developments contributed to this strain. First, a significant portion of the teachers opposed the board's attempt to develop an evaluation scheme. The more militant high school teachers referred to opportunities offered to help design the new system by saying, "We're being asked to help build our own scaffold." Second, the board could not continue to give salary increases to match the special bonus it gave to teachers during the fall of 1973. In the spring of 1974 and again in 1975, the teachers' association just barely voted to ratify the board's final offer for a salary package. The latter year, the proposal carried by only one vote.

Finally, two separate events suggested to teachers that the board would provide only limited support for their attempts to administer stronger discipline. In one case, the board overruled the strong punishment assigned to three truants in the junior high, one of whom was a board member's daughter. Later, the board failed to provide what much of the faculty felt was satisfactory legal support for a teacher who had hit a child and was sued by the child's parents.

Working relations between the board and teachers were not completely severed, however, and the board continued to provide the staff protection from the most coercive measures used previously. The three board members who had most frequent contact with teachers reported that their lines of communication remained open, but there was more reserve on both sides than had existed in 1973/74, and the board continued to push policies that teachers disliked. Still, the board continued to prohibit the use of extreme sanctions on teachers. One principal described the situation in the second year as follows:

> We were put in an unfavorable position last year. . . . If I started working with a teacher who was not doing d/p and I started documenting for dismissal, the board reversed itself once. What's to say they won't do it again?

Even within the context of the new evaluation system, administrators were unwilling to use that strategy to get teachers to work for the project.

Orientations to the Project

The new balance of power in the district led to some shifts in orientations to the project among the school board, the administrators, and the teachers. Student and community attitudes did not change.

The School Board

During the project's second year, the board became more supportive of the project and more impatient with teachers' opposition to it. In the fall of 1974, the Reverend Mr. Maslow said that the board was behind the project and that people "who spent all last year hating John Raleigh will have a difficult time this year." Others were irritated with the militant teachers as well, although Jack Ianetti, an exteacher, continued to defend their position.

However, the board defined the project more broadly than John Raleigh had done. The Reverend Mr. Maslow, who initially feared that the superintendent was turning d/p into a "gospel," became more positively inclined toward the d/p process. In a paper presented to the board, he wrote:

> My first question has always been whether diagnosis and prescription was another form of behavior modification. . . . Manipulation, for whatever purpose, falls short of the educational philosophy which I hold. . . . Now the documentation of behavior appears in a different light. It is a kind of first step in an intervention which promotes growth.

He was very excited about the work Mark Morand was doing with teachers. Another board member took a broad view and suggested the following:

> What I like about the ES project is that the administration and teachers are looking at problems and trying to resolve them in terms of the means available and still turn out quality education.

Board members were also receptive to having new initiatives come from teachers. For instance, they were so impressed with the work of the mathematics coordinator that, when the time came in the fall of 1975 to write a proposal for the last two years of the project, they directed the writing team to establish a set of curriculum areas and to formulate a committee to be charged with the task of coordinating curriculum across grade levels in each area.

The board members were most uniformly impressed with the financial contribution the ES project was making to the district and began to insist on meeting directly with the agency's project officer when he visited the district so they could play an active part in negotiations with Washington. The Reverend Mr. Maslow visited the agency's Washington office in the spring of 1975 and, along with the project consultant, conducted the negotiations for the final year's funding. At the same time, the board became actively concerned with the problems of supporting some of the more expensive parts of the project—like the aide program—after federal funding ended.

Administrators

The principals continued to be unenthusiastic about the project, but they accepted the fact that it would continue. When interviewed, they gave a balanced account of the impact of the project upon their work. One said that the project increased his work tremendously. When asked how, he went on to say:

> The paper work. The d/p process in getting teachers
> oriented to, and using it. . . . Meetings and attendance
> and preparation for them have certainly been time consum-
> ing. I guess I asked for it when I said I'd support the proj-
> ect. One big change, I have become more cognizant of the
> needs of kids, especially those who don't achieve in normal
> ways.

Another principal said:

> The numerous meetings have taken time. However, I be-
> lieve it makes all of us conscious of alternatives. I've
> changed the way I handle discipline. It may not be too
> good. . . . The value of the project is being humanistic.

For principals, the concrete costs in terms of additional work were
balanced to some extent by the intangible benefit of becoming "more
humanistic" in their approach to education.

The superintendent's view of the project remained unchanged.
When asked if the d/p process would survive without federal support,
he responded, "It not only will, it must! It will continue in its complete form as long as I am superintendent!" He explained that the
possible elimination of d/p sheets was "wishful thinking on the teachers' parts. They might be more refined, but you have to have them
for teachers to be accountable."

Teachers

While teachers continued to dislike the ES project, they were
less worried about it after the first year. For instance, the random
evaluation of d/p notebooks that had caused so much anxiety in the
winter of 1974 was only a source of bad jokes and mild discomfort 12
months later. Field notes from that time indicate:

> The date to pick up the d/p notebooks for the mid-year
> quality check has been set for February 14. There seems
> to be a lot less flack among teachers about it this year,
> and the whole thing seems to be a lot more matter-of-fact.
> I noticed during my interviews that teachers aren't looking
> on this upcoming event with trepidation, although a few
> are saying they have done some d/p's just to have in their
> book when the time comes. I saw in the teacher's lounge
> in the high school a sign on the blackboard that looked like
> it had been put up by the principal that said, "The notebooks
> will be picked up February 14 for this check." And under-
> neath somebody had written, "Get to work, Clark."

Generally, teachers viewed the project more as a minor irritant that did little to help them attain their private objectives for their own classes, than as a major impediment to their activities. When asked how the ES project changed their work as teachers, they replied:

> I don't think it has, except that it's increased the paper work. I wish I could get an overhead projector. The project hasn't changed the way I teach. Some things I've always done, but I write them down now.

> The project hasn't changed [my work] that much. I've always done d/p. I just haven't written it down before.

One teacher summarized the views of a number of colleagues by saying, "It's one more thing to worry about. It has little relevance to what I do, and it's a pain in the butt."

In the spring of 1975, the teacher evaluators repeated the survey they had conducted the year before. Two changes were apparent. First, while the intensity of opposition had declined, its pervasiveness increased; 7 to 8 percent fewer teachers said they supported the project and wanted it to continue, and fewer than half the teachers wanted to continue the project for a third year. Second, the issues changed during the second year. Discontent about lack of participation abated, and this was a reflection of the active role played by the board and the ES project officer. Fewer than half the teachers were satisfied with their participation in the project's policy-making procedures, but there was greater satisfaction with participation and a more pervasive feeling that staff recommendations were receiving adequate attention during 1974/75 than the year before. On the other hand, satisfaction with the d/p process declined. Almost 20 percent fewer teachers were convinced that d/p was helping them to help students (see Table 6.1).

One commonality between the first and the second years is that the secondary teachers continued to oppose the project more than their colleagues in the lower grades. Only a quarter of the secondary teachers wanted to continue the project into the third year, while two-thirds of the elementary teachers did. Secondary teachers were less impressed with the educational value of d/p and more concerned with their lack of influence over project decisions than were lower-grade teachers.

Interviews with teachers conducted during the 1974/75 school year indicate their ambivalence about the project. When asked how the project changed their work, their responses, like the principals', were balanced, mentioning both the good and the bad:

TABLE 6.1

Orientations of Teachers toward the ES Project, 1975 versus 1974
(percentage of positive responses)

	1975			1974
	Elementary	Secondary	All	All
To what extent has the d/p technique resulted in a positive direction of change for the students for whom you have diagnosed and prescribed?[a]	54	19	36	55
To what extent are you satisfied with your participation in the policy-making procedures of the ES project?[b]	58	31	48	32
To what extent do you feel that your recommendations for the project have been given adequate attention by the administration?[b]	46	31	40	28
To what extent do you support the ES project?[a]	73	37	55	62
To what extent do you desire to continue the project?	66	25	45	53

[a]Administered in April 1975; 85 percent response rate.
[b]Administered in March 1975; 60 percent response rate.

Note: Based on questionnaires administered by the teacher evaluator committee. Respondents had four choices with numbers 4 and 3 marked positive and numbers 2 and 1 marked negative. Information for 1974 data is taken from Table 5.1.

> We wouldn't have teaming without the ES project. I like
> it and it's good for kids. . . . But, we also have more
> work . . . paper work, d/p sheets.

Students and the Community

While implementation of the ES project caused great consterna-
tion among the district's staff, it had very little additional impact on
the community. In fact, neither students nor the community understood what it was supposed to accomplish. For instance, at the height
of the conflict over the project, the high school newspaper ran the
following story.

WE WANT TO KNOW

> . . . A group of five students met January 14 to discuss the
> question, "Have you realized the effects of the project?"
> Some of the discussion follows:
>
> Junior #1: "As far as I knew, I didn't even know there was
> a project. I think it would help if we would hear more
> about it."
>
> Junior #2: "I heard that it made a lot more work for the
> teachers. I haven't seen what it's done for the students
> yet."
>
> Sophomore: "I heard about it last year, but none of the
> kids know what it is about or what is going on . . . "
>
> The group agreed that the students should be more informed
> about the project so that they might use it to the best bene-
> fit of all.

Most students never did become better informed about the project.
A similar situation existed with respect to the larger community. Surveys conducted by Abt Associates and the teacher evaluators
of community residents and parents indicated that about three-quarters of the district's residents had heard of the project; but, in spite
of considerable newspaper publicity, very few people had any idea of
how the new funds were being used. For instance, at public meetings
organized by the taxpayers' association, the superintendent was asked
about a "rumor I want to check out. Is it true that the school district
is paying a doctor from the . . . School of Mines, who is on the staff?
If so, what do you pay him?" This question referred to the project
consultant, who did not work for that college but did live in the same
city. Other discussions at those meetings indicate that many people
did not understand the project, even if they had heard of it.

PROJECT ACTIVITIES

The new project context required the use of different tactics to build support for it within the district and permitted an important shift in project activities. On the one hand, a more low-keyed approach was used to sell the project, while on the other, teachers ceased to complain so vehemently about their d/p work. However, the displacement process begun the year before continued, reducing not only the work involved but also the impact the project might have on students. The governance and evaluation components became less important, while new activities related to curriculum and construction, often initiated by teachers, were started.

Selling the Project

The task of maintaining support for the project within the district fell to the superintendent, the project consultant, and the principals. In response to new pressures, John Raleigh began taking a lower-keyed approach to obtaining support. This approach avoided unilateral sanctions and emphasized responsiveness to teachers' concerns. In the fall of 1974, Raleigh tried to work out a doctrine of group d/p especially for secondary teachers, and this doctrine, according to him, was "reversing the field on them. It says we'll play your game up to a point." Although this new doctrine, which allowed teachers to group students for the d/p process, did not become widespread, it indicated an attempt to modify project goals and practices to be more responsive to teachers' concerns. Another such development was the attempt at the same time to simplify the d/p process by modifying the sheets so that less writing would be required. In addition, the superintendent became more responsive to staff ideas for the use of federal money.

Mark Morand was extremely proficient at this low-key approach, and his position facilitated supportive relationships with the staff. Having no line responsibilities, he made no personnel decisions and was never linked to threats to fire teachers that had been made during the first year. In fact, he actively avoided being tied too closely with the district's authority structure. His 180-day contract with the district included his working during the summer and allowed him time to pursue smaller consulting assignments with other districts in the area. When the board offered him the project directorship in the superintendent's absence, he tactfully refused, saying, "We don't want to jeopardize my role by making me an administrator." He later accepted the position, but not without misgivings. However, his doctorate, his knowledge of the project, and later, his liaison work with

ES/Washington made him a knowledgeable and important actor in the
district to whom administrators deferred and looked for advice on a
wide range of matters.

His major function continued to be that of working directly with
teachers. In doing so, he avoided any use of sanctions. In a conversation about teachers' "putting kids down," he said:

> When I hear that, I don't tell the teacher she's wrong. I
> ask why and they usually see they're wrong. I don't want
> to do the same thing myself by telling them they're wrong.

Instead, he provided inducements for working with him by helping
teachers with a variety of their own problems. He tried to avoid push-
ing techniques or suggestions on teachers, but followed up when they
asked for help. For instance, he helped a teacher develop a way to
use a tape recorder for a child who could not read. Another time he
offered to help teachers interpret the reading scores of a boy with a
problem that was difficult to diagnose. He usually stepped in where
he felt he could use a particular case to make a point about d/p, and
the teachers appreciated the expertise he could apply to the problems
they faced.

The consultant also provided other services that the teachers
appreciated. In the summer of 1974 he gave a nonmandatory workshop
on learning disabilities that was attended by 83 teachers. One, a well-
known cynic and opponent of the project, said that "the workshop . . .
should have been given last year" because it was so inspiring. Moreover, because the consultant was free to move among the various
buildings and levels of the district, he could elicit and support teachers' ideas that interested him in a way that no one else could. For
example, when implementation of a new curriculum for a grade level
bogged down because the principal neglected to distribute the printed
materials and guides that had been worked out, the consultant volunteered to follow up and see that the job was done.

In his work with teachers, the consultant faced severe time
constraints resulting from the large number of teachers he had to work
with and the part-time aspect of his position in the district. In addition, considerable administrative work connected with the project fell
to him. Besides designing the first d/p sheets, he coordinated the
formulation of summer work programs, attended administrative meetings and consulted with the superintendent and principals, provided
technical assistance to the teacher evaluators, and spent more and
more time reporting to the board and to ES/Washington as the superintendent lost influence. Moreover, the work with individual teachers
became oppressive to him because of the repetition involved.

To optimize his contact with teachers, he tried numerous strategies, but most had the disadvantage of not offering teachers the per-

sonal attention that they had appreciated. These strategies included
a combination of strategic intervention with small and large group
meetings in which he would work with one teacher on a particularly
tricky problem and hope the ideas he suggested would spread by word
of mouth. In addition, he worked with the principals who were supposed to do the same kind of consulting with their own staff that he did
throughout the district.

In spite of time limitations, Morand was well received in the
district. Even the project's most adamant opponents were at least
lukewarm toward him, and most teachers felt he provided a useful
service. At a workshop to recapitulate the summer work done in
1975, he was the only person to receive applause from the teachers.

The principals' ambivalence toward the project limited their
usefulness in obtaining support of others or in providing staff with
help. In spite of coaching and prodding from the superintendent and
the project consultant, most of them never understood the d/p process,
and their instructions contradicted the consultant's and confused teachers. As one teacher put it:

> [My principal] can get us more mixed up on those sheets!
> People who haven't done them don't understand. [The con-
> sultant] understands. [The principal] hasn't done them
> and doesn't understand them.

One exception to this was the principal in the Angels Camp Elementary School. He developed an interest in the d/p process and, as mentioned earlier, his handling of discipline and work with teachers on
classroom organization helped him develop more influence with his
staff than did his peers. As a result of these two factors, the d/p process was adopted by teachers in his school more quickly and with
fewer problems than in the other buildings.

Administrators also inhibited attempts to build from teachers'
ideas about needed changes, as these examples from field notes indicate:

> [A teacher] says he is supposed to go on a trip next week.
> He's having a lot of trouble getting it okayed. He actually
> called the project officer to find out if he could go, and
> the officer said that would be fine and that he would send
> a letter. But the business manager would not okay the ex-
> penditure until he got the letter . . . The teacher thinks
> that people are really afraid of [ES/Washington]. The
> business manager is afraid to do anything that might cost
> the district money.

> [A librarian] said they started working on an audio-visual
> materials catalog some time ago, but they couldn't talk
> [a principal] into buying it until [the consultant] walked
> in on a conference between her and another librarian. He
> told the superintendent about it. The superintendent recog-
> nized the possibilities, and they got [ES/Washington] to
> fund it. They had asked to work during the summer before,
> but they never got the money.

Project leaders acknowledged that administrators were hindering development of the project. The project consultant argued:

> Principals shouldn't have veto power over an idea. If a
> principal can't support it, he should encourage a teacher
> to write a proposal on it. That stops some teachers. With
> others, the principal says, "I tried it and it won't work."

Displacement of the D/p Process

In discussing the d/p process, teachers distinguished between
filling out the sheets and working with students:

> I haven't written down any [sheets] yet, but I have many
> in my mind. I could easily write down fifteen.

> I'm only doing three. . . . There are more I am working
> on, but I'm not writing them down. . . . I looked up the
> records on one boy. His IQ is in the low 80's. I'm not
> doing a sheet on him, but I'm trying to work with him
> every day. I don't expect a big change from him. He is
> overacheiving to be able to read and write at all.

The displacement of d/p consisted of a shift in emphasis from
student treatment to filling out forms, which changed the thrust of the
innovation from a new educational approach to an additional bureaucratic burden. When asked how the project affected their work,
teachers indicated that it increased their sensitivity to individual
children:

> It has made me more aware of the fact that several kids
> need more help than the average student. Without the
> project, I wouldn't concentrate as much on kids with prob-
> lems.

It has formed me to think more about specific individuals.
. . . I never compiled information as thoroughly and
thought as much about a specific person before.

It made me aware of what I have been doing. It created a
tool to measure the effectiveness of what I was doing.

I'm more aware—I was before, but I was not accomplishing
what I wanted to—of the unique needs of different children.

This perceived outcome of the project was mentioned by 16 of the 34
teachers interviewed; and it suggested that the project was beginning
to have its originally expected impact and that many teachers viewed
that change positively.

Actual changes in teachers' classroom behavior were small,
however. Teachers were asked to describe cases where they worked
with students using the d/p process. A selected sample of these
cases shows the kinds of information they obtained and the actions
they took. Teachers distinguished between academic and nonacademic
problems. Academic problems permeated all grade levels:

Case #1: Elementary Social Studies
Some children have trouble with the geography concepts
studied. One girl had "no idea of what an ocean or conti-
nent is." The teacher worked with her individually and
explained them to her. The aide worked with her, and the
teacher gave her work sheets. Now she knows them, says
the teacher.

Case #2: High School Typing
One girl had "a bad habit of watching her fingers." The
alternative was to put her on a blank key typewriter. She
overcame the problem.

Case #3: Fourth Grade
A boy "couldn't read at all or even recognize words like
'a,' 'an,' or 'the.' He liked math but had terrible rever-
sals. He couldn't copy math problems. Orally he did
o.k. . . . He wasn't dumb." The teacher visited with
his mother. Last year he had tests to prove he had normal
IQ and no brain damage. One eye doctor said he was o.k.
The teacher talked the parents into going to a different eye
doctor to check his eye-brain coordination and "there
wasn't any." The child now has special glasses and still
"really wants to learn." The aide, his mother, and the
teacher work with him, teaching him to use his new bi-
focals. He got the third highest grade in science the day

before the interview, and his reading and math are better, though children still read to him.

Case #4: High School Social Studies

A student has reading difficulties. The teacher makes a special effort if he doesn't understand, to re-explain it to him. The teacher helps him read test questions and gives him more explanation of what they ask for. The teacher also gives the student extra maps to use as work sheets and tries to show personal concern.

Nonacademic problems were described more frequently than academic ones, partly because teachers often identified motivational or other nonacademic roots to the academic problems they encountered. These also appeared at all grade levels:

Case #5: Third Grade

The student "is an exceptionally good reader and is almost done with our programmed reading series. He is always lonely because he's way ahead of the others."

The teacher had him tested for fourth grade reading, and he was high, so she talked the fourth grade teachers into letting him go with them for reading. She felt he needed a chance to discuss with other kids, and he enjoys it and is learning a lot. If it becomes a burden, the teacher will pull him out. She had a conference with parents on this too.

Case #6: High School English

The teacher says the student is a "chronic forgetter." She thought about giving the student a K grade but gave him an F instead. This student and others were told that if they would work with the teacher, she would change their grades later. The student doesn't pay attention in class. He loses pencils and things. For a while he worked with upper class tutors. He would almost finish something and then lose it.

The teacher works with the student individually. When he didn't like one exercise she was trying, she tried another, asking him to write about a chess club meeting on the blackboard. They worked over his sentences. She says, "What I am doing is probably nothing except showing concern."

Case #7: Fifth Grade

The teacher says the boy has home problems. His parents were divorced, and his mother retained custody. IQ tests show he has below average intelligence, but he was in a special education class, and the teacher feels he is capable of more than that. When his mother is "on a binge," he has a short attention span. Other people take care of him then. He has poor motor control and may not like writing. He reads below grade level, but enjoys it.

The teacher is working on his attention span by setting a short time limit and checking with him to hold him to that limit and lengthen it. He does better with the things he likes. The teacher is not sure how much she is accomplishing because some days he does better than others.

Case #8: High School Social Studies
The student "lives in a fantasy world." He has been a class clown. He doesn't do well academically although the teacher thinks he is fairly intelligent. The mother says the student doesn't take his work home, and the counselors feel he can do better work than he does.

The teacher worked with the student on the side, familiarizing him with terminology used. The next day, the student dropped out of school.

Case #9: Second Grade
According to the teacher, this girl "doesn't take kindly to authority." The teacher talked to the mother and found the student had been to a school psychologist in another state.

The teacher has tried two techniques: using a timer because the student "is so lackadaisical about getting assignments in," and putting her desk away from those of the other students because she is easily distracted. The teacher has also talked to the girl alone and sent her to the special education class for short periods of time.

Work with most of these children did not require great imagination or variation from former classroom routines. Case 3, where the teacher identified a neurological problem, was an unusually specific and knowledgeable diagnosis. While the treatment did not require changes in classroom procedure, the teacher did talk to the parents and persuaded them to get their child retested. Moreover, before new glasses were tried, she experimented with new instructional techniques like sight vocabularies in the hope of by-passing the suspected perceptual block. The use of short deadlines and the timer in cases 7 and 9 required less specialized knowledge, but took more class time. Other treatments were very standard. The use of the blank keyboard, for instance, was so routine that another typing teacher did not even "d/p" students until that technique had failed. Similarly, most teachers gave special attention to a student with a problem whether or not the child was part of the d/p process.

Nor did teachers themselves feel that the practices they employed were different from what they had done before the project began. The teacher who worked with the vision problem in case 3, for instance, said, "I suppose I would've done it anyway." Unlike most teachers, she had special training in learning disabilities treatment. Another teacher said, "D/p hasn't changed the way I work with [a student]. I would have done the same thing. What I'm doing with her happens to be probably right with the project." This impression of minimal change in classroom procedures is reinforced by teachers' reports that they worked the same way with the students they did not formally include in the d/p process.

The one clear change that d/p created was the addition of more paper work. This work was complicated, but not terribly onerous. The teachers interviewed during 1974/75 were working on anywhere from zero to fourteen sheets, with the average number five or six in the lower grades, and three at the secondary level. Most expected to complete between six and eight by the end of the year. The actual work of filling out the sheets turned out to take less time than anticipated, once the initial confusion about what was required was eliminated. Most teachers hesitated to even guess how much time they devoted to the d/p sheets, but estimates ranged from twenty minutes to one-and-a-half hours, including the time to look up test scores. If one takes the highest of those estimates, the teachers who filled out eight sheets spent only about twelve hours on that task in nine months.

While filling out the sheets did not take a great deal of time, it appeared to offer no intrinsic benefits to teachers. Only 4 of the 34 teachers interviewed said that doing the sheets helped them work with students, while 15 said that the sheets were no help. Some of the ways the d/p sheets helped were minor. For example, they encouraged the teacher to review the student's cumulative folder and test scores and to spend more time thinking about the child's problem. Some teachers believed that the sheets reminded them of the problem student's existence and the nature of the child's difficulty. Others argued that they would remember anyway and that their existing record systems—grade books and special charts—did the same job as the d/p sheets. Some teachers believed that the sheets provided good reports for future teachers working with the same child. Others strenuously objected to this use of d/p sheets, fearing that the sheets contained "good gossip" that might be used against a child.

Because the intrinsic advantages of filling out the sheets were slight, administrative enforcement and surveillance continued to be an important factor in getting them completed at all. This was especially apparent in the secondary schools, where some of the first teachers interviewed had not yet filled out any sheets, although only one upper-grade instructor had done none at the end of the second year. Several explicitly indicated that they were filling out the forms to avoid trouble during the random evaluation. This administrative surveillance was mildly resented. One teacher said, "I dislike that part of teaching: meal tickets, lunch counts, bookkeeping, permanent record writing. I put [d/p sheets] in the same category."

Teachers developed techniques for coping with administrative enforcement while reducing the work required of them. One of the most frequently used was batch processing, the creation of similar or identical sheets for large numbers of students. For instance, one teacher whom the consultant specifically pointed out as having a good grasp of the d/p process and who had done a record number of sheets, explained her procedure as follows:

A. Since I teach arithmetic, all my sheets are on arithmetic; and most of them are on math facts. About half the children have trouble with speed. The other half half just don't know them.

Q. Are there any other children with the same problem that you haven't written down?

A. Another fourteen are not quite as far behind as these. I'm doing the same thing with them, but I'm not writing it down. I picked the ones that needed it worst.

Q. Does filling out the sheets help you work with those students?

A. It doesn't help that much. Most of the time you know what you've got there anyway.

She reported that filling out the sheets did not influence the kind of treatment she gave these students.

There were more and less extreme versions of batch processing. The most blatant example was an upper-grade teacher who spoke of his "carbon copy" d/p sheets. He devised two standard problems, each with a standard treatment. He then filled out ten sheets of each type, changing nothing but the student's name. A less extreme version was to identify several students who needed the same treatment and fill out sheets on all or a few of them. Batch processing was an almost undetectable way to cope with requirements to fill out d/p sheets. If a teacher only filled out a few sheets with the same problem, it looked like he or she was "individualizing," no matter how many children received the same treatment or whether they received it on an individual or group basis.

Faltering of Governance and Evaluation

While d/p became a regular part of life in the district, the governance and evaluation systems set up the first year gradually declined in importance. After the second year, the Tri-Parties, which were supposed to be the vehicle for community involvement, were discontinued. The cabinet continued to operate, but its position in the district was unclear, and it lacked staff support. Similarly, the teacher evaluators continued to do their work, but the information they collected had very little utility for anyone.

Attendance at tri-party meetings remained low during 1974/75. During the first round of meetings in the fall of 1974, attendance by parents ranged from 3 to 24. By midyear, teachers were outnumbering parents, and principals and lay chairpersons began agreeing to skip meetings because attendance was so low.

Two complaints were made about the Tri-Parties. First, they were believed to be dominated by someone, although different people had different perceptions of who that was. Parents who attended meetings said that their neighbors would not come because they feared that any complaints would lead to teacher retribution against their children in class. On the other hand, teachers resented what they felt was harassment at meetings. As one teacher said, "Sometimes I feel like a puppet on a string."

The second complaint was that tri-party meetings did not accomplish anything. This complaint was rarer among laymen. One minister said that, from the beginning during consolidation, Tri-Parties had been a farce and had suffered from lack of leadership and trivial complaints from parents. Teachers agreed with this assessment; 10 of the 34 interviewed complained that the tri-party meetings degenerated into gripe sessions.

Most tri-party meetings were mundane. They included reports on new schedules in the high school and explanations of a new physical education program. Some more controversial topics included steps taken to provide equal athletic programs for high school girls and a proposal to eliminate the use of letter grades in the primary schools. Parents asked why girls had to wear track shoes during meets and requested that more attention be given to flag etiquette in the elementary curriculum. The most controversial educational issue debated in the community that year, the demand to reduce taxes, was not raised at these meetings. The only request that came from the meetings was to expand the elementary swimming program. In the fall of 1975, at the start of the project's third year, the Tri-Parties were discontinued.

After the first year, the district staff became disenchanted with the Curriculum Cabinet. Of the 34 teachers interviewed, 19 volunteered that they did not know what the cabinet had accomplished. The better-informed teachers believed that the cabinet had helped in their attempts to change district policies, but they thought the mechanism was too cumbersome. As one put it:

> Some things coming out of the cabinet are good, but I don't see why it took that kind of body to bring those simple things about.

They believed that it should be possible to achieve such changes through normal administrative channels.

The principals opposed the cabinet, arguing that it was unduly political. Said one:

> The cabinet has been used, viciously at times, by various power groups in the school. A small group will come in with a well-researched proposal they can talk for. . . . Lay people have no more idea about the value of third-grade swimming [a recently passed proposal that most administrators had opposed] than I do about flying to the moon.

They wanted the cabinet to operate in a rational, problem-solving manner and argued that the district should have a clear set of objectives. The cabinet could help set these objectives, but its major function would be to determine whether or not change proposals were congruent with, and facilitative of, those objectives.

The major source of support for the cabinet was ES/Washington; the project consultant was in close contact with the project officer. When a group of teachers and principals considered modifications to the cabinet's structure in the spring of 1976, the project officer warned that any modifications would have to be carefully thought out and justified in order to be well received in Washington.

The cabinet's functions and jurisdiction were never clarified. For instance, during the 1975/76 school year, two groups of teachers representing grades 1 through 3 and grades 4 through 6 from all elementary schools met to consider revising report card formats. The first group presented its proposal to the cabinet, but the second did not, and no criticism of this procedure was made. What clarifications did exist were often ignored. For example, the project plan specified that proposals for summer in-service work had to be reviewed and coordinated by the cabinet, but this task was actually performed by district administrators and the project consultant.

The cabinet clearly did not have formal authorization to approve projects or allocate funds. Hence, discussion of most programs focused on where money would come from to support them. Several proposals were not passed until the cabinet had verbal assurance that ES/Washington would approve the expenditure. Even then, proposals were usually approved "contingent upon the availability of funds."

In spite of these problems, the cabinet served as a mechanism to redirect the project. It passed proposals to start a Special Learning Disabilities Program and to hire two special teachers for it, to redesign report cards in grades 1 through 3, and to change the elementary swimming program. The only proposal it vetoed was one to give counselors performance incentives on their contracts, a proposal that most staff saw as a subterfuge to get salary increases.

Like the Curriculum Cabinet, the teacher evaluators were a source of great interest to ES/Washington. Program staff saw this teachers' group as an interesting departure from typical evaluation staffing patterns. They encouraged the district to expand the committee's functions so it could provide general policy-making information to decision makers. Mark Morand also encouraged the committee to take on new tasks, such as evaluating new programs passed by the cabinet.

However, there were three barriers to expansion of the evaluators' function. First, in spite of informal encouragement from Morand and ES/Washington, the evaluators were never authorized to deviate from the evaluation design. Whenever their work had ramifications beyond simple data collection, their authority was limited. During the project's second year, the evaluators revised the checklist used to rate the quality of d/p sheets. Their revision was criticized; principals felt the list was still too ambiguous, and the superintendent asked that a second revision be made by a committee including both evaluators and principals. "Otherwise," he argued, "the teacher evaluators are put into a position of making decisions and prioritizing and doing things they shouldn't do."

Second, the evaluators had the impression that their reports were ignored, complaining that no one in the district, or in Washington, read them. During their three years of operation, their data were used in the formulation of only one decision. (In the first year, an evaluator survey was used to verify that aides were being used as substitutes.) The committee felt that future decisions about the project and district administration would depend more on financial constraints than on any information they could provide.

Finally, the evaluators had no experience in conducting evaluations. They had taken the committee assignments reluctantly and had no interest in changing their assignments. When pressed to revise their procedures, they deleted some tasks, but they decided not to take on any new ones until instructed to do so by the school board. Throughout the time this research was conducted, no such instruction was ever given.

New Activities

The new distribution of power in the district facilitated the addition of new activities to the ES project, but these additions were somewhat misleading because of confusion about the project's purposes and boundaries. Although the major emphasis was always on d/p, and the superintendent had insisted in early cabinet meetings that all new developments be related to that process, what was actually not included in the project was never clear. Ambiguity about project boundaries was apparent in the superintendent's statement the first year that the new program had become "a way of life" that would characterize all district activity, as well as in the tendency to report on a wide variety of things, including the regular attendance of conferences on such topics as civil defense and driver education, in quarterly reports to Washington, as if they were activities connected with the project. Reflecting on this tendency, one teacher argued, "It's all right to do non-ES things with ES money, but it's not fair to say we wouldn't do them without the ES project."

From the very beginning, this ambiguity permitted project planners to incorporate budget items that benefited staff and thus could be somehow justified in terms of d/p. As mentioned previously, 45 percent of all funds spent during the project's first year went for teachers' aides and curriculum materials. These items constituted 40 percent of expenditures in the project's second year. Similarly, approximately 15 percent of the federal funds spent each year supported counselors' interest in expanding their staff and mandate so that more work could be done with the families of troubled children.

After the first year, a variety of new activities appeared in the district under the auspices of the ES project, many of which increased benefits for staff. These activities took the forms of summer work or ongoing projects, and they varied in both their source of initiation and their relationship to d/p. The change in summer work began with the arrival of the third project officer. Before then, district administrators believed they were required by ES/Washington to hold a series of mandatory summer workshops for all staff with a uniform content clearly related to d/p. That assumption had guided their planning for the first year's summer work in 1973. The new project officer encouraged the district to avoid standardized, mandatory summer work and to allow teachers to develop their own proposals for summer work to be approved by Washington. About $32,000 of the $43,000 spent that summer went to teacher-initiated projects. It is difficult to know how closely teachers intended to relate their activities to the project, since most anticipated administrative criticism and tried to justify their work in terms of d/p. As one said the following spring after he had been asked to revise his proposal, "You have to play politics. You have to tie it in with d/p." Still, most proposals, including those to revise an Indian education course, to collect more material for the junior high bioethics course at the Spokane World's Fair, and to develop an elementary career education program, had no connection to the main theme of the project. Similarly, about $39,000 of the $80,000 spent on summer work the following summer was for course revisions in high school mathematics and English, elementary swimming and other curriculum changes.

Project leaders did initiate some summer work. For instance, the original objective of cataloging useful educational alternatives that the teachers had developed through the use of d/p became the task of an alternative notebook committee in 1974, and was continued the following year. In order to institutionalize the task of training new staff members in d/p and related activities, after the consultant left the district, two different workshops were developed to prepare teachers to fill that role.

In addition to activities initiated by teachers to improve the curriculum and those initiated by project leaders to meet project objectives, there was a third area of summer work consisting of voluntary workshops in areas that enhanced staff competence to do d/p. These included the consultant's own workshop on learning disabilities in 1974, another on multisensory learning, and an especially popular one on perceptual-motor development that stimulated a one-year curriculum development activity in that area the following year. Some of these, such as the perceptual-motor project, were initiated by teachers.

Most year-round subprojects had no relationship to the project's original goals. The mathematics coordinator and environmental education proposals passed by the Curriculum Cabinet in the spring of 1974 had no relation to d/p. The idea of curriculum coordinators gained support, especially among board members, and in the fall of 1975, a proposal to fund a permanent committee to serve that function in the reading area was also approved by the cabinet. The development of a kindergarten-through-grade-12 Indian education program began when the new project officer became interested in teachers' attempts to revise and upgrade a course on the American Indian in the high school.

The program most closely tied to d/p did not initially receive ES money. During the summer of 1974 a mother with a retarded child in the district's preschool program began prodding the board and, at

its direction, the cabinet, to increase services for children with severe handicaps. The cabinet set up a committee with her as chairwoman that ultimately recommended that the district hire two teachers to treat children with severe handicaps and special learning disabilities and to help classroom teachers learn how to better work with
the latter. These later became known as SLD teachers. The first
position was supported by Title I funds. Not until several months after the chairwoman began working did administrators, at the prodding
of the board, approach ES/Washington to fund the other position.

CONCLUSION

The Butte-Angels Camp ES project underwent a transformation
when the existing plans for implementation proved inadequate. The
central component of the project, diagnosis and prescription, was sub-
verted through a process of displacement because, rather than helping teachers to work more effectively on a one-to-one basis with their
students, it became largely a time-consuming exercise in filling out
forms. Other project components such as the governance system and
the teacher evaluators committee were seen as useless because their
roles were so ill defined, and all of the new committees, except the
cabinet, were disbanded before project funding was terminated. A
variety of new activities focusing on curriculum and instruction—from
the revision of old courses to the addition of new kinds of specialists
such as learning disabilities teachers—were funded by the project after the first year. These activities were initiated by teachers and
parents as well as by project leaders.

Because the issues of rational planning, resistance, participation, and comprehensive change were not adequately dealt with, the
ES project precipitated a struggle for power. The original project
leaders, especially John Raleigh, lost that struggle. In fact, Raleigh
lost his job. Those who gained control of the project had a broader
view of its potential, and changing conditions in Washington facilitated
this more liberal view. Once this struggle in the district was resolved,
the quality of resistance shifted from near-open revolt over project
management to mild discontent with its busywork elements.

An adequate explanation of the transformation of the district's
project must incorporate both the problems of managing change and
the initial conditions in the district. Such an explanation underscores
the continuity between the ES project and the rest of the district's recent history. Failure to resolve the issues of how to promote change
increased the demands on the district's staff through added work, confusion about what was required, and threats to individual autonomy.
At the same time, the project offered limited incentives because it

simply did not address the educational problems that concerned teachers. Vocational education was ignored, and d/p did not offer teachers anything new that seemed helpful. In effect, the project was part of a history of increased demands and reduced rewards that can be traced through the five years of special projects, discipline problems, and declining salary increases that preceded it.

The history of the Butte-Angels Camp ES project illustrates the perils of embarking on federally initiated change projects. In describing the complexities of the implementation process, and of the local and federal settings for change, it also throws light on some common assumptions about how change does or should take place. As such, it offers some useful lessons for educators, change agents, and policy makers. The following chapter turns to those lessons.

7

CONCLUSION

The Butte-Angels Camp ES project underwent an extensive transformation. Initially intended to be a districtwide effort to introduce diagnostic and prescriptive instructional techniques derived from the field of special education, it evolved into a number of disparate efforts designed to meet a multitude of ends. Its side effects included a new balance of power in the district and a new superintendent. In tracing these changes, the effort has been to identify conditions in Washington and the district that contributed to ineffective planning and tumultuous implementation.

While the history of the project highlights what can go wrong with federally funded change efforts, it also suggests a number of lessons about how to conceptualize and organize such efforts. Most of these concern the assumptions about the usefulness of rational planning, the benefits of staff participation, the effectiveness of the federal role as a catalyst for change, and the feasibility of comprehensive change. After discussing these assumptions, this chapter will distinguish between project implementation and school or district reform. It will identify some of the tasks required for the latter effort and draw implications of the study for the role of school administrators, teachers, and community residents in the change process. The final section highlights the diversity and politics inherent in the change process.

CONCLUSIONS ABOUT THE FOUR ASSUMPTIONS

The four assumptions introduced earlier have to do with rational project planning, participation and resistance to change, the effectiveness of the federal government as a catalyst for change, and the utility of the comprehensive change strategy.

Rational Project Design

The essence of rational planning is the formation of a technically adequate decision based on clear goals and accurate information. The planning process includes both the identification of discrepancies between goals and performance and the selection of alternative procedures, that is, innovations that will help reduce those discrepancies. This process requires clear and agreed-upon goals, accurate information on progress toward meeting goals, and the capacity to identify useful alternatives. Usually, this process is assumed to take place within the changing organization. The process is essentially dispassionate and analytical.

The case study suggests that at least three new assumptions about planning are needed to replace or supplement the assumption about rational planning. First, planning is an advocacy process more than disembodied, rational analysis. The Butte-Angels Camp District did not have a set of generally agreed-on goals. Formal statements of goals were largely collections of platitudes that were not based on the views of the community or staff. They were more like general lists developed for special purposes than guiding principles. The task of assessing the extent to which goals were being met had never been addressed. Individual or group interests took the place of organizational goals. While some interests were selfish and personal, many were job related. For instance, the high school mathematics teachers wanted to improve curriculum integration to raise test scores, while home economics teachers sought to introduce more up-to-date methods to a broader range of students to keep up with standards of good practice in their field. Some interests were in finding solutions to specific problems. However, these problems were identified through staff work experience rather than through formal needs assessment. Other interests are better described as solutions for which the problems were not clearly specified. One principal's interest in team teaching and John Raleigh's fascination with diagnosis and prescription are clear examples of such solutions. These innovations were selected more on the basis of chance encounters than on systematic search procedures. For instance, Raleigh's ideas about diagnosis and prescription might never have developed if he had not met Mark Morand.

A great deal of planning time was devoted to persuasion as well as data collection. Community-planning meetings were forums where the superintendent presented his ideas for the project and the community aired a number of major and minor grievances about the school's program. Similarly, staff meetings were used by the superintendent to build support for his programs with some repackaging to make them more palatable. Staff used the sessions to press for initiatives in vocational education and a variety of other concerns.

The results of such advocacy will depend on a number of factors, including the persuasiveness of different parties, their control over the formulation of the final plan, and their ability to generate creative compromises or syntheses. In Butte-Angels Camp, the final plan was written by a committee dominated by allies of the superintendent. The unifying theme of the plan, personalized education, clearly reflected his interests. While intended by some as an umbrella under which a variety of parochial interests could be addressed, it was not so perceived by most teachers. Still, many items in the final plan—from support for team teaching in one building to requests to purchase 17 overhead projectors—were included to please different special interests. The project's plan was a conglomeration designed to please many people, which effectively satisfied very few.

While the outcome of internal advocacy was questionable in Butte-Angels Camp, that need not always be the case. Even in this district, internal advocacy was an effective needs-sensing device. Most of the important programmatic issues the district faced seemed to be raised, but not all were fully addressed, partly because special interests controlled the final plan-writing activity and partly because district administrators believed they were involved in a rational planning activity in which advocacy and bargaining are not legitimate activities.

The second new assumption suggested by this case is that when implementation is contingent on the receipt of outside funds, planning is an interorganizational process, and fund raising can drive out other activities. Both rational analysis and internal advocacy are often supplemented or supplanted by "grantsmanship"—the effort to get support for a change project. When this happens, planning becomes a game in which district staff try to anticipate the wishes of the funding agency. In Butte-Angels Camp, considerable energy was devoted to anticipating ES/Washington's wishes. Some of the staff's more specialized interests were not addressed because the program wanted a comprehensive plan. Satisfaction of other interests seemed to be prohibited, at least in part by various program regulations.

While fundamentally a game, the extent to which the competition for funding can contribute to effective internal planning will depend on such factors as the skills of players in the district and the way the game is structured by the source of funds. Although some staff in Butte-Angels Camp were familiar with federal programs, the district lacked experience in this area. The overall absence of experience of the rural ES districts was commented on by federal project officers who had the opportunity to compare ES rural and urban districts (Corwin 1977).

The role of the federal agency raises the third assumption about planning for change, which is that federal agencies are no more rational than rural school districts. While there is a growing body of literature testifying to the irrationality of school districts (Meyer and Rowan 1978; Weick 1976), somewhat less attention has been given to federal agencies.* Yet, many of the observations about planning in Butte-Angels Camp apply to the ES Program as well. Its own goals were not clearly articulated. The title "Experimental Schools" helped the program respond to the diverse interests of its early backers, but its meaning was never clearly specified. The idea of comprehensive change was too poorly articulated for program staff to know how to apply it when reviewing proposals. Moreover, the federal program became involved in its own advocacy process within the National Institute of Education (NIE), with its continued survival at stake. This process affected local planning efforts by contributing to the ambiguity of federal guidelines. The pressure bargaining tactics in final contract negotiations with Butte-Angels Camp and other districts was also a response to events in Washington. It seems probable that the district could have played the grantsmanship game more effectively and had more opportunity to conduct serious planning if the rules of the game had been clearer.

Resistance and Participation

Resistance is often viewed as the primary barrier to planned change, and participation is seen as an effective way to overcome it. This case has identified four misleading assumptions about resistance and one form of participation that actually increases opposition to a change project, but it also suggests other means to build support for a change effort.

Resistance

Resistance to change is assumed to be irrational, concentrated in the lower staff of a school or district, only a response to a specific change project, and passive. Each of these assumptions was incorrect in Butte-Angels Camp. First, to the staff resistance to the ES project was quite rational. Teachers believed the project added to their burdens by increasing paper work and meeting time without substantially improving their instructional effectiveness or providing them with adequate compensation in the form of assistance or materials. Moreover, many teachers in the district were innovative in their own fashion. While not supportive of centrally mandated change projects, they initiated many of their own innovations.

---

*For an exception, see Sproull, Weiner, and Wolf (1978).

Second, in addition to teachers, this project required the active support of principals and the consent, or at least noninvolvement, of the school board and the community. The community ignored the project because its relationship to the interests of taxpayers and parents was unclear. However, principals shared many of the teachers' reservations so they did not actively support the project. Similarly, the school board raised questions and acted to redirect the project.

Third, resistance to the project was in large measure a response to other issues. The project brought to a head growing discontent with John Raleigh's administration—including his failure to support teachers' salary increases and proposals to innovate—as well as with his projects, which increased work for staff.

Finally, resistance became quite active. The most important opposition was the direct appeals to the school board. When coupled with previous electoral activity, this strategy was effective in unseating the superintendent and in redirecting the project.

In sum, resistance is not an isolated phenomenon. It is part of the ongoing political life of a school district. A specific proposal for change will be viewed by different groups in the light of both its specific impact on their interests and their general sentiments toward the proposal and their working conditions. Their response will be conditioned by their ability to influence decision making and decision implementation.

"Mock Participation"

One result of the stress on participation in the literature on planned change is that school administrators and federal program managers now believe that it is important to involve key participants, like teachers and the community, in decision making, but there is very little guidance on the consequences of different forms of involvement. One such form is mock participation where teachers or parents are brought together under conditions implying that they can make decisions, but where the final decisions do not clearly reflect their views. There is the promise of influence without substance. This phenomenon occurred most obviously in Butte-Angels Camp when teachers were brought into planning for the ES project and during the early meetings of the Curriculum Cabinet. The result was increased opposition to the project on the part of those who were most sensitive about their own influence.

Mock participation did not stem from conscious efforts to manipulate. Instead, federal requirements to employ more open decision-making structures than were typical for the district, combined with administrative insecurity and misunderstandings about the consequences of different ways to involve staff, created a situation that no one anticipated.

Other Alternatives

Although mock participation can build opposition to a project, three other ways to build support are suggested by this study. First, planners and administrators should anticipate and respond to barriers to implementation. These barriers increase the costs of taking part in an innovative project. Some are technical, resulting from failure to plan the project in sufficient detail. These include work with no obvious payoff (the curriculum catalogs required by ES/Washington), confusion about what is expected (misunderstandings about how to do d/p and the conditions under which it is useful), and incompatibilities (the conflict between the need for thorough knowledge of a child to diagnose and prescribe, on the one hand, and the multiclass schedule in the upper grades that brings teachers into contact with so many children, on the other). Other barriers are more political in that they represent threats to staff autonomy and authority. Fears that d/p will lead to teacher evaluation and that the committee system will undermine principals' prerogatives are examples of political barriers. The reduction of such barriers to implementation will not build support for a project, but it will reduce grounds for opposition.

Second, situations characterized by extensive conflict should be avoided unless the innovation is designed to help work out staff differences. As long as a staff is polarized or in conflict with a community, there is a strong probability that the conflict will become attached to the project.

Finally, support for a project will increase when the relevant actors see a connection between the innovation and the problems they face. For a connection to be seen, it must be both present and demonstrated. One way to ensure that a connection is demonstrated is to allow staff to influence the planning process. When representatives of relevant constituencies are allowed to help devise final plans, they are likely to ensure that their groups' interests are met and, where those interests are not met, to communicate reasons for noninclusion back to the group.

Shared influence can be counterproductive where leaders of a school or district are already committed to a project because relevant groups will raise issues the project cannot address. Then project leaders might be better advised to centralize control of planning as much as possible and to devote special attention to demonstrating the connection between the proposed project and recognized problems and, where possible, to look for new ways to resolve problems that cannot be addressed by the project in question.

The Government as Catalyst

The federal government has been viewed as the primary catalyst for educational change in the United States. Indeed, most of the financial support for reform comes from the federal level. However, the whole Experimental Schools Program raises serious questions about the extent to which the availability of funding will generate attempts at change and the ability of agencies to ensure that funds will be spent for constructive purposes. The fact that less than 5 percent of the districts eligible for the rural ES competition even applied for funding suggests that without the stick of regulation, the carrot of funding competitions will not motivate a great deal of activity. However, in some districts where there are active entrepreneurs, grant programs will be a spur to action.

A number of factors limit the extent to which an outside agency can ensure that its funds are used constructively. One of these is the federal system of government that places control over education with state government and grants substantial autonomy to local school districts. When one agency must compel the cooperation of another to ensure that its mission is accomplished, the implementation of that mission is often problematic (Elmore 1978). A shift from the use of grants to contracts as the legal instrument for the relationship, as occurred with the ES Program, is not enough to overcome the force of custom and law and thus shift the balance of control.

Distance is another limiting factor. Project officers located in Washington or a regional office simply cannot be in close enough touch with a district to contribute to the day-to-day activities through which plans become reality. The distance problem was especially apparent in Butte-Angels Camp where the ES Program lost touch with the district for extended periods of time. Hence, the effectiveness of local change efforts seems to depend primarily on the skill of the people in school districts who identify the changes that are needed, select the funding competitions to enter, develop the plans for new projects, and put the plans into practice.

Still, the politics surrounding a funding agency and the way that agency administers its competitions and resulting grants and contracts can have some impact on local project management. The history of the Experimental Schools Program strongly suggests that an agency under siege has difficulty supporting local school improvement because all attention is turned toward survival. The ES Program always suffered from wavering support, but its political problems were exacerbated by the transfer from the Office of Education (OE) to the NIE. At the OE, the program was relatively small so it did not attract a great deal of attention. Moreover, it had substantial support, for a while at least, from the commissioner of education. At the NIE, how-

n was relatively large, and it had no support. In
agers at the NIE were under severe pressure from
same time they were looking for discretionary funds
n programs. The ES Program was one of a number
vities that came under fire in the NIE's early history
r, and Wolf 1978), and the pressure on the program
lly related to its own merits as a change effort. Nevertheless, ... pressures the program experienced were transferred
to the local districts during planning. Later, Washington politics and
declining travel funds kept ES project officers from adequately monitoring or providing assistance to local projects. The program apparently did not become aware of the severe internal conflict in Butte-
Angels Camp until the struggle was almost over.

The NIE's attacks on the ES Program are an extreme example
of the instability and opposition that a new idea can face within the
federal bureaucracy, but they are not unique. From the very beginning, the idea of an experimental schools program attracted the attention of a wide variety of White House aides and functionaries from the
Department of Health, Education and Welfare, all of whom had different ideas about what such a program should do. Moreover, the cast
of characters kept changing. The multitude of ideas and actors contributed to the difficulties in specifying the program's mission. The
resulting ambiguity created difficulties for selecting and monitoring
local change projects, but it may have been a major contributing factor to the program's early survival.

For a program to be administered effectively, it must have support within the federal government, but there are other requirements.
First, the program must have a clear sense of purpose or direction.
The major purpose of the ES Program was to examine the utility of
comprehensive, long-term change strategies, but the concept of comprehensiveness was never clarified to the satisfaction of program
staff or district leaders. This clarification is partly a writing task:
ensuring that the numerous mission statements, announcements of
competition, and regulations the program produces specify and contribute to its ends. However, considerable staff development is also
needed. Project officers must make numerous judgmental decisions
in describing a program orally, reviewing documents produced by
districts seeking funds, and making site visits to funded projects
(CPI Associates 1977). These decisions require more than memoriz-
ing written statements. The ability to apply program purposes to new
contingencies is also needed. Such application requires thorough understanding of the program's direction.

Second, the program must have means to monitor project development that match program requirements. Newer or more innovative
programs often require closer monitoring than older, more established

ones. The capacity to monitor a project is a function of the number of projects an officer must oversee, other commitments, stability of the project officers, and travel funds. While ES project officers initially had relatively light loads when compared with other programs, priorities stemming from conflicts at the NIE, the loss of old project officers without replacement, and severe cuts in travel funds inhibited communication with local projects.

Finally, project officers must have sufficient autonomy and experience both in their program's content area and in the tasks of monitoring and assisting projects. As a result of pressures from outside the agency, the first ES program director apparently intervened frequently in the interaction with districts. However, some project officers had relatively little experience in education, and many were new to the federal government.

Comprehensive Change

The Experimental Schools Program defined comprehensive change for its rural projects as affecting all the school system from kindergarten through high school and the system's curriculum; staff training; use of time, space, and facilities; relations with the community; and governance and administration. The program's cycles of funding added a third implicit requirement: that all changes be implemented at once after an initial planning phase. This multicomponent, one-shot approach to change is the alternative of grandeur. It is a high-risk approach to systemwide reform that is intended to overcome and take advantage of interdependencies among the system's parts.

One of the many questions the program did not answer was how to integrate the diverse elements of a comprehensive change project. At least two mechanisms for integration are possible. One is standardization, the use of identical procedures and materials in all situations. The other is functional integration, where one or a limited number of problems are identified and the factors contributing to each problem are specified or classified by setting. Then new practices are proposed to address different facets of the same problem. The practices adopted may vary substantially from setting to setting.

Butte-Angels Camp's ES project plan called for extensive standardization. Diagnosis and prescription were to be uniformly applied at all levels of the district. Beyond that, the project at its inception was a congeries of separate parts with the relations among them poorly specified. Functional integration was conspicuously absent. If a comprehensive change project is an integrated effort, then this project was not comprehensive at the outset. The extent of integration, and therefore comprehensiveness, declined over time.

In Butte-Angels Camp, the comprehensive approach failed largely because there was a lack of interdependence among the district's parts. Junior high school teachers reported that they could cope with the use of different mathematics curricula in the two elementary schools because curriculum-related variation in what students could do was washed out by individual differences. Moreover, the problems in different parts of the district also varied. For example, the high school teachers' interest in strengthening vocational education was not shared in the lower grades. Because interdependence was low, attempts to tighten coordination, for instance, through some forms of teaming or joint scheduling, were resisted. In sum, the problem that the alternative of grandeur is designed to overcome simply did not exist. The acceptance of standardized techniques depended in part on their compatibility with existing practices. In the content-oriented high school, diagnosis and prescription was resisted. The same technique caused much less opposition in the elementary schools, which were more oriented to working with individual children.

Still, the effort at comprehensive change raises a question that has received little attention until recently: how does one manage the reform of a school or district? Researchers have looked at the dissemination of single ideas (House 1974), the management of single projects (Smith and Keith 1971), and adoption rates in single schools (Daft and Becker 1977). In these studies, the focus of attention has been the idea or project, not the district. Yet, some schools and even some districts perform better than others (Bidwell and Kasarda 1975; Spady 1973). The next section addresses the question of how to improve district performance.

FURTHER IMPLICATIONS FOR
EDUCATIONAL CHANGE

Since most educational change activity takes place in schools and school districts rather than federal bureaus, this section addresses the question of how to stimulate school or district reform and then identifies implications of this case study for the role of school administrators, teachers, and community residents in planned-change efforts.

School and Districtwide Change

The problems of project management and school or district change are conceptually distinct. Single projects rarely suffice in accomplishing district change for several reasons. A single district encompasses too many different kinds of problems related to different client groups (for example, the gifted, the handicapped, those whose socioeconomic background creates an educational deficit), subject areas, and community interests (for example, sports programs and cost reduction). Moreover, a variety of interest groups in the form of subject matter specialists, special occupational groups, and different collections of parents and other segments of the surrounding community give different priorities to the solution of each problem. Finally, school administrators, school boards, and the public all lack the means to control and coordinate the change process or to concentrate efforts in one area. Hence, many districts find themselves carrying out a multitude of changes simultaneously.

The management of school or district reform, then, hinges on the way this multitude of changes is orchestrated. Three separate tasks are involved. First, it is important to create conditions conducive to the initiation of separate change efforts. Even in Butte-Angels Camp, where many staff-initiated change proposals were stifled, there was no shortage of ideas. However, conditions can be created to facilitate the initiation of improved practice. Research on innovative organizations suggests that a number of structural and cultural conditions appear together where changes are frequently initiated (Berman and McLaughlin 1979; Daft and Becker 1977; Guest 1962; Rosenblum and Louis 1978). Hage and Aiken (1970), for instance, identify two organizational styles—the static and the dynamic. They suggest that dynamic organizations are characterized by the following attributes:

- High complexity or a multitude of occupational groups;
- Decentralization or broad distribution of power;
- Low formalization or control through the use of rules;
- Low stratification or a limited number of levels in the organizational hierarchy and little differentiation between levels;
- An emphasis on quality, as opposed to quantity, of production;
- Deemphasis on efficiency or cost cutting; and
- High job satisfaction.

Berman and McLaughlin (1979) add the following attributes:

- An emphasis on diversity in the services delivered,
- The primacy of improved educational service over "bureaucratic or political" concerns,
- Open boundaries to the environment, and
- A climate characterized by mutual trust and encouragement for risk taking.

The common theme of such lists is that school districts that facilitate access to new ideas protect innovators in the system from being punished for advocating the new and the different and encourage people to seek out changes that will improve their educational programs are most conducive to the initiation of constructive innovations.

Some of these characteristics are not easily controllable. The Butte-Angels Camp District, for instance, had relatively few occupational groups when compared with more urban districts, and it could not add many more because of its small size and economic considerations. Moreover, the community's low-tax ideology was conducive to an emphasis on cost cutting. Many others can be changed, however. For instance, the district's administrative style emphasized the centralization of power and the maximization of distance between the superintendent and staff. When combined with other administrative actions, these conditions created a climate of low job satisfaction, a primacy on political concerns, and low trust. A different administrative style could have done a great deal to change the climate of the district.

The second task in managing district reform is to screen suggestions for change. This task creates a dilemma because, on the one hand, not all change ideas are constructive or really contribute to the solution to local problems. Moreover, ideas that are good in principle may be badly worked out leading to severe implementation problems. On the other hand, aggressive screening procedures can inhibit the initiation of ideas by reducing job satisfaction, the emphasis on service diversity, and the level of trust in the district. Screening procedures that (1) include clear criteria for acceptance and support, (2) place the burden on the proposer to show how the project will enhance the district's functioning, (3) are simple, (4) are fair, (5) prohibit penalties for the suggestion of new ideas, and (6) err in favor of accepting new ideas rather than rejecting them would seem to be the most effective.

The final task is to provide administrative support for the change effort. This support includes assistance where appropriate, with grantsmanship. Not all change ideas require financial support. Where such support is needed, however, the assistance of someone who is aware of the range of special programs that provide funding and of the procedures for writing applications or proposals and for negotiating and administering agreements with the funding source can be an important help. Where the people with knowledge of grantsmanship are facilitators rather than advocates of specific changes, the emphasis on service diversity can be increased and internal politics reduced.

Perhaps more important than grantsmanship is assistance with planning for implementation. Supportive administrators can help innovators within the district identify where new training is needed, where additional materials and personnel are required, and what existing policies or schedules impede the innovation. They can also help devise ways to overcome such barriers. At the same time, administrators can build in reporting procedures to allow them to follow the development of the innovation and provide assistance when plans go awry and unanticipated barriers appear.

The kind of multiproject district reform that would result from following these three steps would be quite slow. School districts are too diverse and "loosely coupled" to be changed rapidly (Weick 1976). Such change would also look very different from the single-project comprehensive change advocated by the Experimental Schools Program. While each separate project might be better planned than the Butte-Angels Camp project was, the total effect would look rather unplanned. Different schools would have different projects aimed at solving different, but locally identified, problems. The common thread would not be a single procedure or theme, but a general concern with improving practice and a general willingness to take risks.*

Implications for School Administrators

This case study suggests at least three implications for school administrators. First, it is important to recognize the limits of one's authority. Administrators have more control over financial matters, scheduling, and the coordination of groups of instructors than they do over the day-to-day decisions concerning what material will be taught or how specific children will be treated. Even authority over decisions on what courses will be taught and what course objectives are typically are shared with teachers. Administrators lack the mandate, the means to observe the process and outcome of instruction, and the sanctions to control instructional behavior. These limits seem to be more extreme at the secondary level where teachers are more militant and have more specialized content knowledge to increase their own authority.

Second, while formal authority is limited, administrators have a number of sources of influence at their disposal that are often overlooked. Administrators can gain the esteem of their staff by provid-

---

*There are conditions where the proposed approach would not be appropriate. The most obvious situation is one where there is consensus that draconian measures are needed to overcome a specific problem. This situation seems to be the exception rather than the rule, however.

ing support with disciplinary problems, improving teachers' working conditions, and handling allocation decisions fairly. These tasks are required of all administrators; how they are handled will determine an individual's influence.

Finally, the administrative role is more conducive to the orchestration and facilitation of change than it is to the advocacy of specific reforms. Administrators simply lack the influence to mandate specific changes except within their own zones of authority. However, the burden of achieving the tasks required for district reform outlined above falls on administrators, and these tasks are not simple ones. This observation applies more to line positions, like principals and superintendents, than it does to staff positions. One might expect educational psychologists, special education teachers, and subject matter specialists to advocate changes relative to their specialty, but it is still necessary to sell these ideas rather than impose them. Moreover, the higher the position in a district hierarchy and the broader the responsibility, the more one serves as a facilitator and the less one can advocate specific changes.

Implications for Teachers

Teachers are important arbiters of what changes will be made in schools. Through passive resistance and following the letter, rather than the spirit of directions for a change, they can contribute to the displacement of an innovation from an approach to instruction to a series of empty procedures. Their collective action can put an end to a special project or redirect it. In the process, they can cause the innovator to be removed.

On the other hand, teachers can be agents for change. In Butte-Angels Camp, teachers were not radical reformers bent on the wholesale restructuring of their district, but they did have a number of modest ideas about how to do their own work better. An important element in any change effort will be stimulating and taking advantage of teachers' interests in being more effective instructors.

Implications for Parents and Community Residents

This case study suggests that concerted action on the community's part can have significant results. In Butte-Angels Camp, the school board and top administrators anticipated the community's interest in holding down costs. When the community indicated its displeasure with the district's fiscal policies, additional steps were taken to reduce spending.

There are two further observations for those who see community residents as a possible force to motivate reform. First, at least from the school district's perspective, community interest appears sporadically and residents' concerns may be contradictory. The one major episode of community interest that occurred during the four years covered in this case study of the Butte-Angels Camp schools was actually a response to actions taken by the county commissioners, and the taxpayers' revolt that resulted died out before its leaders could elect a member of the school board. Moreover, administrators point to instances where community residents want contradictory things. For example, some want more control of students while others want less.

Second, the interests of community residents and professional educators may be at odds. The community will apply a set of general interests in government having more to do with fiscal responsibility and community integration than anything that is specifically relevant to education. By contrast, educational specialists advocate changes related to developments in their fields. They may develop and employ modes of student treatment that are at odds with general community norms. The values of the local community are not necessarily better or worse than those of professional educators, but they are different. As a result, community-motivated reform could take a very different direction from that instigated and controlled by district staff.

DIVERSITY, POLITICS, AND CHANGE

If there is a single theme running through this volume, it is that the cast of characters in the change process is exceedingly diverse. One change project in one school district entailed at least some involvement of teachers, school administrators, the school board, community residents, project officers, and program managers, not to mention assorted White House aides, commissioners of education, and secretaries of health, education and welfare. These individuals and groups shared a general interest in education improvement, but the strength of that interest, and the way it was interpreted, varied considerably. Their special interests and responsibilities stand out more than what they had in common. At the same time, no one group in Washington or the district was able to dominate the process except for short periods of time, yet joint decisions were required for the project to take place at all.

This diversity lends an inherently political cast to the change process. Conflict and compromise cannot be avoided. Modes of thinking about change that accept diversity and politics as natural will help to avoid some of the misconceptions and mistakes that plagued this project and seem to be endemic to educational change efforts in the United States. To that end, this case has been used to question the assumptions that change can be planned rationally by central decision makers in a school district or in Washington; that participation can build support for change without entailing shared influence; and that comprehensive, one-shot change is possible in education. It has also suggested ways to take advantage of diversity in orchestrating change. Hopefully, it will sensitize future innovators and change managers to the complexities and risks of planned change and to the limits of what is possible.

APPENDIX A:
CONDUCTING THE STUDY

Like most other researchers who have conducted case studies, I relied primarily on participant observation to learn about the organization and dynamics of the Butte-Angels Camp School District and its ES project. In this kind of research what is learned depends in large measure on the relationships that are established with people in and around the district and how those relations are maintained. When I arrived in the district, I had survived a complex selection procedure intended to identify young researchers with the potential to manage field relations and write descriptive reports, but my actual experience was limited. Twenty-seven years old, I was fresh out of the education department at the University of Chicago. I had done field work in urban ghettos and among the countercultures that started parent-run free schools, but that was never the kind of live-in field work practiced by anthropologists and required for this multiyear study. Nor did my upbringing in a small, west-coast city provide much background for the rural mining community in which I would spend the next three years.

I was not playing the conventional role of anthropologist studying a primitive culture, however. Instead, I was caught up in a web of interorganizational relationships among the district, ES/Washington, and my employer—Abt Associates—that was fundamentally modern. These relationships engendered issues of autonomy and authority between federal and local agencies and of contract and grants management that affected my access to information. Moreover, the Experimental Schools' literature described our research function as that of evaluation. As much as Abt Associates tried to downplay that label, through the use of techniques like giving me the title of on-site researcher (OSR), the question of the appropriate role of an evaluator inevitably arose.

These issues all affected my attempt to play a role, initially endorsed by both ES/Washington and Abt Associates, of neutral observer. As Pelto (1970) explains, this role is useful for learning about economic, social, and political strategies of interpersonal interaction and for uncovering the special secrets and failures that are usually hidden. A neutral observer can learn the viewpoints of all

---

*The problems of conducting this study and the way I coped with them are also described in Firestone (1975) and Wacaster and Firestone (1978).

sides in internal conflicts and can penetrate the backstage life of an
organization that is normally withheld from public view. However,
this ability to penetrate the facade rests ultimately on membership
in a different and distant society: the observer is neutral precisely
because he or she is not competing for anything on the local scene and
is not making moral judgments. The observer is outside the action.
He or she provides the possibility for social interaction in which normal rules are relaxed. Friendship and interaction come with little
risk to the informant because the observer is not competing for a
better position and because she or he has promised not to divulge information that would have a bearing on the informant's local role or
reputation.

   Although I tried to remain neutral, the people in Butte-Angels
Camp expected me to provide technical assistance and to report to
ES/Washington. Technical assistance was badly needed because of
the confusion created by the ES project. However, Abt Associates
recognized that providing technical assistance creates affiliations in
the local setting. Ultimately, the assister risks taking sides and
losing his or her neutrality (Center for New Schools 1976). The Abt
Associates-ES/Washington contract was negotiated to relieve us from
any responsibility for providing technical assistance. Our obligation
not to provide assistance created some mild resentment locally because district staff had assumed that we could provide help. Ultimately, this problem was alleviated because the ES/Washington-
Butte-Angels Camp contract stipulated that the district must accept
the residence of an on-site researcher as one of the conditions for
getting funded and because I maintained a low profile and did not flaunt
my background as expert.

   The technical assistance problem was easier to resolve than
the reporting issue. Everyone in the district knew that I reported to
their funding agency. When I first arrived, many people mistakenly
assumed that I worked for ES/Washington, or at least that I reported
to the agency frequently. John Raleigh seemed to be afraid that I
would report the project's internal difficulties to ES/Washington, and
many teachers hoped that I would. In the battle shaping up between
the superintendent and the militant teachers, my testimony could be
extremely useful.

   At the outset, I carefully explained to the superintendent, to
teachers, and to others who asked or needed to know, that short-term
monitoring was not part of my responsibility. I would write a report
on the project, but not until after it was over. The Abt Associates
staff had explained that I would submit a final report, but that no interim reporting on project progress would be required. In fact, the
Cambridge office was very concerned with maintaining the confidentiality of field data.

However, the ES/Washington-Abt Associates understanding that allowed OSRs to protect their data and withhold tentative conclusions violated responsible research monitoring that require that some evidence be provided to demonstrate that competent work is in progress before the funding period is terminated. * To some extent, the initial understanding was forgotten or ignored. More important, ES/Washington was in a battle for its life, and it was losing. Field data could provide the basis for interim reports that would prove to the program's external constituencies that it was actually producing competent research. These data could be extremely useful to ES/Washington's project officers as well. These people were responsible for the local districts' progress, but their interaction with the districts was impaired by turnover in Washington, changing assignments, competing responsibilities, and limited travel funds. The OSRs could provide them with useful information, but doing so could affect future funding for the districts and would eliminate any possibility of maintaining a neutral role.

During 1974 the confidentiality issue led to a protracted series of negotiations between ES/Washington and Abt Associates in which the OSRs from all ten rural sites played an intermittent but active role. Ultimately, the impasse was resolved through three decisions. First, Abt Associates agreed to require that OSRs produce annual reports in the form of narrative pieces that could be incorporated into their final reports. ES/Washington appointed a representative of NIE who was an experienced field researcher with no responsibility for monitoring local projects to review those reports and provide an assessment of quality. He agreed to share his assessment but not the actual contents of the reports. Second, Abt Associates offered to generate a number of interim reports from other data sources that might help ES/Washington with its internal problems. Finally, a meeting was held in which the OSRs and ES/Washington project officers explained their responsibilities and shared, in very general terms, observations about the sites. This meeting broke the ice and offered us some limited insights into the problems ES/Washington faced. Thus, substantive information was kept out of the hands of people with program responsibilities, but we OSRs were required to go back on at least the letter of our promises.

Interim reporting problems characterized the first two years of implementation. By the project's third year, my final report became a minor issue. People in the district knew that I was not sharing information locally, and believed that I was not reporting to Wash-

---

*For a more extensive discussion of this issue, see Herriott (1977).

ington, but they were also aware that I was disappearing for long periods of time to put together my report. They knew something of what I had seen and heard, and they wanted to know how I assessed the situation. Some people probed indirectly, "I'm not going to ask you what you think about . . . , but—." Others asked more directly, and the ploy I had used earlier of turning their questions around no longer worked. Their response would be, "Don't give me that 'What do you think?' routine!"

Attempts to determine my opinions and conclusions were all the more effective because of the time I had spent in the district. After two years, it was getting to the point where I was not inclined to be quite so neutral any more; many of my informants were friends. Most of my colleagues and I avoided such revelations, but at some personal cost. In retrospect, the termination of funding for OSRs two years before the local projects ended had the advantage of forcing us to leave before more incidents occurred, even though we were unable to witness the final developments of the local projects.

As I began the study I relied heavily on participant observation, and I continued to collect information through this means until the end of the project's third year. At the early organizational meetings, I became known as the "man with the yellow pad." I attended training sessions and committee meetings, and I openly took notes on all that transpired. I also attended routine district meetings of administrators and the school board. I was present at special events as well, including a special meeting from which administrators were excluded to determine if teachers would drop out of the NEA and join the AFT. I did some classroom observation, but I spent more time talking to teachers after school, or during their free time at lunch, or their preparation periods. To some extent I did the same thing with administrators and school board members. I was never as well accepted by the administrators as by teachers and board members. Administrators' reticence, even after my reporting responsibilities were clarified, probably reflected the pressure they were under at the time. But I do not think more information was withheld from me than from anyone else. However, the principals and superintendent probably anticipated my final report with some trepidation about its effects on them.

In addition to my observation, I used two other means of obtaining information. First, I was responsible for assisting the Abt Associates Cambridge office with local data collection by assessing records needed for separate comparative studies of changes in the community, in the organization of the district, and in students. These tasks broadened my contacts in the community and the district. I also conducted interviews with selected informants to learn about project planning. These informants included John Raleigh, Mark

Morand (the project consultant), six teachers from different levels of the system, and two community residents. All were chosen for their knowledge of the planning process.

By the second year of project implementation, I was formulating a number of questions on which I needed somewhat comparable information from respondents throughout the district. I was also aware that I was falling into a rut in that I had a set of favorite informants and I risked ignoring some perceptions of events in the district. To get out of my own habitual data collection patterns and to collect this other information, I initiated a set of semistructured interviews. Some questions were varied or eliminated, depending on the position of the respondent. The interviews were conducted between December 1974 and March 1975, and the respondents included all 5 school board members, 4 former members, the superintendent, all 6 principals, and one quarter of the elementary and secondary teachers (18 and 16, respectively). These interviews provided a valuable addition to my less structured observation and questioning. *

Although I relied primarily on data I collected myself, these were supplemented with two surveys conducted by Abt Associates for other studies and by an extensive array of documents available in the district. These data sources included:

- A questionnaire that Abt Associates sent to all district staff in the fall of 1973 that had a response rate of 92 percent. It provided a useful picture of staff attitudes at that important time and was used to verify hypotheses generated by direct observation.
- Another questionnaire sent from Cambridge to all community residents. It only had a 17 percent response rate. Responses to two open-end questions were used to examine some hypotheses about community interests in the school.
- Minutes of planning meetings available in the district. At ES/Washington's direction, a staff of nine teachers developed a massive record of planning meetings and reports of telephone conversations to Washington. What they lacked in clarity, they made up for in volume, and they were extremely useful when combined with interviews.
- Less extensive records of earlier attempts to plan for change and of previous activities of the school board and local teachers' association.
- Newspaper articles. The district's active public relations director placed as many as 600 releases a year in the local paper. Some of these became events in their own right.

---

*See Appendix B.

• Other surveys conducted by the district's own ES-supported evaluation staff and by the local teachers' association. These included useful questions with high response rates. They were used when access was possible.

This appendix has reviewed the opportunities and problems I faced in conducting this study. The primary opportunity was access to a school district conducting an extensive educational change project. I worked in an interorganizational context that provided a wealth of qualitative and quantitative data, and that gave me entry into a great variety of settings within the district and the local community. Access to so many parts of a school district and its surroundings was one of the most unusual and welcome features of the Abt Associates Experimental Schools study.

The problems revolved around the contradictory demands for reporting and maintaining confidentiality that stemmed from contractual obligations, personal ties, and the fatigue of three years of continuous field work in the same setting. Two comments on this complex of problems are in order. First, while the vicissitudes of the NIE-Abt Associates relationship required that I (and my colleagues at the other nine rural sites) leave well before the project terminated, that move was probably for the best. It seems unlikely that I could have maintained my role for another two years or that doing so would have made a major contribution to the study. Second, the way we resolved the contradiction between the expectation of confidentiality (that we generated) and the obligations to report that were thrust on us after the project was under way was messy. However, our solution did allow us to maintain the substance of the obligation we undertook to avoid the role of assistant project monitor as well as to complete our research. The reader can tell whether our struggles were worth the effort from reading the case study.

APPENDIX B:
TEACHER AND SCHOOL BOARD
INTERVIEW SCHEDULES

INTERVIEWS

In the fall of 1974 it became apparent that there were some issues where I would need to elicit information or opinions from a large
number of people in a fairly systematic way. To get this kind of information, I conducted interviews with teachers, administrators, and
past and present board members. A partly randomized procedure
was used to select teachers in order to ensure that I would contact a
variety of people, not just those I used as informants most frequently.
It was not completely randomized because some interviews were conducted before the selection was made, and two individuals who I felt
would not give me an open, honest interview were deleted. One
quarter of the teachers—18 of the 71 elementary instructors and 16
of the 63 in grades 7 through 12—were approached and all agreed to
be interviewed. In addition, interviews were conducted with all principals, the superintendent, all present board members, and four people who had recently been board members—two from Butte, one from
Angels Camp, and one who had served on both the Angels Camp and
the Butte-Angels Camp boards.

Different forms were used with teachers, administrators, and
board members. Those used for teachers and board members are
reproduced here. The administrator form is a composite of those
two.

TEACHER INTERVIEW SCHEDULE

When did you first come to the Butte-Angels Camp area?

How many years have you lived in the Butte-Angels Camp area?

How old are you now?

What school did you get your B.A. from?

What is the highest degree you have?

How long have you worked in this system?

Do you belong to the Butte-Angels Camp Educational Association?
Why?

What other educational organizations, if any, do you belong to?

197

What are some of the most important things that you try to accomplish with your classes?

How has the NIE project changed your work as a teacher? (Better-worse? Easier-harder? Changed effectiveness?)

How many students have you diagnosed and prescribed this year?

Will you please tell me about a student you have diagnosed and prescribed? (Is this process helpful? Simple-difficult? Time consuming? How long? What did you do differently from before?)

Have you ever used the Curriculum Catalog? Alternatives Notebook? AV Catalog? (Why? How often? How helpful?)

Have you even attended a TAPS or Tri-Part meeting? Curriculum Cabinet meeting? (Done anything to affect your work? Easier or harder to change things now?)

Have you met with the ES project consultant this year? Last year? (How often? Helpful? How?)

Are there programs or services that the district should offer to students that it is not now offering? (What about vocational or career education?)

There has been a debate in recent years about whether or not teaching is a profession. In what ways would you say teaching is a profession?

In what ways would you say teaching is not a profession?

What kinds of supervision or support should teachers receive from administrators? What role should they play in classroom work, evaluation, discipline, materials, allocation of aides, parents? What do they do?

What kinds of supervision or support should teachers receive from the school board? What do they do? (Salary evaluation, relations with administration, kinds of communications.)

Some teachers seem to take a more active part in systemwide affairs by serving on committees, speaking out at meetings, and so forth. Those that speak out hold different views about the rights and responsibilities of teachers. Who are a few of these more active teachers that you agree with?

Who do you disagree with?

Regardless of how much they speak out, who are the teachers you talk to most often?

Five years from now what do you expect your major occupational activity to be?

SCHOOL BOARD INTERVIEW

How many years have you lived in the Butte-Angels Camp area?

How old are you now?

Do/did you have any children in the school system (when you were on the board)?

What is/was your occupation (when you were on the board)?

What is the last grade of school you completed or the highest degree you hold?

Where did you go to elementary school? High school? College? Where did you get your highest degree?

What clubs or organizations do/did you belong to (when you were on the board)?

What political party do you belong to?

Do you expect to run for the school board again?

Do you ever expect to run for any other elective office?

Would you please describe for me the steps you went through to be-come a school board member? (Who asked by? Who helped? Issues of concern?)

What were the critical problems the district faced while you were on the school board? What happened and how resolved? (Negotiations. Hiring superintendent.)

What are some of the most important things teachers should try to accomplish with their classes?

Are there programs or services that the school district should pro-vide that it is not now providing? (What about vocational or career education?)

Are there programs or services the district provides that it should eliminate?

What sources of information about attitudes of people in the district are useful to you as a board member? (Superintendent, principals, teachers, BACEA, written records, community people.)

Do representatives of community groups or organizations ever con-tact you personally to seek your support for their positions or ideas? (Examples.)

Do members of the school staff ever contact you personally to seek your support for their position or ideas? (Examples.)

Do you ever feel any conflict between your responsibility to the public and to the school system? What about conflict between responsibilities to different parts of the school system? (Examples.)

(Besides NIE) what are some of the most important state or federal agencies that affect your work as a board member? How?

What kinds of supervision or support should teachers receive from administrators? What do they receive?

What kinds of supervision or support should teachers receive from the school board? What do they receive?

What kinds of supervision or support should administrators receive from the teachers? What do they receive?

What kinds of supervision or support should administrators receive from the board? What do they receive?

When did you first hear about the NIE program?

What role, if any, did you play in planning the NIE program?

As you see it, what kinds of progress and problems has the project stimulated?

What changes have you seen in teaching practices, materials, and personnel, what students learn, staff morale, relations with the community?

How would you describe the district's relations with Washington? How have they changed over time?

What aspects of the project do you expect to remain once federal support has ended?

BIBLIOGRAPHY

Alford, Robert. 1960. "School District Reorganization and Community Integration." Harvard Educational Review 30: 350-71.

Allison, Graham T. 1971. Essence of Decision: Explaining the Cuban Missile Crisis. Boston: Little, Brown.

Argyris, Chris. 1969. "Explorations in Consultant-Client Relationships." In The Planning of Change, edited by Warren Bennis, Kenneth Benne, and Robert Chin, pp. 437-57. New York: Holt, Rinehart & Winston.

ASCD Yearbook. 1964. Individualizing Instruction. Washington, D. C.: Association for Supervision and Curriculum Development.

Becker, Howard S. 1953. "The Teacher in the Authority System of the Public School." Sociology of Education 27: 128-41.

Berman, Paul E., and Milbrey W. McLaughlin. 1979. An Exploratory Study of School District Adaptation. Santa Monica, Calif.: Rand.

_____. 1975. Federal Programs Supporting Educational Change, vol. 1. Santa Monica, Calif.: Rand.

Bidwell, Charles, and John Kasarda. 1975. "School District Organization and Student Achievement." American Sociological Review 40: 55-70.

Blau, Peter M. 1964. Exchange and Power in Social Life. New York: John Wiley & Sons.

_____. 1955. The Dynamics of Bureaucracy. Chicago: University of Chicago Press.

Carlson, Richard O. 1972. School Superintendents: Careers and Performance. Columbus, Oh.: Charles Merrill.

Center for New Schools. 1976. "Ethnographic Evaluation in Education." Journal of R&D in Education 9: 3-11.

Chesler, Mark, R. A. Schmuck, and R. Lippitt. 1975. "The Principal's Role in Facilitating Innovation." In Managing Change in Educational Organizations, edited by Terrence E. Deal and J. Victor Baldridge, pp. 321-27. Berkeley, Calif.: McCutchan.

Clark, Burton R. 1966. "Interorganizational Patterns in Education." Administrative Science Quarterly 10: 224-37.

_____. 1956. "Organizational Adaptation and Precarious Values: A Case Study." American Sociological Review 21: 327-37.

Coch, L., and J. R. P. French. 1968. "Overcoming Resistance to Change." In Group Dynamics, edited by Dorwin Cartwright and Alvin Zander, pp. 336-50. New York: Harper & Row.

Cohen, Elizabeth et al. 1976. Organization and Instruction in Elementary Schools: First Results, 1973. Stanford, Calif.: Stanford Center for R&D in Teaching.

Corwin, Ronald G. 1977. Patterns of Federal-Local Relationships in Education: A Case Study of the Rural Experimental Schools Program. Cambridge, Mass.: Abt Associates.

_____. 1973. Reform and Organizational Survival: The Teacher as an Instrument of Educational Change. New York: John Wiley & Sons.

CPI Associates, Inc. 1977. The Roles and Functions of Project Officers in DHEW Region VI Program Agencies. Dallas: CPI Associates.

Cremin, Lawrence A. 1961. The Transformation of the School. New York: A. A. Knopf.

Daft, Richard, and Selwyn Becker. 1977. The Innovative Organization. New Holland, N.Y.: Elsevier.

Doyle, Denis. 1975. "Final Report of the ESP Review Committee." Unpublished memorandum to Emerson Elliott.

Doyle, Walter et al. 1976. The Birth, Nurturance and Transformation of an Educational Reform. Portland, Ore.: Northwest Regional Educational Laboratory.

Dreeben, Robert. 1970. The Nature of Teaching: Schools and the Work of Teachers. Glenview, Ill.: Scott Foresman.

Dunn, William N., and Frederic W. Swierczek. 1977. "Planned Organizational Change: Toward Grounded Theory." Journal of Applied Behavioral Science 13: 135-58.

Elmore, Richard F. 1978. "Organizational Models of Social Program Implementation." Public Policy 26: 185-228.

Emrick, John A., and Susan A. Peterson. 1977. A Synthesis of Findings Across Five Recent Studies of Educational Dissemination and Change. Menlo Park, Calif.: Stanford Research Institute.

Firestone, William A. 1975. "Contract Shop." The Generator 3: 3-15.

Ford Foundation. 1972. A Foundation Goes to School. New York: Ford Foundation.

Fullan, Michael, and A. Pomfret. 1977. "Research on Curriculum and Instruction Implementation." Review of Educational Research 47: 335-97.

Gamson, William A. 1968. Power and Discontent. Homewood, Ill.: Dorsey.

Gearhart, B. R. 1973. Learning Disabilities: Educational Strategies. St. Louis: C. V. Mosby.

Giacquinta, Joseph B. 1973. "The Process of Organizational Change in Schools." In Review of Research in Education 1, edited by Fred N. Kerlinger, pp. 178-208. Itasca, Ill.: F. E. Peacock.

Gideonse, Hendrik D. 1979. "Designing Federal Policies and Programs to Facilitate Local Change Efforts." In The Dynamics of Planned Educational Change, edited by Robert E. Herriott and Neal Gross, pp. 298-327. Berkeley, Calif.: McCutchan.

Goss, Mary E. W. 1961. "Influence and Authority Among Physicians in an Outpatient Clinic." American Sociological Review 26: 39-50.

Gross, Neal, Joseph B. Giacquinta, and Marilyn Bernstein. 1971. Implementing Organizational Innovations. New York: Basic Books.

Gross, Neal, and Robert E. Herriott. 1965. Staff Leadership in Public Schools. New York: John Wiley & Sons.

Guest, Robert H. 1962. Organizational Change. Homewood, Ill.: Dorsey & Irwin.

Hage, Jerald, and Michael Aiken. Social Change in Complex Organizations, pp. 94-95. New York: Random House.

Halperin, S. 1975. "ESAA Ten Years Later." Educational Researcher 4: 5-9.

Herriott, Robert E. 1979. "The Federal Context: Planning, Funding and Monitoring." In The Dynamics of Planned Educational Change, edited by Robert E. Herriott and Neal Gross, pp. 49-75. Berkeley, Calif.: McCutchan.

_____. 1977. "The Rural Experimental Schools Program: Some Implications for Federal Reformers." Paper presented at the American Educational Research Association, New York.

_____. 1974. "Sociological Research for Educational Policy by Independent Research Firms." Paper presented at the American Sociological Association, Montreal, Canada.

Herriott, Robert E., and Neal Gross, eds. 1979. The Dynamics of Planned Educational Change. Berkeley, Calif.: McCutchan.

Hirschman, Albert O. 1970. Exit, Voice and Loyalty. Cambridge, Mass.: Harvard University Press.

Homans, George C. 1961. Social Behavior: Its Elementary Forms. New York: Harcourt Brace Jovanovich.

House, Ernest R. 1974. The Politics of Educational Innovation. Berkeley, Calif.: McCutchan.

Hughes, Everett C. 1958. Men and Their Work. New York: Free Press.

Iannaconne, Laurence, and Frank Lutz. 1970. Politics, Power, and Policy. Columbus: Charles Merrill.

Kirst, Michael W. 1974. "The Growth of Federal Influence in Education." In Uses of the Sociology of Education, edited by C.

Wayne Gordon, pp. 448-77. Chicago: University of Chicago Press.

Leavitt, Harold J. 1965. "Applied Organizational Change in Industry." In Handbook of Organizations, edited by James G. March, pp. 1144-70. Chicago: Rand McNally.

Lindblom, Charles E. 1959. "The Science of 'Muddling Through'." Public Administration Review 19: 79-88.

Lortie, Dan C. 1969. "The Balance of Control and Autonomy in Elementary School Teaching." In The Semiprofessions and Their Organization, edited by Amitai Etzioni, pp. 1-53. New York: Free Press.

Merton, Robert K. 1968. Social Structure and Social Theory. New York: Free Press.

Meyer, John W., and Brian Rowan. 1978. "Notes on the Structure of Educational Organizations." In Studies on Environment and Organization, edited by Marshall W. Meyer et al. San Francisco: Jossey-Bass.

Miles, Matthew. 1965. "Planned Change and Organizational Health: Figure and Ground." In Change Process in the Public Schools, edited by the Center for Advanced Study in Educational Administration, pp. 11-34. Eugene: University of Oregon Press.

Morris, R., and R. H. Binstock. 1966. Feasible Planning for Social Change. New York: Columbia University Press.

Morse, N., and E. Reimer. 1956. "The Experimental Change of a Major Organizational Variable." Journal of Abnormal and Social Psychology 52: 120-29.

National Center for Education Statistics. 1978. Digest of Education Statistics, 1977-78. Washington, D.C.: U.S. Government Printing Office.

National Society for the Study of Education. 1961. Individualizing Education. Chicago: University of Chicago Press.

Nelson, Margaret, and Sam D. Sieber. 1976. "Innovation in Urban Secondary Schools." School Review 84: 213-31.

Ouchi, William G. , and Mary Ann Maguire. 1975. "Organizational Control: Two Functions." Administrative Science Quarterly 20: 559-69.

Pelto, Perti J. 1970. Anthropological Research: The Structure of Inquiry. New York: Harper & Row.

Perrow, Charles. 1970. Organizational Analysis: A Sociological View. Belmont, Calif.: Wadsworth.

Rogers, David. 1968. 110 Livingston St.: Politics and Bureaucracy in the New York City School System. New York: Vintage.

Rosenblum, Sheila, and Karen S. Louis. 1978. A Measure of Change: The Process and Outcomes of Planned Change in Ten Rural School Districts. Cambridge, Mass.: Abt Associates.

Rosenthal, Alan. 1969. Pedagogues and Power. Syracuse: Syracuse University Press.

Schattschneider, E. E. 1960. The Semi-Sovereign People. New York: Holt, Rinehart, & Winston.

Simon, Herbert A. 1957. Models of Man. New York: John Wiley.

_____. 1964. "On the Concept of Organizational Goals." Administrative Science Quarterly 9: 1-22.

Smith, Louis M., and Pat M. Keith. 1971. Anatomy of Educational Innovation. New York: John Wiley & Sons.

Spady, William G. 1973. "Impact of School Resources on Students." In Review of Research in Education 1, edited by Fred N. Kerlinger, pp. 135-78. Itasca, Ill.: F. E. Peacock.

Sproull, Lee, Stephen Weiner, and David Wolf. 1978. Organizing an Anarchy. Chicago: University of Chicago Press.

State of New Jersey. 1976. T & E: A Primer for School Improvement in New Jersey, pp. 8-12. Trenton: Department of Education, State of New Jersey.

Sussman, Leila. 1977. Tales Out of School: Implementing Organizational Change in Elementary School. Philadelphia: Temple University Press.

Thompson, James D. 1967. Organizations in Action. New York: McGraw-Hill.

Tumin, Melvin. 1973. "Foreword." In Reform and Organizational Survival: The Teacher and an Instrument of Change. New York: John Wiley & Sons.

Vidich, Arthur, and Joseph Bensman. 1968. Small Town in Mass Society. 2d ed. Princeton, N.J.: Princeton University Press.

Wacaster, C. Thompson, and William A. Firestone. 1978. "The Promise and Problems of Long-Term, Continuous Fieldwork." Human Organization 37: 269-75.

Watson, Goodwin. 1969. "Resistance to Change." In The Planning of Change. 2d ed., edited by Warren Bennis, Kenneth Benne, and Robert Chin, pp. 488-98. New York: Holt, Rinehart, & Winston.

Weick, Karl E. 1976. "Educational Organizations as Loosely Coupled Systems." Administrative Science Quarterly 21: 1-19.

Zaltman, Gerald, and Robert Duncan. 1977. Strategies for Planned Change. New York: John Wiley & Sons.

Zeigler, L. Harmon, and M. Kent Jennings. 1974. Governing American Schools. N. Scituate, Mass.: Duxbury.

INDEX

ABOUT THE AUTHOR

WILLIAM A. FIRESTONE is Coordinator of Field Studies at Research for Better Schools, an educational laboratory in Philadelphia. He worked previously for Abt Associates, a private, policy research firm in Cambridge, Massachusetts.

Dr. Firestone has published widely in the areas of sociology and education. His articles have appeared in such journals as Sociology of Education, the Journal of Applied Behavioral Science, and School Review. He holds a B.A. from Antioch College in Yellow Springs, Ohio, and an M.A. and Ph.D. from the University of Chicago.